GAWAIN: KNIGHT OF THE GODDESS

By the same author:
The Aquarian Guide to British and Irish Mythology (with Caitlín
    Matthews)
The Aquarian Guide to Legendary London (with Chesca Potter)
An Arthurian Reader
The Arthurian Tarot
The Grail-Seeker's Companion (with Marian Green)
Hallowquest: Tarot Magic and the Arthurian Mysteries

GAWAIN: KNIGHT OF THE GODDESS

Restoring an Archetype

John Matthews

Foreword by Mildred Leake Day

THE AQUARIAN PRESS

First published 1990

Cover illustration: Walewein (*West-Vlaanderen*),
from Leiden University Library, Holland (ms. Ltk. 195, f.120v).

British Library Cataloguing in Publication Data

Matthews, John
Gawain: knight of the goddess.
1. Legends. Characters : Arthur, King
I. Title
398'. 352

ISBN 0-85030-783-X

The Aquarian Press is part of the Thorsons Publishing Group, Wellingborough,
Northamptonshire, NN8 2RQ, England.

Printed in Great Britain by Mackays of Chatham, Kent
Typeset by MJL Limited, Hitchin, Hertfordshire

1 3 5 7 9 10 8 6 4 2

For Freya Reeves Lambides
who without knowing it sparked off this book in 1987.

Gwalchmai, who pursued his quarry
to the end of the wide world and back,
could change at will to swan or wren,
win further names, saunter in and out
of the Other World, live forever on
the lips of bards.

Peter Vansittart: Parsifal.

...Gawain, with his old curteisye,
Though he were come ageyn out of Fairye...

Chaucer: The Squire's Tale.

Contents

Foreword

Sir Gawain, nephew of the great King Arthur, figures in much of the extensive literature of the Arthurian legend. Although this body of material was written down long after the pagan era had ended, the tales preserve hints of the ancient story that celebrated the heroes and rituals of the pre-Christian ages. Anthropologists, folklorists, and archeologists working with the Celtic traditions have identified many gods and goddesses, but perhaps the most pervasive is the Goddess of the Land, sometimes called the 'Sovereignty', sometimes 'The Great Mother', and often represented as a triple figure. Although Gawain serves no person identified specifically as 'The Great Goddess', he is involved with women of mysterious characteristics — Morgan (sometimes called a Goddess), Lady Bercilak, Dame Ragnell, even Guenivere. These ladies can be identified by name or by story motifs with Irish and Welsh pagan figures of an earlier time, as can Gawain himself. Behind these stories is a compelling feminine power dimly remembered in Western culture as 'Mother Nature', 'The Mother Country', 'the Muse', and even 'Lady Luck'.

Beginning with the massive work of Sir James Frazer almost a century ago, scholars have tried to reconstruct the largely lost pagan cultures. Frazer, in *The Golden Bough* (1898), presents a pagan past based on the agricultural year with rituals for increasing the fertility of soil and flocks. His research on the sacral kingship and the battles between summer and winter have done much to increase our understanding of the relationship between the king and his land that appears in the Arthurian legend as the Wounded King and the Wasteland. Frazer does not deal as extensively with the feminine principles, although he does touch on the Corn Goddess in her two aspects of hag and bride, which he explains as a variation of the Demeter Persephone concept:

> Judged by these analogies [the customs he has recorded] Demeter would be the ripe crop of this year; Persephone would be the seed-corn taken from it and sown in autumn, to reappear in spring. The descent of Persephone into the lower world would thus be a mythical expression for the sowing of the seed; her reappearance in the spring would signify

the sprouting of the young corn. In this way the Persephone of one year becomes the Demeter of the next ... (Theodore H. Gaster, ed., 1959, p. 422)

Although Frazer's golden mistletoe bough may now be considered merely a green branch broken by a suppliant and much of his collection of folklore and ritual frowned upon as not collected with proper professional discipline, Frazer's influence on twentieth century scholars and artists is immeasurable. Jessie Weston, T.S. Eliot and John Boorman, to name but a few, have touched on fertility, the king, and the wasteland.

C.G. Jung, perceiving that the patterns of the ancient mythology continue to recur in modern literature as well as in the dreams and hallucinations of his patients, proposes that these myths exist as archetypes in the unconscious, providing modern man with the patterns for coping with the great crises of human birth, puberty, and death. Jung identifies the feminine principle as the 'anima', dividing her into mirror aspects, the 'Good Mother', and the 'Terrible Mother'. He explains that the creative principle of great art is in the evoking of the archetypes and that it is generated from the unconscious of the artist:

> It makes no difference whether the artist knows that his work is generated, grows and matures within him, or whether he imagines that it is his own invention. In reality it grows out of him as a child its mother. The creative process has a feminine quality, and the creative work arises from unconscious depths — we might truly say from the realm of the Mothers. ('Psychology and Literature' (1950) in *The Spirit in Man, Art, and Literature* p. 103.)

Robert Graves, whose primary thesis in *The White Goddess* (1948) is not so much anthropology or psychology but poetry, presents a poet's description of the Goddess as Muse:

> The Goddess is a lovely, slender woman with a hooked nose, deathly pale face, lips red as rowan-berries, startlingly blue eyes and long fair hair; she will suddenly transform herself into sow, mare, bitch, vixen, she-ass, weasel, serpent, owl, she-wolf, tigress, mermaid or loathsome hag. Her names and titles are innumerable. In ghost stores she often figures as 'The White Lady', and in ancient religions, from the British Isles to the Caucasus, as the 'White Goddess'. I cannot think of any true poet from Homer onwards who has not independently recorded his experience of her. The test of a poet's vision is the accuracy of his portrayal of the White Goddess and of the island over which she rules. The reason why the hairs stand on end, the eyes water, the throat is constricted, the skin crawls and a shiver runs down the spine when one writes or reads a true poem is that a true poem is necessarily an invocation of the White Goddess, or Muse, the Mother of All Living, the ancient power of fright and lust — the female spider or the queen-bee whose embrace is death. (2nd ed., p. 24)

Joseph Campbell, in *The Hero with a Thousand Faces* (1949), describing the adventure of life to which all are called, asserts the inevitability of meeting the Goddess:

> Woman, in the picture language of mythology, represents the totality of what can be known. The hero is the one who comes to know. As he progresses in the slow initiation which is life, the form of the goddess undergoes for him a series of transfigurations: she can never be greater than himself, though she can always promise more than he is yet capable of comprehending. She lures, she guides, she bids him burst his fetters. And if he can match her import, the two, the knower and the known, will be released from every limitation. Woman is the guide to the sublime acme of sensuous adventure. By deficient eyes she is reduced to inferior states; by the evil eye of ignorance she is spellbound to banality and ugliness. But she is redeemed by the eyes of understanding. The hero who can take her as she is, without undue commotion but with the kindness and assurance she requires, is potentially the kind, the incarnate god, of her created world. (2nd. ed., Bollingen series, p. 116)

Miranda Green, in *The Gods of the Celts* (1986), adds to our visualization of the Great Goddess in a triple form through her richly illustrated archeological study:

> The mother-goddess is perhaps the commonest type of Celtic divinity treated in this way [triplism] and the triadic form appears to have played an important role in her worship and cult-expression. The Three Mothers or *Deae Matres*, as they are frequently called in inscriptions, were known also as *Matronae*, especially in Cisalpine Gaul (North Italy) and lower Germany ... The iconography of the Three Mothers gives us valuable information as to how they were looked upon by their devotees. The vast majority are seated side by side, fully draped. But within this framework, there are many variations, all of which stress the maternal, nourishing and fertility role of the goddesses. The commonest attributes are baskets of fruit, *cornuacopiae*, loaves, fish and children. (pp. 78-81)

Jaan Puhvel, in *Comparative Mythology* (1987), does not discuss the Celtic gods until he has covered chapters on the gods of India, Persia, Greece and Rome. Then following his account of various Roman attempts to explain the Celtic pantheon in terms of the Roman one, he describes the Celtic Goddess:

> 'Minerva', with the epithet *Belisama*, 'Brightest', is the cover term for a great goddess. Powerful female types stand out in Celtic mythical lore at both the divine and the saga levels. The transfunctional goddess has here come into her own. 'Minerva' had a temple with 'eternal flame' in the third-century C.E. Britain and is identifiable with the British Celtic theonym Brigantia, formally identical with the Sanskrit feminine adjective *brhati* 'great, lofty' and with the Irish Brigit, the later saint with her feast day

of *Imbolc* (1 February) and her monastery with perpetual fire at Kildare. (Unlike the usual overlay, e.g., with the Virgin Mary superimposed on the sanctuary of Aphrodite at Cypriot Paphos, the Celtic deity was simply Christianized, name and all.) Triplicity or triunity is in evidence among the Celtic mythical females: Brigit herself had two synonymous 'sisters', there was the triad of Irish Machas, Gaul had the triple Matres or Matrae or Matronae. Just as the Greek three-by-three Muses did not perturb Homer's Muse, the Matronae did not preclude a single great Matrona, embodied in a river (Matronae = Marne), whereas in Ireland the mother-goddess was the land itself . . . Matrona was the mother of the 'Divine Son', Maponos, matching Modron and her son Mabon in Welsh saga . . . (pp. 173-174)

Before these modern authorities from folklore, psychology, anthropology, and archeology are construed as presenting a tradition of the Goddess completely independent of the Arthurian legend, it must also be said that each of these authorities uses aspects of the Arthurian material to support their theories. Frazer cites the episode of Lancelot in the burning city from the *High History of the Holy Grail* as evidence of the representation of the sacral slaying of the king in legend (pp. 237-240). C.G. Jung's wife and collaborator, Emma Jung, wrote *The Grail Legend*, illustrating the Jungian interpretation of the Arthurian material in a volume completed posthumously by Marie-Louise von Franz in 1960. Robert Graves makes extensive use of the early Arthurian poem 'The Spoils of Annwm' to support his answers to the Gwion's riddles in *Hanes Taliessen* (pp. 97-112). Joseph Campbell illustrates his description of the Goddess quoted above with the Irish tale of how Niall gave a kiss to a hag in exchange for water, only to have her turn into a beautiful woman and declare herself the 'Royal Rule of Ireland', an analogue of the tales of Gawain and Dame Ragnall (pp. 116-118). Miranda Green acknowledges not only Irish but also Welsh sources, particularly the four branches of the *Mabinogion* and the *Tale of Culhwch and Olwen* (p.16). Jaan Puhvel works primarily with the Irish sagas and the *Mabinogion*, but cites parallel episodes in the Arthurian material (p. 185). The possibility of a circularity of logic exists between contemporary studies of the mythology of pagan Celts and a study of pagan mythology in the Arthurian legend.

Yet if one goes back to texts of the twelfth century, the pagan qualities of the Arthurian material can be affirmed. Even if Nennius records that Arthur carried the Blessed Virgin's image on his shoulders and Geoffrey of Monmouth tells of Arthur's investiture by the Archbishop Dubricius, other writers writing in Latin are clear about the pagan aspect of the Arthurian material. Etienne de Rouen, writing *Draco Normannicus* for Henry II in 1169 or 1170, tells how the Bretons were hard pressed by Henry's forces and called on King Arthur for his promised aid. Arthur, in turn, writes a letter to King Henry, threatening to return and save his people. Etienne does not hesitate to make Arthur a pagan. Arthur calls upon the triple Goddess by her classic names of the three fates: Clotho, Lachesis and Atropos. His very immortality is a state of suspended animation induced by the ministrations of his sister Morgana, a nymph He awaits the call of his people in the Antipodes. (It is interesting that the Latin term *fata* for the Three Fates apparently becomes singular, as in 'Fata Morgana', and passes into French as *fée*, 'fairy'. This may be evidence of the simplification of grammar in process in medieval Latin, but the triplicity of the Celtic Goddess may also have had its influence on the ambiguity of the form.)

The author of *Historia Meriadoci regis Cambrie* 'The Story of Meriadoc, King of Cambria' (twelfth century), who also wrote *De Ortu Waluuanii*, 'The Rise of Gawain', states unequivocally that the Arthurian adventures took place in Britain in the pre-Christian era. He names the Goddess who controlled the destinies of men 'Fortuna'. Fortuna also appears as the Goddess in *Wigalois, The Knight of Fortune's Wheel*, in *Diu Crône*, and in a number of other Arthurian romances. The choice of Fortuna as the name of the Goddess by these early authors is particularly appropriate: Fortuna shares many of the attributes of Matrona or the Celtic Sovereignty. In the statue now in the Vatican, Fortuna holds a cornucopia in her left hand, a rudder in her right. The rudder is the *gubernaculum*, the steering mechanism that is the metaphor behind our term 'government'. Her cornucopia, symbol for fertility, good harvest and plenty, is also a recurring motif in the depictions of the Three Mothers. It passes into Arthurian literature as an ivory horn and as the food-giving grail. Not only that, but since the highly respected Boethius, *De Consolatione Philosophiae* (524) had portrayed Fortuna as the handmaid of Philosophia and the agent of God's will, she remained a proper subject for a Christian author.

But though her name is Fortuna, her attributes remain those of the Celtic Great Goddess. In *Historia Meriadoci*, her palace appears on a plain where no building had been seen before. She entertains her people with chess. She tells the hero Meriadoc that she has long awaited his coming. She feeds the hero at a feast more splendid than anything he has experienced before. She wants the hero to remain, but he breaks a taboo by asking questions and, terrified, flees the palace. Later, after many trials, she reappears as the Weeping Lady and provides the hero with a horse. The hero is then able to leave the Otherworld and return to the world of men. Many adventures later Meriadoc rescues the Emperor's daughter from the King of the Land From Which No One Returns. A folklorist would recognize the episode as analogous to other tales of the Sovereignty, making the Emperor's daughter another human manifestation of the Goddess. Fortuna favours Meriadoc, but he never realizes this. Instead he continues to defy what he sees as 'misfortune' with courage, following in this Latin romance the Roman code of behaviour. Although Fortuna dominates his story, Meriadoc never becomes the knight of the Goddess.

It is Gawain, with his Celtic code of honour, who becomes the champion of the Goddess, as John Matthews demonstrates. More of the Arthurian legend is accessible today in printed editions and translations than ever before. Matthews has taken this immense body of literature and, concentrating on the episodes in which Gawain appears, put together the recurring elements into a pattern of what must have been the core of the Gawain story. This core he then elucidates from what is known of the pre-Christian pantheon and culture. He restores our understanding of the character of Gawain to the premier hero and Grail-winner that he was before the innocent Perceval, the wise Bors, and the saintly Galahad pursued the quest, sweeping all other contenders behind them. Yet even though Gawain is portrayed in the later romances as a failure in the Christian quest and his character is degraded in comparison to Lancelot and Galahad, he remains in the Arthurian tradition one of Arthur's foremost companions: a knight of gallantry, courtesy, and prowess — and a champion of women. That he was also, as Matthews demonstrates, the recognized champion of the Goddess — the feminine creative principle of the Sovereignty, the Great Mother, the Muse — will not surprise those of us who have studied his story.

Mildred Leake Day
Quondam et futurus
Gardendale, Alabama, USA
March, 1989

Acknowledgements

There is simply no way to express my debt to my wife, Caitlín, who not only found time to listen to my ravings in the midst of her own busy work schedule, but also helped shore up my flagging energies time after time, opened many of the secrets of the Goddess to me, and generally shared her own not inconsiderable understanding of the Matter of Britain.

My thanks must also go to Prudence Jones for her excellent translation of *L'Enfances Gauvain*, for which all Gawain scholars should be grateful, and for her stimulating conversation on this and other topics.

To Dick Swettenham for his timely translation and summary of *La Pulzella Gaia*.

To my friend Richard Blackford, whose operas of *Gawain and the Green Knight* and *Gawain and Ragnall* have remained a deep source of inspiration to me.

To all those legions of explorers and commentators who went before — naturally the mistakes are mine not theirs.

I have tried to look at every text, though several are in antique and sometimes unreliable editions. Where this was the case I have relied upon the exhaustive commentaries available, especially those of Professor Bruce, Alfred Nutt, and H.O. Sommer. For much of the background to Chapter 1 I owe an especial debt to the work of R.S. Loomis, whose detailed research into the origins of Gawain proved some valuable links. Also particularly helpful was Keith Busby's exhaustive study of the French Gawain texts, without whose sharp eye and excellent scholarship, Chapters 6 and 7 would have been much the poorer.

Grateful acknowledgement also to the Scottish Academic Press Ltd, for permission to reprint the text of *The Great Sorrow*, which originally appeared in Volume 5 of *The Carmina Gadelica* by Alexander Carmichael.

Thanks also to Tim Cann, for the photo of Wetton Mill which appears on p.190.

Finally I would like to thank Mildred Leake Day for her encouragement and for her generous foreword, and of course for her translation of *De Ortu Waluuanii*,[39] a contribution without equal in Gawain scholarship.

John Matthews, London, 1989

Introduction

Gawain was once the most important knight at Arthur's court, a shining example of all that was best in the chivalry of the time; yet as the popularity of the Arthurian romances grew throughout the Middle Ages, so Gawain's star waned, until by the time Sir Thomas Malory wrote his great book *Le Morte d'Arthur* in 1485, he had become little more than a stock character, noted more for his cavalier attitude to women than for his chivalry. How this transformation came about, and more importantly the reasons for it, are explored and charted in this book.

The answers are inextricably bound up with the question of Gawain's real identity and of his allegiance to the great sovereign Goddess of Britain, facts which became steadily obscured with the passage of time. In showing how this came about we shall need to examine the evidence contained in the many stories where Gawain features as hero (or anti-hero) including Celtic hero-tales, elegant medieval romance, and the justly famed Middle English poem *Sir Gawain and the Green Knight*.

From this we shall endeavour to chart the course of Gawain's rise and fall, of his great middle years when he outranked all other knights (including the latecomer Sir Lancelot du Lac) at Arthur's court. And we shall show that he once attained the greatest heights to which an Arthurian hero could aspire — the achievement of the Grail, and how his service to all ladies once stood for service of another kind.

Finally we shall attempt to unravel the mystery of Gawain's original role in the great mythic cycle of Camelot, thus restoring him to his once unchallenged position as the foremost of the Round Table knights.

Considering this importance it is surprising that comparatively little has been written about Gawain, despite the fact that, 'apart from Arthur himself, the two ubiquitous characters are Arthur's nephew, Gawain, and Kay the seneschal'.[112] These two are with Arthur from the start. As Gwalchmai (the Hawk of May) and Kai, they are among the foremost warriors of the Arthurian court in the earliest surviving versions of the mythos.[121]

Later, during the heyday of Arthurian literature, Gawain occupied more space and has more adventures attributed to him, than any other knight. Even Perceval, who as a successful quest knight in search of the Grail features in numerous texts, is secondary to Gawain in the number of appearances he makes.

A number of commentators have drawn attention to the way in which Gawain's character undergoes such a significant change throughout his literary career. It is a far cry from the description found in the early Welsh tale of *Culhwch and Olwen*, where it is said of him that,

> he never came home without the Quest he had gone to seek. He was the best of walkers and the best of riders He was Arthur's nephew, his sister's son, and his first companion.[31]

to the account, in *Le Morte d'Arthur*, of his part in the murder of King Pellinore (or for that matter of his slaying of an innocent woman in the early pages of the same text).

Scholars such as J.D. Bruce,[77] Jessie Weston,[152] R.S. Loomis, J.B. Whiting[154] and Raymond Thompson[147] have all drawn attention to this curious state of affairs; however, with the exception of Miss Weston, none have so far come up with a satisfactory reason, being content to assume that the appearance of Lancelot, as the representative of fashionable Courtly Love, ousted Gawain from his premier position. In reality it was another rivalry, more fundamental than literary fashion, which was responsible for Gawain's downfall. The present author hopes to show that it was in fact Gawain's original role as Champion of the Goddess which lies at the heart of the mystery. Her own history precludes that of her knight, for as Christianity became the dominating force in the land, so belief in the ancient goddesses changed, faded and finally went into hiding. They became, rather than figures of worship and adoration, objects of vilification and symbols of evil.

All of this makes it very difficult to say with any degree of certainty just what the Celts themselves understood by the term Goddess, or what, for that matter, it meant to certain other people in the Middle Ages. Celtic religious beliefs are still little understood, though we do know that they worshipped deities of wood and water, sky and sea — indeed that each of the elements was of prime importance to them. So that when they spoke of goddesses they were probably thinking of what we would call an abstract principle, represented in the form of a woman.

The best example of this is the Goddess of Sovereignty, with whom Gawain, as we shall see, had a particular relationship. For the Celts, particularly the Irish, the concept of sovereignty, as of kingship, was of a unique kind of link with the earth itself. Thus the king was believed literally to mate with the Goddess of the Land — the otherworldly representative of the particular area over which he reigned. Without the sanction of sovereignty thus gained he could not rule wisely or honestly, or ensure that the kingdom remained strong and virile. This is all part and parcel of a much older idea concerning the sacredness of the land itself — which perhaps in some distant foretime gave birth to the people who walked upon it — hence the concept of Mother Earth.

By the period of the Middle Ages much of this had been forgotten — or at least reassimilated. The fact remains that it takes many hundreds of generations for a new set of religious beliefs to supersede an earlier strata and while the process is taking place a situation exists in which the shadowy forms of earlier traditions mingle with those of the new.

This is the situation which existed during most of the time the Gawain romances were being composed and reactions to it came in two distinct forms. There were those who took the stories that came to them, mostly from wandering singers and story-tellers, and who simply turned them into medieval romances by dressing them in the fashions of the time. And there were those who saw these same stories as an opportunity to put forward the tenets of Christianity in a unique form and who recognized the 'pagan' origins of much of what they saw. It is to these writers that we owe the degraded view of Gawain, who saw in him a champion of the old ways and sought to discredit him in the eyes of the world.

In considering this view we must not allow ourselves to forget that the subject of belief, of faith and theological teaching, was much more to the fore in educated society than it is today. Although it was among the so-called 'ordinary' people that the stories that went into the making of the Matter of Britain originated, in the process of becoming literary creations they underwent a considerable degree of change and adaptation, to suit both the era and the audience.

Thus, since the majority of that audience was made up of knightly or noble classes, who loved to hear about chivalrous adventure above everything, so the epics of the Middle Ages concerned themselves with battles and tournaments and single combats. And when later on the concept of Courtly Love appeared on the scene, so that element also was tossed into the melting pot to add its flavour to the already heady brew.

The final element was the religious one evidenced by the sudden outbreak of interest in the Grail story, which until the beginning of the twelfth century had existed as part of an obscure collection of Celtic tales and Christian apocrypha, but which by the end of the fourteenth century had become one of the most important, most widely written about themes of the time.

Gawain, as the Champion of the Goddess, underwent a form of

character erosion similar to that of the Goddess herself — though in his case it was more subtle, hence the frequent failure of earlier writers to perceive the truth. Yet there is, as we shall see, a significant body of evidence connecting Gawain with the Goddess and showing not only his original role as her champion, but the stages by which he became demoted to the kind of Victorian rake pictured by Tennyson in the nineteenth century. It has been argued that Gawain was ousted from his position of supremacy by the new code of Courtly Love[77] which preferred the illicit passions of Lancelot and Tristan to the more casual amours of Gawain. Certainly Gawain was no courtly lover, despite his famed *courtesy*; indeed, it is more than likely that finding him intractable material in the new literary *genre*, the medieval authors simply sought elsewhere for their heroes and that Gawain's career suffered as a result. Yet it is curious, not to say ironic, that his reputation remained primarily that of a lover.

As Jessie Weston remarked as long ago as 1898 in her book *The Legend of Sir Gawain*:

> It ought not to be impossible to single out from among the various versions of Gawain's adventures certain features which, by their frequent recurrence in the romances devoted to him, and their analogy to ancient Celtic tradition, seem as if they might with probability be regarded as forming part of his original story. It is scarcely to be hoped that we can ever construct a coherent account on which we may lay our finger and say 'This, and no other, was the original Gawain story'; but we may, I think, be able to specify certain incidents, saying, 'This belongs to Gawain and to no other of King Arthur's knights. That adventure is a necessary and integral part of his story.'

It is in belief that this is the case that the present writer has undertaken this study, for although it has become customary to criticize Miss Weston for her flights of fancy, in this instance (as in others) she was close to the truth. While this current investigation frequently diverges from her own, it is very much to the spirit of Miss Weston's pioneering study that the present work is dedicated.

Another writer, in more recent times, dedicated his study of Gawain to 'bringing him out of Fairyland into the world of real men and their affairs.'[112] On consideration it is the opinion of the present writer that there is no evidence to suggest that Gawain ever had *anything* to do with the real world, except in as far as it affected his role in the Matter of Britain. He seems to have been born in 'Fairyland', lived most of his life within its confines, only to have emerged long enough to die. Otherwise his whole character, deeds and behaviour mark him out as an otherworld figure, more properly described as a 'Green Knight' than his actual adversary of that name. Gawain was indeed, as I shall hope to show, the Green Knight at Camelot, the representative of the Goddess-upon-Earth — Sovereignty's Champion, the Son of the Mother.

John Matthews

Chapter 1.

The British Cuchulainn

MODENA: ON THE ROAD TO THE GREEN CHAPEL

Our search for the truth about Gawain begins far from Britain, in the medieval city of Modena, in northern Italy. There, above the north-facing porch of the cathedral, known as the Porta della Pescheria, instead of the usual angels, saints or Old Testament prophets, we find a surprisingly secular scene sculpted on the archivault.

In the centre is a moated castle with twin towers, in which are two people, a man and a woman, Mardoc and Winlogee. From the left three mounted knights, Artus de Bretania, Isdernus and an unnamed man, charge with lowered lances, to be met by a huge churl wielding a kind of pickaxe called a *baston cornu*. To the right a battle is taking place between two mounted knights, Carrado and Galvagin, while two more knights, Galvarium and Che, spears at rest, gallop up from behind.[104]

Much debate has raged over the precise dating and subject matter of this sculpture, but most scholars now accept, from evidence furnished by details of armour and the architecture of the castle, that it was executed some time between 1090 and 1120. There is little doubt, either, that the main characters in the piece, whose names appear in what seems to be Breton, are in fact more familiar to us as Guinevere (Winlogee), Melwas or possibly Mordred (Mardoc), Arthur (Artus de Bretania), Yder (Isdernus), Caradoc (Carrados), Gawain (Galvagin), and Kay (Che). Only the names Galvarium and Bermaltus have no exact equivalents in Arthurian legend; although, as we shall see, the characters they represent are well known therein.[108]

The story told in this enigmatic tableau has been reconstructed several times, the most likely (with certain reservations, which will appear later) to date being that of Roger Sherman Loomis in 1927. The story as he gives it is as follows:

Winlogee, Arthur's queen, escorted only by the unarmed knight Isdern, has gone out to a meadow. Suddenly there gallops out, from a wood near by, a giant knight, Carrado, who swings her from her palfrey to his horse. . . Carrado rides away with the Queen. Isdern goes back and gives the alarm . . . and starts in pursuit. There set out after him. . . Galvarium, Galvarin, Artus and Che. At length they arrive before a castle, surrounded by a marsh and approached by two opposite barbicans. Before one of them stands a huge ruffian, swinging a baston cornu, whose name is Burmalt. At the other entrance, Galvagin, Galvarium and Che are met by the giant Carrado. Probably Che and Galvarium are overthrown. Galvagin, however, encounters Carrado and pursues him into the castle. When Galvagin breaks his sword, a damsel whom Carrado has abducted places Carrado's own sword, with which alone he could be killed, within Galvagin's reach, and with this Galvagin dispatches him. The hero then proceeds. . . finds at last Winlogee with Mardoc, who has long loved her and to whom Carrado has delivered her. What is the fate of Mardoc is uncertain, but probably he throws himself on the Queen's mercy and is pardoned. Galvagin then brings her back to her husband.[104]

The central theme of this story, and one which we shall meet again throughout this book, is that of the rape and subsequent rescue of the Flower Bride, an aspect of the otherworldly queen or Goddess with whom Gawain is seen to be consistently connected.

What interests us particularly about the version of the story given here, which is reconstructed from several texts, is the role of Gawain as the rescuer of Guinevere, a task normally reserved for Lancelot; and the fact that it probably marks the earliest recorded appearance of the name Gawain (Galvagin) anywhere. Before this time, though we may assume that stories featuring the hero were in circulation, we have no definite evidence to support the claim. Though there is, as we shall see, plentiful indication of a much earlier Gawain figure.

The story depicted on the Modena archivault is familiar from more than one major Arthurian source. In Malory's *Le Morte d'Arthur*[32] Guinevere is abducted by Meleagraunce and rescued by Lancelot; in the medieval Latin *Life of St Gildas*[59] Melwas, Lord of the Summer Country, is the abductor and Arthur himself the putative rescuer, aided by the Saint, who brings about a peaceful settlement. In three other texts, *Iwein* by Hartmann von Aue, the *Diu Crône* (The Crown) of Heinrich von dem Turlin,[22] and the *Livre d'Artus*,[60] Gawain is named as the hero, though the identity of the abductor varies in each case.

Other characters in what we may for convenience call the *Modena version*, appear in a variety of roles. In the thirteenth-century poem *Durmart le Gallois*[45] the hero rescues Guinevere from the castle of an aggressor, aided by Yder (Isdernus). Durmart himself is probably the same name as Bermalt, though in this case he is an attacker rather than a defender. While the full significance of this story will be discussed later (see pp. 47-52) we should note that in four out of the eight texts mentioned above Gawain is the hero, while in the *Vulgate Lancelot*[60] he is himself rescued, and that he is depicted in the *Modena version*, together with a giant, axe-bearing churl — the first of many such encounters that we shall meet.

The further importance of the Modena carvings lies in the evidence they offer both for the importance of the Arthurian mythos at a time substantially *before* any of the great romances had appeared, and for the presence of such stories far afield from their place of origin in Celtic Britain. This is not the place to go into the complex matter of transmission, by which the stories of Arthur and his knights were disseminated across the Western world. However it is important to grasp certain salient points.

The stories were almost certainly carried across the English Channel to Brittany by wandering bards and story-tellers at various times after the general exodus which followed upon the Saxon Wars of the fifth-sixth centuries — not long, in fact, after the disappearance of Arthur himself. Once there they were carried deeper into Europe, where they became cross-fertilized with native tales, finally returning to Britain with the Normans.

Often the tales were changed so much that even those who knew the original versions would have been hard put to identify them. Isolated episodes were taken up, transformed, applied to other people, so that a single story could reappear in as many as a dozen new forms, embedded in much larger tales, and often attributed to a completely different set of characters.

We will observe this happening throughout Gawain's literary and mythical career. It is one of the main reasons why his true story has remained obscured for so long, and it reflects the changes which took place in the medieval world during the heyday of Arthurian romance.

But it was long before this that the story really began, in the richly peopled and magical realm of Celtic myth and legend. Although many of the texts to be considered here were not written down until after the carving of the Modena archivault, the material they contain dates from much earlier. It is here that we first learn of Gawain.

The *Trioedd Ynys Prydein* (Triads of Britain)[56] although not collected until the twelfth century, remain one of the most reliable sources for the lost Celtic hero sagas. We find, altogether, eight mentions of Gawain there, under the Welsh version of his name, *Gwalchmai*, which may be translated as The Hawk of May — though the name itself, as we shall see, has caused problems of its own.

In Triad 4, 'Gwalchmai son of Gwyar' is described as one of the 'three well-endowed men of the Island of Britain'. Triad 75 names him one of the 'Three men of the Island of Britain who were most courteous to guests and strangers'; and Triad 91 as the first among the 'Three Fearless Men of the Island of Britain'. Triads 42 and 46a further mention his horse *Meingalet* (translated as 'Slender-Hard' by Rachel Bromwich) or *Keincaled* (translated as 'White and Hardy' by R.S. Loomis).

To this may be added one further reference. The late medieval work known as *The Twenty-Four Knights of Arthur's Court*[36] refers to the 'three Golden-Tongued Knights [who] were in Arthur's Court: Gwalchmai son of Llew son of Cynfarch . . . [etc.] . . . and there was neither king nor lord to whom these came who did not listen to them; and whatever quest they sought, they wished for and obtained it, either willingly or unwillingly' (Trans. Bromwich).

These may well be the earliest surviving references to Gawain we possess, for though we must not forget that they are of medieval origin, there is little doubt that they derived from much earlier sources. We may note, also, that the references to Gwalchmai already possess a certain unity and that they clearly refer to one person, rather than several. Gwalchmai is rich (well-endowed), courteous, fearless, and possessed of a golden tongue — all attributes which we may see reflected in the later romances.

The theme of Gwalchmai's ability as a conciliator is taken up again in three of the major Arthurian stories contained in the *Mabinogion*.[31] In 'The Lady of the Fountain' he is clearly shown to be Arthur's confidant, walking with him and advising him as to the best course of action to take over a missing knight. In 'Geraint and Enid', he acts as an intermediary between Arthur and Geraint, when the latter is wounded and unwilling to appear before the king. Finally, in 'Peredur', he awakens the hero from a trance into which he had fallen and during which he had absent-mindedly unhorsed two other knights who had approached him.

In each of these tales, which we shall examine in more detail later, we see Gwalchmai acting in a noble, as well as a heroic, manner. He is a respected courtier whose ability to smooth the path between contending factions is widely recognized.

The reference in the *Twenty-Four Knights* to Gwalchmai's ancestry are of particular importance since they lead us directly into the genealogical tangle surrounding Gawain's original identity. We note here that he is the son of Llew ap Cynfarch, a figure who has been identified with Loth or Lot of Lothian and Orkney, a major figure in the Arthurian romances. He it was who, according to these later stories, married Arthur's half-sister, sometimes called Morgause, sometimes Anna, thus establishing Gawain as Arthur's nephew, an important relationship as we shall see.

The fact that Lot is known chiefly in the later French texts has led some scholars to the belief that the reference to him in *Twenty-Four Knights* is also late, and was influenced by the continental stories. In much the same way, the name Gwalchmai has been put forward as an attempt, by a Welsh story-teller, to Anglicize the French name *Gauvain*. However, there seems to be no real justification for this other than a desire to claim French origin for all the Matter of Britain. Sufficient references exist in *The Mabinogion*,[31] *The Stanzas of the Graves*,[56] and the *Ystoria Trystan*,[85] as well as *The Triads*, to indicate the presence of an established Gawain tradition. And as we shall see, there are further reasons for choosing to see the name Gauvain as deriving from another direction altogether.

⌘

THE THREE SONS OF LUGH: GAWAIN, CUCHULAINN AND GWRI

The great Celtic scholar Sir John Rhys first advanced the theory that Gawain was to be identified with the Irish hero Cuchulainn and that both were solar heroes.[135,134] He based this in part on certain points of similarity between their careers, and from the fact that both had a specific quality — their strength waxed and waned with the rising and setting of the sun, being at its height at midday. This has been a popular theory with critics of the Arthurian legend, and R.S. Loomis in particular made much of it in his brilliant early book *Celtic Myth and Arthurian Romance*[104] and in various articles which followed it. In all of these he found further evidence to support the identification and in so doing added considerably to our understanding of Gawain.

Loomis' argument may be summarized thus.

1. Gwair, a rather mysterious figure whose name appears several times in the *Mabinogion* and elsewhere,[114] is the son of the Welsh hero Llwch Lleminawc.

2. Cuchulainn is the son (or possibly the reincarnation) of the Irish god Lugh Loinnbheimionach.

3. Gwalchmai is the son of Llew ap Cynfarch (Lot or Loth in the later romances).

4. Numerous incidents from Gawain's career coincide with those in the life of Cuchulainn, and also with those of Gwair under the names Gwri and Goreu.

5. The name of Gawain's son in the romances, Guinglainn, sounds like an attempt to Anglicize the name Cuchulainn.
6. Two names which appear in the warrior list in *Culhwch and Olwen*, Gwri Gwallt-Avwyn and Gwri Gwallt-Euryn, transpose easily into the names of Galvagin and Galvarium, as found on the Modena archivault.
7. The epithets attached to the name Gwri both mean Golden Haired.
8. Cuchulainn had a halo of golden hair.
9. Both Cuchulainn and Gwri are precocious at birth and are put out to fosterage.
10. Both are connected with the birth of a foal which is to provide them with a steed in later life.
11. Another rebirth of Lugh is as the huge and heroic warrior Curoi mac Daire, who plays the Beheading Game (see pp. 65-7) with Cuchulainn in the same way that an identical figure, Bercilak, who will be discussed in Chapter 3, plays it with Gawain. To this we must add,
12. Both Curoi and Bercilak can be identified as playing similar roles to that of Bermaltus in the *Modena version*.

We are looking then, at an overlay between the careers of Gawain and three different heroes: Cuchulainn, Gwri Gwallt-Euryn and Curoi mac Daire. We must now look at all three in more detail to see how they enlarge our understanding of Gawain's original role.

Cuchulainn perhaps needs least by way of introduction. He is the premier hero of Ancient Ireland and one of the most extraordinary figures in Celtic myth. His mother, Dechtire, was spirited away to the Otherworld on the evening of her wedding to Sualtaim mac Roth and while there the god Lugh fathered Cuchulainn upon her (or was reincarnated through the birth according to a more primitive version of the story). The child was named Setanta bec, the Little One, but received the name *Cu Chulainn* (The Hound of Cullan) when he killed the giant dog of Culann the Smith and promised to act as watch-dog until another animal could be trained.

He had many loves but the first and greatest was Emer, daughter of Forgall the Wily. When Cuchulainn presented himself as a suitor Forgall indicated that he would only look with favour on someone who had been trained by Domhnall the Warlike of Alba. Having swiftly learned all he could from Domhnall, Cuchulainn went on to the woman warrior Scathach, who trained him further, until he was the greatest warrior in all Ireland. Returning to Forgall, Cuchulainn again presented himself as a suitor for Emer, and on being refused yet again attacked and slew so many men that Forgall jumped from the ramparts rather than face the angry warrior. Cuchulainn married Emer but had many other loves, including the fairy woman Blathnat, whom he abducted from Curoi's revolving fortress in a story reminiscent of the abduction of Guinevere. We shall return to this episode in more detail in a moment.[11]

Cuchulainn's career is a catalogue of remarkable adventures, but his most famous exploit was his virtually single-handed defence of Ulster against the invading armies of Connacht. The story is told in full in the epic poem *The Tain*[54] and is one of the great hero-tales of all time. He was only finally killed after he rejected the love of the Morrigan, the terrible battle goddess of Ireland, and this too will prove to be part of the story of Gawain.

The second in this trio of heroes Gwri, under his recognized aliases, Gwair, Goreu and Pryderi, has a similarly remarkable life.[114] In the *Mabinogion* of *Pwyll, Prince of Dyfed* his story is as follows:

When a son is born to the goddess Rhiannon and her husband Pwyll, she is accused of the infant's murder when he is stolen from her side on the night of his birth. At the same time, in another part of the land, a man named Teyrnon Twrf Lliant had a mare which bore a splendid foal every May Eve, but which always disappeared. Determined to find out the cause of this, Teyrnon lies in wait and sees a huge arm and claw come in through the window of the stable. He successfully cuts this off and gives pursuit of the wounded monster. Returning from the chase, he finds a newborn child in the stable, wrapped in rich clothes. It is, of course, Rhiannon's child, the implication being that he had been stolen by the same monster and dropped in the struggle. Teyrnon and his wife adopt the boy and name him Gwri Gwallt-Euryn (Gwri Golden Hair). He grows rapidly and becomes so attached to the colt born on the night of his discovery that Teyrnon gives it to him. Soon after they learn that Rhiannon has been banished from the court and made to wait outside the gate to carry guests inside on her shoulders, and noticing the likeness of the growing Gwri to Pwyll, they take him to court. Both refuse to be carried inside by Rhiannon, and Teyrnon relates the story of Gwri's discovery. Rhiannon declares that she is released from anxiety (*pryder*) and the boy is named from this 'Pryderi'.[31]

The second instance of Gwri's appearance is also in the *Mabinogion* in the story of *Culhwch and Olwen*. This long and complex tale is really a compendium of ancient stories bound together by Culhwch's quest for Olwen, the daughter of the giant Yspaddaden Pencawr. In this he is aided by a glittering array of heroes from Arthur's court, who assist him in performing a number of impossible tasks set for him by the giant. Among those who offer outstanding help is Goreu, the yellow-haired son of Custenin, Yspaddaden's herdsman, and possibly of the giant's sister. It is told of him that his mother hid him in a cupboard for fear of the giant, who had already killed 23 of her sons, but that the hero Cai (Kay) came and made him his companion and page. He is said to be a cousin to both Arthur and to Culhwch. He acquits himself with outstanding bravery in the stealing of a magical sword from another giant, Gwrnach, and it is then that he is named Goreu, which means 'the best'.

He appears again in Triad 52 which lists the Three Exalted Prisoners of the Island of Britain:

> Llyr Half-Speech, who was imprisoned by Euroswydd,
>   and the second, Mabon son of Modron,
>   and third, Gwair son of Geiriodd.
> And one [prisoner] who was more exalted than the three of them, was three nights in prison in Caer Oeth and Anoeth, and three nights imprisoned by Gwen Pendragon, and three nights in an enchanted prison under the stone of Echymeint. This Exalted Prisoner was Arthur, and it was the same lad who released him from each of these three prisons — Goreu, son of Custenin, his cousin.[56]

The meaning of this enigmatic Triad has been successfully established by Caitlín Matthews in her book *Mabon and the Mysteries of Britain*[114] and need only be summarized here. Gwair, Goreu and Gwri are all aspects of the Celtic Divine Child, Mabon son of Modron, who, like Gwri/Pryderi, is stolen from his mother's side within three nights of his birth, and who must be released rather in the same way that the waters of the Waste Land in the Grail tradition must be released in order to heal the wounded land. Mabon is the imprisoned splendour and beauty of the world, which remains dark and desolate until he is set free. His mother, Modron, is the Goddess of the land and together these two archetypal figures reappear again and again throughout Celtic and Arthurian myth. As we have seen, Gawain also appears in Arthurian romance as a conciliator — one who frees people from difficult situations in which they have become embroiled through meddling in otherworldly affairs, and he is, almost certainly, the son of a Goddess.

Under the name Gwair, Mabon-Gwri-Goreu appears in perhaps the most genuinely ancient Arthurian text, the *Preiddeu Annwn* (Spoils of Annwn), where the lines appear: 'Perfect is the captivity of Gwair in Caer Siddi, According to the testimony of Pwyll and Pryderi'[120] another reference to the captivity theme which is a concomitant of the Mabon story. Loomis believed that Gwair was the son of the Welsh hero Llwch Llemenawc which, as we shall see, provides a further link between the three figures under discussion. Gwair's name certainly passed into Arthurian romance, in a mutated form, attached to Gawain's brothers

Gareth and Gaheries. He is also involved in a quest for a magical sword, which became a key motif of the Gawain saga.

The third of this trio of Celtic heroes is Curoi mac Daire, who is a curious blend of historical character and mythic being. He was probably a real king of Munster sometime during the Heroic period (roughly equivalent to the Iron and Bronze ages), but he is best known through the Cuchulainn saga where he begins as Cuchulainn's friend and ends as his bitterest foe when they quarrel over the fairy woman Blathnat. Here he plays a far more otherworldly role, as two further incidents from his life indicate.

A detail from the early Irish text, *Compert Cuchulainn*,[11] instanced by Loomis, offers a clue to Curoi's original identity, and ultimately, to that of Gawain. The story concerns an incarnation of the god Lugh, and how in the same night two colts were born (as in the story of Gwri). This particular incarnation was unsuccessful, the child dying in infancy, but Lugh appeared to the mother of the dead child and instructed her to keep the two colts until she should bear another son. This is to be Cuchulainn himself, another incarnation of Lugh.

Loomis' inference is that the first incarnation was, in an earlier version, Curoi, which he backs up with the knowledge that Daire himself had a well-founded identification with Lugh or Lugaid, and that both Curoi and Cuchulainn seem to have been, on separate occasions, the father of the same son, Legaidh mac na tri-con.

The second episode from Curoi's career is told in *Fled Bricriu*[13] (Bricriu's Feast). It has him appearing as a giant, who offers to play the Beheading Game with three heroes: Conall Cearnach, Laoghaire, and Cuchulainn himself to establish the championship of Ireland. The game consists of each one of the three being allowed to cut off Curoi's head in return for allowing him to do the same to them. Expecting no possible retaliation, both Laoghaire and Conall Caernach strike their blows, but in each case Curoi replaces his head. Both heroes flee, Cuchulainn alone being prepared to accept the return blow, which is withheld and Cuchulainn pronounced a worthy champion.

As with the related theme of the rape of the Flower Bride, we shall meet this most important incident in one form or another throughout this study. Its most famous appearance is in the Middle English poem *Gawain and the Green Knight*[49] in which Gawain takes the role originally assigned to Cuchulainn, while Curoi's role is played by the monstrous Green Knight, who challenges the knights of Arthur's court to the Beheading Game. We shall be examining the evidence of this text, and others where the motif appears, in Chapter 3. For the moment it is enough to say that it is this test which helps establish Gawain as the Champion of the Goddess, though this has been obscured in the later versions of the story.

For a text in which both the rape of the Flower Bride and the Beheading Game appear side by side, though in confused form, we have to
look only at *The Tragic Death of Cu Roi Mac Daire*.[13]

Blathnat is part of the spoils of the siege of Fir Falge in which Curoi
had fought bravely in disguise. Because no one knew him, he received
none of the spoils, and in anger seized the cows of Tuchna, together
with the three birds which perched in their ears, causing them to give
the milk of 30 cows into a great cauldron, and putting the birds into
his belt, Blathnat under one arm, the cows under the other and the
cauldron on his back, he fled. Cuchulainn gave chase but was overcome by Curoi, who shaved his head and buried him up to his armpits
in mud and anointed him with cow dung. So angry was Cuchulainn
that he followed Curoi and, discovering at last who he was, secretly
planned his death with Blathnat, with whom he was in love. Blathnat
bathed Curoi in a river into which she poured milk to alert her lover,
then she bound Curoi to the bed by his hair and Cuchulainn burst in
and slew him, cutting off his head.

The idea of the hero fighting incognito could come from almost any
one of a hundred Arthurian stories, including several featuring Gawain.
But there are several more important points in this story. Not only is
it, as already remarked, similar to the abduction stories associated with
Guinevere, (and thus with the Flower Bride), but we find Cuchulainn,
who as we have seen is a precursor of Gawain, acting as her rescuer.
There is also the matter of Blathnat being Cuchulainn's lover, which
seems to look forward to the later situation where Lancelot is both
Guinevere's rescuer and her lover. The nature of Curoi himself, as abductor, is very similar to that of both Mardoc *and* the giant churl Bermaltus
in the *Modena version*. Add to this the method of Curoi's death, by
beheading, and we are once again back at the story of the Beheading
Game, though this time all the dice are weighted in favour of Cuchulainn.

More importantly, perhaps, is the clue this story offers to another
aspect of Gawain's original role, in which he undertook various tasks
in order to win the favours of the Goddess. The theme of the abduction of the Flower Bride, of which both Guinevere and Blathnat are
types, will be examined in more detail later (see pp. 86-91). For the present
it is important to recognize that Cuchulainn/Gawain/Curoi act as both
abductor *and* rescuer within the texts examined above.

For the sake of clarity it may now be as well to summarize again the
parallels between Cuchulainn, Gwri and Curoi, and their relationship

to the story of Gawain.

1. All four are in a certain sense sons of the god Lugh or Llwch. Both Cuchulainn and Curoi being sons of Lugh Loinnbheimionach; Gwair (who has been identified with Gwri and Goreu) is the son of Llwch Lleminawc; Gawain is the son of Llew ap Cynfarch (or as he becomes in the later texts Loth or Lot, who in the medieval romance of *Erec* (v.1737) is called Loth 'le Irois', (the Irishman).

2. Cuchulainn, Curoi and Gwri are all associated with horses born at the same hour as themselves.

3. Gwri and Goreu are both called 'Golden Haired'; Cuchulainn has a halo of golden hair.

4. Both Gwri and Cuchulainn are precocious at birth and both are put to fosterage.

5. Both Cuchulainn and Curoi are involved in the Beheading Game which afterwards is a crucial part in Gawain's career;

6. Gawain and Cuchulainn are both involved in abduction/rescue stories, in which the object of their efforts is an aspect of the Flower Bride and hence of the Goddess.

All three characters in one form or another have influenced the name and character of Gawain to a lesser or greater degree. They establish him as a mythic archetype whose father may have been a god and whose task is to become the champion of a Goddess, and who epitomizes the figure of the Hero.

Before we pass on to look at the later career of Gawain, it remains to examine the evidence for his possible place of origin, which will be shown to have been a part of the country where the kind of cross-fertilization between Irish and British story-tellers we would expect to give rise to the kind of overlay in the career of Gawain and the other heroes, could easily have taken place.

GAWAIN OF GALLOWAY: THE BIRTH OF A HERO

In one of the many fugitive poems contained in the *Four Ancient Books of Wales*,[15] a fragment known as 'The Porter at the Gate', an unnamed character is referred to as 'a nephew (of Arthur) who would cause reconciliation'. This can surely be none other than Gawain, as both the references to him in the *Mabinogion* and another early text, the *Ystoria Trystan*,[85] bear witness.

This fragment deals with the flight of Trystan and Esyllt (Isolt) to the wood of Celyddon, and their pursuit by her jealous husband March

ap Meirchion (the King Mark of the later romances), who has claimed
the assistance of Arthur and his warriors rather in the same way that
Culhwch does in his quest for Olwen. However, Trystan has certain
special properties, which were

> that whoever drew blood from him would die, and whoever he drew blood
> from would die despite all the doctors in Christendom . . . (Trans. J. Hill)

Understandably, therefore, neither March nor his borrowed men are
eager to attack Trystan, even though they have the guilty lovers surrounded. Therefore Arthur advises that he send 'singers with verses
of praise to praise him [Trystan] and bring him out of his fury and anger.',
and that they also send 'the chief of peace, that is to say Gwalchmai
ap Gwyar, to talk to him.'[85]

This is done, and the following exchange takes place:

> G: Fierce is the unbounded wave
> When the middle sea doth rave.
> Who art thou, O warrior brave?
>
> T: Fierce are the thunder and the flame,
> Though they be no whit the same.
> In battle Trystan is my name.
>
> G: Trystan I can nowhere see
> Blemish in thy Chivalry.
> Gwalchmai once was friend to thee.
>
> T: If Gwalchmai in the day of blood
> Needed me, for him I would
> Do more than a brother could.
>
> G: Trystan, noble prince of light,
> Sore they buffets. I am hight
> Gwalchmai, Arthur's nephew wight.
>
> (Trans. R.S. Loomis)[10]

Thanks to Gwalchmai's golden tongue Trystan is persuaded to submit
to Arthur's judgement, which is that one man should have Esyllt while
the leaves are on the tree and the other while they are not, and that
the husband should have the choice. March chooses winter, 'because
the nights would be longer at that time', but of course he thereby for-
feits all rights to Esyllt because of the evergreen 'holly, ivy and yew,
which keep their leaves as long as they live.'

This episode owes something to the ancient battle of the lords of summer and winter for the Flower Bride (see Chapter 3) traces of which
are also to be found in the abduction stories of Guinevere and Blathnat. But what is even more interesting is the part played by Gawain,

who is referred to as 'the chief of peace', and the setting of the story
in the forest of Celyddon in Scotland. This northern link points us
towards the probable birthplace of the Gawain legends, to a place also
associated with Trystan where, as already stated, there was opportunity for shared information by both British and Irish story-tellers.

This is Galloway, on the western side of Scotland, and it has consistent associations with Gawain. According to Professor Chadwick[82] in
the ninth century, when the earliest Gawain stories were probably written and told, *Gall-Gaidil* extended over all the islands and coastline
of the Western Highlands. It was here that a well-founded Gaelic-
speaking community existed, to which travellers from Ireland found
welcome.

Here, until the seventeenth century, a Castell Gwalchmai was
recorded, and here, in a significant number of later French texts, Gawain
was said to have his abode. In both the continuations of Chrétien de
Troyes' *Conte del Graal*[12] and the slightly later *Perlesvaus*[23] Gawain's
home is said to be in 'Galvoie', while in the English *Awntyrs of Arthur
at Tarn Wathelin*[21] Gawain is awarded the lands of 'Galeron of Galloway' for his services.

All this may add up to nothing more than a scribal confusion between
the name Gawain, or Gwalchmai, and the place name Galloway, which
appears in Middle English texts under such variant spellings as:
Galeweoie, Galeweie, Galvoyne, and Galvoye. The last is an almost exact
approximation of the Old French *Galvoie*, and clearly suggests that
there was a well-founded tradition of Gawain's association with the area.
In the *Vulgate Merlin Continuation*[60] there is even mention of a
detachment of men from Galloway, fighting for Arthur under the command of one 'Bertelot' — a name significantly similar to Bercilak (the
Green Knight in *Gawain and the Green Knight*) to uphold yet another
link with the area.

Finally, if we turn to William of Malmesbury's *De Gestis Regum
Angelorum* (Deeds of the Kings of the Angles) (1125) we find the following passage:

> At the time (1066-1087) in a province of Wales called Ros [modern
> Pembrokeshire] the tomb of Walwein [Gawain] was found who, by no
> means unworthy of Arthur, was a nephew by his sister. He reigned in that
> part of Britain still called Walweitha [Galloway], a soldier greatly celebrated
> for valour, but driven from the kingdom by the brother and nephew of
> Hengist, of whom I spoke in Book I, he made them [the Saxons] pay
> severely for his exile. (Trans. L.B. Hall)[21]

Whatever theory one accepts finally, there is enough evidence to suggest that Gawain's point of origin may have been the North. (Later

medieval texts place him in Orkney). And since this has long been accepted as the probable home of many of the most prominent figures of the Arthurian cycle (Peredur and Cai are notable among these) we may believe with some justification that Gawain also first saw the light of day there. For the story of his birth, and more importantly his parentage, we must refer to later texts, and to the next stage in the development of Gwalchmai into Gawain.

Chapter 2.

The Rise of Gawain

THE SON OF THE GODDESS

On the night that Aurelius Ambrosius, King of the Britons, lay dying from a poisoned draught administered by a Saxon spy, there appeared in the sky 'a star of marvellous bigness and brightness', from which issued a ray of light ending in a ball of fire in the shape of a dragon. From its mouth issued two further rays, one of which reached beyond the regions of Gaul, and the other, stretching towards the Irish sea, ended in seven lesser rays.

This account, from Book VIII of Geoffrey of Monmouth's celebrated *Historia Regum Britanniae* (History of the Kings of Britain),[19] describes a portent which Merlin is on hand to interpret for the King's brother, Uther:

> Thou shalt be king of the whole of Britain!
> For yon star doth betoken thee, and the fiery
> dragon that is under the star! The ray, moreover,
> that stretcheth forth towards the region of Gaul,
> doth portend that a son shall be born unto thee that
> shall be of surpassing mighty dominion, whose power
> shall extend over all the realms that lie beneath the
> ray; and the other ray signifieth a daughter whose
> sons and grandsons shall hold the kingdom of Britain
> in succession. (Bk VIII, Ch. 15)

The first part of this prophecy clearly relates to Arthur; the second is more puzzling. Even Geoffrey seems uncertain about it, and gives conflicting information about Uther's daughter and grandsons. As we read on, it becomes apparent that he is actually referring to Gawain's family, though the prophecy remains unfulfilled since neither Gawain himself, nor any of his brothers or offspring, actually inherit the crown in any obvious sense. It may be that Geoffrey is referring to a source now lost, but this remains uncertain. Another possibility, which we shall examine later, is that Gawain's relationship to the sovereignty-bestowing Goddess of the Land makes Geoffrey's statement more accurate than he could have supposed.

Layamon, in his *Brut*,[61] which followed Geoffrey but adapted it in various ways, modifies the original prophecy to say that Uther's grandsons shall be great warriors. However, the importance of establishing Gawain's parentage is at once apparent from the moment we plunge into the complex dynastic framework of the Latin Romances and their associated texts, which established the next stage in Gawain's literary career.

Geoffrey of Monmouth is clear in his statement that Gawain (Walganus) is Arthur's nephew — a relationship already well established both in the early Celtic texts and oral tradition. Another important text, *De Ortu Waluuanii Nepotis Arturi*[39] (The Rise of Gawain, Nephew of Arthur) makes it clear, by its very choice of title, that this relationship was seen as important.

To see the reason for this, one need look no further afield than Scotland, which at the time the author was writing (1175-1186) was still ruled by kings who inherited through the female line.

As the historian Ronald Williams remarks in his book *The Lords of the Isles*:

> In the elder days, when the succession passed through the female line, the Sovereignty resided in the person of the queen, who, as high priestess, was also the reincarnation of the Great Earth Mother and chose from among her warriors a man to mate with, lead her warband, and after the cycle of seven years, become the king-sacrifice and die to ensure the fertility of the soil and prosperity of the tribe. (Chatto & Windus, 1984)

The significance of this for our own argument need hardly be stated. Certainly in England, where the Normans had introduced primogeniture, this was looked upon as both outmoded and dangerous — despite the fact that in Europe Henry II had also succeeded through the female line. The whole question of the ancient Pictish custom of matrilinear descent had been discussed by the historian Bede, and this would have almost certainly been known to the author of *De Ortu*.

The story of Gawain's birth and parentage is told in five major texts: the *Historia Regum Brittaniae*, *De Ortu Waluuanii*, *Perlesvaus*,[23] *Les Enfances Gauvain* (of which a new translation will be found at the back of this book), and the *Conte del Graal* of Chrétien de Troyes.[10] To these may be added the *Chronicles* of Wace and Layamon,[61] and the Welsh *Bruts*, which contain significant variations of their source, Geoffrey of Monmouth, and a fragmentary fourteenth-century text known as *The Birth of Arthur*.[4]

Each of these gives a remarkably homogeneous portrait of Gawain's birth and parentage, as well as his subsequent rise to greatness. The

Historia Regum Brittaniae is perhaps the earliest text to chronicle these events. In Book IX, Ch. 9 we read that there were

> ...three brethren born of blood royal. Loth, to whit, and Urian, and Angushel, that had held the principality of those parts before the Saxons had prevailed. Being minded, therefore, to grant unto them... their hereditary rights, he [Uther] restored unto Angushel the kingly power of the Scots, and conferred the sceptre of the people of Moray upon Urian. Howbeit, Loth, who in the days of Aurelius Ambrosius had married Arthur's own sister, who had born unto him Gawain and Modred, he did reinstate in the Dukedom of Lothian... (Trans. S. Evans)

The name of this 'sister' of Arthur is given as Anna, and so it remains in *De Ortu Waluuanii* and the *Bruts* of Wace and Layamon. The sequence of events, as agreed upon by all of these texts, is that Uther and Igerna had a son named Arthur and a daughter named Anna, who was married to Loth (Lot) as a reward for faithful service. They, in turn, had two sons, Gawain and Modred, whom Layamon has Arthur call 'the dearest children to me in all the kingdom'.

This is a far cry from the later, darker version of the story, in which Modred has become Arthur's *son* by his sister Morgause (or Morgain) — though even this may have its foundation in Gawain's own story, as we shall see.

But, is this the correct family tree of Gawain? The *Historia* also mentions another nephew of Arthur, Hoel of Brittany, who fights side by side with Gawain in the Roman wars. The descent of this character is cloudy; however the implication that he is a second son of Anna's, perhaps by a previous husband, is lessened by the fact that he is said later to come to Arthur's aid in the wars of succession, though he could not in fact have been old enough, unless Anna was a daughter of Ambrosius rather than Uther. Nonetheless, the importance of this putative relationship is the way it throws light on the importance of Gawain's family. It makes Gawain himself the grandson of a king (Uther), the son of a king (Loth) and a princess of the royal blood (Anna), and a nephew of Arthur — as well as a possible cousin to the royal house of Brittany — surely a splendid enough pedigree for any hero!

Gawain's genealogy then, according to Geoffrey of Monmouth, is as shown in Fig 1 overleaf.

In *De Ortu Waluuanii* the story is subtly different, and more fully developed.

Uther, having subjugated the kings of neighbouring provinces to his authority, took their sons as hostages. Among these was Loth, nephew

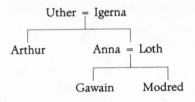

Figure 1: *Gawain's Family Tree according to Geoffrey of Monmouth.*

of King Sichelm of Norway, 'a young man of striking appearance, strong of body and manly of spirit'.[39] He used often to visit Uther, his son Arthur and his daughter Anna, a great beauty, who still lived with her mother in private chambers. Loth and she used often to laugh and joke together, and in time fell in love with each other, at first hiding it from each other but finally declaring it. 'With both their prayers answered, they yielded to their desires, and soon Anna conceived a child. When she was near term carrying the child, she feigned illness and retired to a private bed chamber with only her lady-in-waiting knowing why.'[39] When the child was born — a strong son — its mother gave it into the care of some wealthy merchants with whom she had previously arranged matters. They were to take the child to their own land and bring him up. As well as a large sum of money, Anna also entrusted to these men letters establishing beyond doubt that her son, whom she named Gawain, was the child of the nephew of Norway's king and the sister of Arthur.

Anna is here Arthur's full sister, which she remains throughout the texts under discussion. She gives as reason for sending her child away and hiding the fact of his birth, 'fear of the king' — that is, Uther. Loth is a high-born youth, who is a hostage for the good behaviour of his father — though he is, significantly as we shall see — the nephew of the King of Norway. It is this relationship, along with Anna's to Arthur, which is considered important.

　　Further details of this story can be gleaned from the thirteenth-century French *Les Enfances Gauvain* and the fourteenth-century Welsh *Birth of Arthur*, both of which retain traces of earlier material. The first of these adds significantly to the outline of the story told in *De Ortu Waluuanii*.

Arthur's sister is called Morcades, and when she becomes pregnant, apparently by Loth, she goes not to Uther but to her brother, Arthur (who may or may not be party to the plot) and requests that she be allowed to retire for a time to the castle of Belrepair, accompanied only by her handmaid, her squire — who is in fact Loth — and a small household, the porter being given instructions to admit only such persons known to her, or Arthur himself. Arthur assented to this and seven months later Morcades was delivered of a son, Loth assisting at the birth. Had circumstances been other she would have been happy to raise the boy herself, but decided that she could not lose the standing of a virgin.

Nearby lived a wise knight named Gauvain le Brun (Gawain the Brown), who often sent game from his hunting to Morcades, whose handmaid he longed to marry. Loth and Morcades decided to be rid of the child and requested the handmaid to take the boy away secretly. However, she met with Gawain the Brown on her way and, knowing it could not be hers, he asked to be allowed to care for it, since he was without wife, child or heir. Moved by this, the handmaid promised to marry the knight as soon as the child was baptized. Gauvain gave the boy his own name and took especial care of the rich embroidered shawl in which he had been wrapped. When the child was weaned the knight prepared to follow Morcades' instructions, which were to put the child into a barrel and set him adrift in the sea (a barbarous-seeming custom which was nonetheless much practised in the Middle Ages as a way of ridding oneself of unwanted byblows). In Gawain's case, as we shall see, his fate was to be different.

Here we have a far more fleshed-out version of the story, in which Arthur plays a significant role. Indeed, the text is oblique in its language to the extent that it is possible to believe that the author was implying that Arthur himself may have been Gawain's father (despite a later statement to the effect that it was Loth who had made her pregnant) — a conjecture which, in the light of the later history of Arthur's incestuous union with his sister Morgause (a later version of the name Morcades) is not as improbable as it may seem. It is also worth noting that in the case of Modred, his fate is similarly to be cast adrift upon the sea, and that like his brother Gawain he is fated not to drown but to become a significant figure in the later story of his uncle/father.

Further evidence for this line of reasoning, as well as for the significant change in the name and history of Gawain's mother, is to be seen in the fact that in the intervening years between the two versions of the story, Anna has become Morcades. Anna persists from Geoffrey, while the oral tradition goes its own way. The name Anna can be shown to derive from the more familiar Morgain or Morgause, who are sometimes known as queens of the Orcades or Orkneys, part of Loth's kingdom, and who, in later texts, become half-sisters of Arthur — Morgause continuing to be known as Gawain's mother, as well as the mother of

Gareth, Gaheries and Agravain, and of Modred by her half-brother.

Robert Graves, in *The White Goddess*, his classic study of mythopoic themes, has this to say about Anna:

> Anna probably means 'queen', or 'Goddess-mother'; Sappho uses *Ana* for *Anassa* (queen). She appears in Irish mythology as the Danaan goddess Ana or Anan, who had two different characters. The first was the beneficent Ana, a title of the Goddess Danu... (glossed as 'Good Mother')... The malificent Ana was the leading person of the Fate Trinity, Ana, Badb, and Macha, together known as the Morrigan, or Great Queen. Badb, 'boiling', evidently refers to the Cauldron, and Macha is glossed... as meaning 'raven'... indeed if one needs a single, simple, inclusive name for the Great Goddess, Anna is the best choice. (The White Goddess. Faber & Faber, 1948.)

All of this merely strengthens the identification of Morgain with Anna and Morcades, and shows that we are here dealing with a figure of considerable importance whose role we shall see gradually unfolding throughout our study of Gawain.

The *Conte del Graal* of Chrétien de Troyes,[10] in which Gawain figures as a major character, names his mother as Morcades, while in *Perlesvaus*, though she is unnamed, the story is essentially the same as in both *De Ortu Waluuanii* and *Les Enfances Gauvain*.

Arthur and Gawain come to a once magnificent castle, now in ruins and with only an old priest and his clerk living there. They stay there and next morning hear mass in a splendid chapel. There are pictures on the walls, painted in gold and blue, and Arthur and Gawain are delighted by them. The priest notices their attention and when mass is over tells them about the nobleman, Galobrun, who had them made, and who 'dearly loved the lady and her son in whose honour they were made.' The story told by the picture is of Gawain himself, who was born there. His mother had fallen in love with King Lot, and when her child was born she did her best to conceal the fact. She placed him in a 'beautiful vessel' and begged the lord of the castle to take him away and leave him to die. But the good man would not do so evil a deed. Instead he hid sealed letters inside the child's clothing, declaring him of royal descent from both father and mother, put a great sum of money in the vessel with him and, wrapping him in a rich cloak, took him to a distant land. There he gave him to a childless couple and rode away.

The couple cared for Gawain until he was grown to manhood, at which point they took him to Rome and showed the Pope the letter written by Galobrun. The Pope saw that he was a king's son and had him cared for and given to believe he was of the Pope's own family. In time he rose so high that he was chosen Emperor, but declined because he did not know the truth about his birth. At length he left Rome and is said to be one of the best knights in the world, and no one dares take the ruined castle, which the nobleman left to his foster-son and which the old priest was to guard until his return.

Gawain, realizing that this is his own story, is cast down to learn of his birth, but Arthur points out that the same could be said of himself, and the priest points out that Loth had married his mother, thus making him legitimate.[23]

This story is firmly in the mould of the majority of the texts at which we have been looking. The name of the knight who saves Gawain, Galobrun, is clearly a corruption of Gauvain le Brun who performs the same function in the *Enfances*.

Turning next to the fourteenth-century Welsh text *The Birth of Arthur*[4] we find the following:

> ...he [Uther] caused a feast to be prepared for the nobles of the island, and at the feast he married Eigyr [Igraine] and made peace with the kinsmen of Gwrleis [Gorlois] and all his allies. Gwrleis had two daughters by Eigyr, Gwyar and Dioneta. Gwyar was a widow, and after the death of her husband Ymer Llydaw she dwelt at her father's court with her son Hywel. [Hoel?] Now Uther caused Lleu, the son of Cynvarch [Lot] to marry her, and they had children, two sons Gwalchmai and Medrawd [Modred], and three daughters, Gracia, Graeria, and Dioneta. The Duke's other daughter, Uther caused to be sent to the Isle of Avallach, and of all her age she was most skilled in the Seven Arts. (Trans. J.H. Davies)

There are several interesting hints within this text, which although it bears the unmistakable marks of influence from later versions, retains something of the earlier traditions concerning Gawain. Here, his mother is called Gwyar, who is the daughter of Gorlois rather than of Uther, though the marriage is arranged as in Geoffrey of Monmouth; and Modred is still Gawain's full brother. The name Gwyar, according to Professor Rhys, was a word used in early Welsh poetry to signify the shedding of blood. This, he suggests, implies that Gawain's mother may have once been recognized as a kind of battle-fury or war goddess. The references to Gorlois' other daughter, here named Dioneta, who was sent to 'the Isle of Avallach' where she became skilled in the Seven Arts, seems to predict Malory's statement, in *Le Morte d'Arthur*, that Morgan le Fay, also Gorlois' daughter, was 'put to school in a nunnery, and there she learned so much that she was a great clerk of necromancy' (Bk I, Ch. 3).

Morgan (or Morgain as she is more properly called) led a chequered career. Her origins have been traced back to the goddess Matrona, worshipped from northern Italy to the Rhine. She is called 'Morgane the Goddess' in *Gawain and the Green Knight*, and receives the same epithet in a twelfth-century text by Giraldus Cambrensis, the *Speculum Ecclesia*[49] and again in the thirteenth-century *Vulgate Lancelot*.[60] Both Professor Loomis and Robert Graves have successfully established her as deriving from the Celtic war goddess Morrigan (Great Queen) who, as we saw earlier, was responsible for the death of Cuchulainn after he had refused to become her lover. Dr Helaine Newstead[125] in an illuminating article, has shown that she is related both to Modron and to the Irish goddess Macha. Modron was, of course, the mother of Mabon, who is himself an aspect of the putative Gawain character Gwri/Goreu/Gwair.

The fact that Uther and Igraine, as well as Gorlois, have a daughter named Dioneta is interesting. It may simply be a slip of the copyist's pen, or it may be a memory of an earlier tale in which it was the daughter of *Uther* who was sent to the Isle of Avallach, and became skilled in the magical arts. Or it may suggest the influence of another text *The Vita Merlini* of Geoffrey of Monmouth,[29] in which we hear of nine sisters ruling over 'The Island of Apples' (*Insula Pomorum*). They are named as Morgen (Morgan), Mononoe, Mazoe, Gliten, Glitonea, Gliton, Tryonoe, and Thiten — a list which sounds not unlike that of Loth and Gwyar's children.

As it is, the very mention of Avallach is itself important, since this is generally understood to be a variation of the name for the very same Island of Apples referred to by Geoffrey — Avalon, the mystic isle where lived the Lady of the Lake, or Morgan le Fay herself.

Avallach, as a personal name, refers to a shadowy figure who seems to have been a king of the Otherworld, and also, in certain ancient genealogies, the father of Eigyr, thus making Gawain himself of otherworldly descent if we accept the evidence of *The Birth of Arthur*. We may remember also that the earliest (or at least, the most primitive) of the texts we have been examining, *Culhwch and Olwen*, gives a similar genealogy, in which Eigr (Igraine) is the daughter of Amlaut Wledig (Hamlet?) and Gwen the daughter of Cunedda, the great early king of Wales. If Amlaut and Avallach are one and the same, or even aspects of the same archetype, as textual evidence would seem to suggest, we have a reasonable alternative genealogy for Gawain, which in all probability predates Geoffrey of Monmouth (see Fig 2).

In each of the texts discussed above, the emphasis is upon Gawain's descent from his mother. Later on, this changed as the Continental authors, having little or no understanding of matrilinear descent, altered the emphasis to Gawain's relationship with his uncle, Arthur. The pattern seems increasingly to be that Arthur's family is continually enlarged

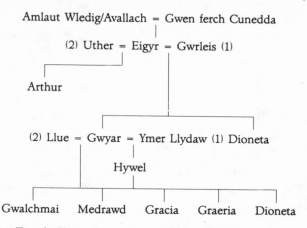

Figure 2: *The Family Tree of Gawain according to* The Birth of Arthur *and* Culhwch and Olwen.

by the addition of further sisters, whose sole function is to bear heroes who feature in the later romances. Originally, in the Celtic stories, this would have reflected the importance of the sister-son relationship; the change is all part of the subtle alteration in Gawain's original status and his subsequent fortunes.

The evidence points, then, to Gawain's original mother having been of otherworldly stock, and the weight of evidence from the foregoing texts point to Gwyar being confused, at some point, with either Morgain, Morgause or Morcades, full sisters of Arthur rather than the half-sisters they become in later texts. We may remember that the name Gwyar itself probably referred to a battle goddess (see Fig 3 overleaf).

This brings us full circle to Morgain as an aspect of the Morrigan. Before we can understand fully how this relationship came about, and know more of the nature of the role these otherworldly women played in the shaping of Gawain's destiny, we must look further at their relationship to certain other characters in the story.

꙳

THE BESIEGED LADY AND THE KINGLY CHAMPION

Towards the end of *De Ortu Waluuanii*, shortly before Gawain's real

Text	Mother	Father	Putative Father Guardian	Siblings Brothers
Historia	Anna	Lot	The Pope	Modred
Wace	Anna	Lot	The Pope	Modred
Layamon	Anna	Lot	Bishop of Llyndain	Modred
De Ortu	Anna	Lot	Viamundus/The Emperor	None
Perlesvaus	Unnamed	Lot	Galbrun/The Pope	None
L'Enfances Du Gauvain	Morcades	Lot	Gauvain le Brun/ The Pope	None
Chrétien	Morcades	Lot	None	Agravaine Gaharret Guerrethet
First Continuation	Morcades	Lot	None	None
Birth of Arthur	Gwyar	Lleu	None	Medrawt
Old Welsh Trystan	Gwyar	Lleu	None	None
Chulhwch and Olwen	Gwyar	Lleu	None	None
Of Arthur and Merlin	Belisent	Lot	None	Agrevain Gaheriet Modred
Morte d'Arthur	Morgause	Lot	None	Agravain Gaheries Gareth Mordred

Figure 3: *The Family of Gawain*.

identity is revealed, there appears the following episode:

Arthur learns that a lady of whom he is particularly fond is besieged in *Castellum Puellarum* by a certain pagan king, who has repeatedly defeated Arthur in battle. Nevertheless, the King at once sets out to rescue the lady, only to be put to flight by his enemy. Gawain, observing this from a hilltop, meets Arthur and his army in retreat, and castigates the King for fleeing. Gawain then rides alone against the enemy, strikes down the pagan king and carries the lady to safety. He then singlehandedly routs the rest of the enemy force, and cutting off the head of the pagan king, returns to Arthur's court with the head on his spear and the lady at his side.[39]

The central theme of this episode, that of the Besieged Lady, has been traced by Helaine Newstead[125] through a number of texts in which Gawain, or an aspect of Gawain, acts as rescuer, and in which the various identities of the lady requiring rescue, and the name of either the castle or the country in which she is imprisoned, bear witness to her identification with a goddess or otherworldly queen whose champion Gawain became. It also relates closely to the stealing and rescue of the Flower Bride, of which we saw a version in the earliest adventure attributed to Gawain in the Modena archivault carvings (see Fig 4).

Text	Besieged Lady	Rescuer	Name of Castle or Country
De Ortu	Unnamed	Gawain	Castellum Puellarum
L'Enfances Gauvain	Morcades	Gawain	Belrepair
Of Arthur and Merlin	Belisent	Gawain	Belrepair
English Syr Percevale	Lufamore	Perceval	Maydenlande
Lanzalet	Queen of Meidenlant	Gawain	Meidenland
Sick Bed of Cuchulainn	Fand	Cuchulainn	The Otherworld
Owein	Unnamed	Owein	Unnamed
Conte del Graal	Igraine/Anna/ Clarisant	Gawain	Castellum Puellarum
Yvain	Lady of Nrison (Morgur le Sage)	Gawain	Unnamed
Diu Crône	Queen of Meidenlant	Gawain	Meide lant
Erec	Morgain le Fay	Guingamore	Avalon

Figure 4: *The Besieged Lady and Her Rescuers.*

The story as related in *De Ortu Waluuanii*, is itself almost certainly of primitive origin, predating Geoffrey of Monmouth and deriving from a source, no longer extant, in which the relationship between the Besieged Lady and her rescuer was other than it appears in the later versions.

Initially, it is interesting to note that the name of the castle in which the lady is held prisoner is given as *Castellum Puellarum* (The Castle of Maidens), which is the ancient name for Edinburgh (and in fact appears as such in a document of c.1142). Edinburgh was, of course, the capital of Lothian, over which both Loth and Anna ruled. This made Anna the Lady of Lothian, who in other stories is named Morgain or Morcades as we have seen. It would appear, then, that the confusion between these two characters originates here and that the theme of the Besieged Lady, which was originally attached to Morgain, was transferred to Anna (or to Gawain's mother, by whatever name she was known at the time) at some point *before* Morgain/Morgause was herself identified as the mother of Gawain and his brothers.

Professor Loomis, in an article published in *The Proceedings of the Society of Antiquaries of Scotland* (vol. LXXXIX, 1955-6) quotes further evidence for the identification of Morgain with the mistress of *Castellum Puellarum*.

It was, he writes, the author of the thirteenth-century Breton Lai of *Doon* (which itself tells a story not unlike that of Gawain's birth and *Enfances*) who first identified the 'Chateau des Pucelles' with 'Daneborc', an earlier name for Edinburgh. Loomis continues:

> So we know that the Castle of Maidens was Edinburgh. We know that the mistress of the Castle of Maidens was Morgain la Fée. We know that, though she had various lovers and at least two husbands, one of them was King Loth of Lothian. As Queen of Lothian, Morcades or Morgain could have dwelt in several castles with her attendant maidens, but none would have suited her so well as the great fortress of Edinburgh. Once the tradition was established that Morgain la Fée was wooed and won by Loth, the eponymous king of Lothian, it was a matter of plain logic that Edinburgh was the Castle of Maidens.

Later in the same article Loomis points out that the heroine of *Doon*, the wife of Loth, and the lustful temptress of a late Scottish ballad known as the *Queen of Scotland* (*The English and Scottish Popular Ballads*, edited by F.J. Child, Dover Publications, 1965, vol v. p176ff) bear a marked resemblance. 'Can it be', he asks, 'that these were all at one time the same, were all avatars, as it were, of Morgain la Fée?' As we have seen, the only answer to this is a simple yes.

In Chrétien's *Conte del Graal* Gawain again visits a castle named *Castellum Puellarum*, where he finds not only Igraine but Morcades also, his mother and grandmother, both of whom he rescues. Later in the same text Perceval, the actual hero of the poem, rescues a maiden named Blanchfleur from a castle named Belrepair, which in both the *Enfances de Gauvain* and the later English text *Of Arthour and Merlin*, is given to the castle in which Morcades retires to give birth to her son.

This is interesting because the personal name Blanchfleur has been proved to derive from an earlier form, Fleur, who was once a goddess. And since Morgain herself has been derived, by both Professor Loomis and Dr Newstead, from the Irish goddesses Macha and Morrigan, as well as from the Welsh Modron, we may safely assume that the Besieged Lady herself was once recognized as such. This relates back to the theme of the Flower Bride, which we first observed carved on the archivault at Modena Cathedral. This, as will be seen shortly, is an important clue to the actual identity of the Besieged Lady.

We may also assume that her rescuer, as he has become in later stories, was once more than this (in fact her lover *and* her champion). Evidence which supports this belief is to be found in the anonymous English redaction of Chrétien's poem known as *Syr Percevale of Gales*,[52] the *Diu Crône* of Heinrich von dem Tulin[22] and the *Lanzelet* of Ulrich von Zatzikhoven.[58]

In *Syr Percevale* the hero encounters Lufamore, Queen of Maydenlande, who is besieged by a certain 'Sowdane' (a word generally understood to mean a pagan lord). Percevale routs the besieging army exactly as does Gawain in *De Ortu Waluuanii* and is rewarded by marriage to the lady, with whom he stays for a year before setting out to search for his mother. As we shall have cause to see, this remaining for a year with the lady is a significant motif in Gawain's relationship with the Otherworld queen or Goddess; the fact that is is here applied to Percevale does not invalidate the idea since it can be shown that these two figures frequently exchanged roles and adventures throughout the tales in which they feature.

In the Middle High German *Diu Crône* Gawain encounters the Queen of *Meide Lant*, who dwells on a floating island. She gives him a vessel containing a mysterious substance which grants eternal life — a further reference to the hero's one-time status as Grail knight (see Chapters 5-7) — along with an offer of love. Gawain prudently declined the latter, while accepting the gift of the magic vessel.

Although the name of the Lady in this text is different (she is called Levenet) and although she is not in fact besieged, she is nonetheless clearly an aspect of the primal figure whom we recognize in Morgain and her siblings. Confirmation of this is to be found in another German text, *Lanzelet*. In this, the hero (whom as we have seen was Gawain's successor and the inheritor of various aspects once attributed to him) is brought up by the Queen of Meidenland, who has a natural son named Mabuz (Mabon). Since, in Welsh tradition, Mabon is the son of Modron, daughter of Avallach or Avallo, and the mother of the hero Owein by Urien; and since both Morgain and Gwyar — Gawain's mother in Celtic tradition — are said to be daughters of Avallach and mothers of either Owein by Urien or Gawain by Loth, we are once again brought back to the central fact that Morgain at some point became confused with Gawain's original mother (then named either Anna or Gwyar) and that along with this identification she brought the attributes and characteristics of several Goddesses (see Fig 3).

Confirmation of this, together with further evidence of the original relationship of Morgain and Gawain, is to be found in several other texts, which, though only tangentally related to the central Gawain complex, nevertheless throw light on this and other questions.

In the *Mabinogion* text *Owein ap Urien*[31] as well as in its French concomitant *Yvain, ou le Chevalier au Lion* (Yvain, or the Knight of the Lion) by Chrétien de Troyes[8] we find an episode in which the hero has been driven mad and is discovered running naked in the woods by the Lady of Noroison (in *Owein* specifically the location is *by the margin of a lake*) who restores his sanity with an ointment which in *Owein* is said to be of her own making, but in *Yvain* she had from 'Morgue le Sage', and which is clearly similar to the mysterious life-preserving substance offered to Percevale by the Queen of Maydenlande on her floating island.

If we turn to the cycle of stores concerning the Irish hero Cuchulainn, whom we saw in Chapter 1 shares many of the attributes and adventures of Gawain, we find a text known as *The Sick Bed of Cuchulainn*[13] in which the story is substantially the same as the episode in *Owein* and *Yvain*, but with certain significant variations:

Failing to capture two magical birds which settle on the waters of a lake, Cuchulainn falls asleep and in his dreams sees two otherworldly women who laughingly beat him with twigs. When he wakes he has lost the power of speech and is in a trance-like condition. This continues for a year, at which point a man appears by Cuchulainn's bedside and offers to restore him to health if he will visit Fand, an otherworldly woman who has seen the hero and fallen in love with him. Cuchulainn recovers the power of speech and visits the place where he first had the dream. There he encounters Liban, Fand's sister, who brings him a message of love and word that Fand's husband, Manannan mac Lir, has deserted her, leaving her at the mercy of her enemies. At first Cuchulainn does not wish to go into the otherworld and sends his charioteer Loeg instead. Finally however, he does go and defeats

Fand's enemies single handed. He remains with her for a month, then returns to Ireland having arranged a meeting with Fand. Later, Cuchulainn's wife Emer hears of this and plans to kill her rival. Fand prepares to give him up rather than cause further pain and Manannan, hearing of this, takes her away with him. Cuchulainn, grief-stricken, goes mad for a time, until he is caught by druids and given a drink of forgetting. Emer is also made to forget the whole episode and Manannan shakes his cloak between the two lovers so that they may never meet again.[13]

Here, then, just as Gawain in the other Besieged Lady texts discussed above, Cuchulainn enters the otherworld to see Fand and there defeats her enemies. Further, Cuchulainn's sickness is described in similar terms to that of Owein or Yvain. Similarly, he is restored to health by a servant of Fand's, just as Owein/Yvain is healed by the Lady of Noroisand or *her* servant. Fand herself is associated (through her husband Manannan who is a god of the sea) with water, as are both the Morrigan and Macha, the earlier archetypes of Morgain, who is also frequently associated with a lake or an island upon a lake.

A further implication of the *Sick Bed of Cuchulainn* is that the hero goes mad after being separated, or sent away from, or having refused the love of an otherworldly woman, Goddess or fée. In much the same way Lancelot, in the later stories, goes mad after being rejected by Guinevere — which, if we are correct in supposing that Gawain once fulfilled the role of Guinevere's lover, would be fully in keeping with the story. This also points to Gawain having, at some point in his career, abandoned for a short time his devotion to the otherworldly queen. This is discussed more fully in Chapter 3.

To summarize the foregoing argument we may now say that the theme of the Besieged Lady of *Castellarum Puellarum*, as identified by Dr Newstead, is at various times attributed to Gawain's mother, either as Anna (the Lady of Lothian), or as Morgain le Fee, both of whom, as we have seen, were identified as sisters of Arthur, and that, in each case, Gawain is the rescuer.

Morgain, under her various guises as the Morrigan, Macha, or Modron, is associated with water, has a mortal lover to whom she gives a divine vessel (or in some instances supernaturally fast — otherworldly — horses), and is the provider of an ointment which, either directly or indirectly, restores the lover she has rejected (or who has rejected her) and who has consequently run mad, to sanity.

In *The Sick Bed of Cuchulainn* this same story is told, in which the elements of the Besieged Lady, her otherworldly love, and the healing ointment are combined, Cuchulainn himself is an archetype of Gawain.

From the foregoing we may therefore propose the following recon-struction:

A hero (later identified as Gawain) rescues, or visits, a Goddess, whose love he wins. He then leaves, or is sent away by her, which causes him to go mad and to wander in the wilderness until he is found, either by the Goddess herself or by her agent, by whom is is healed. This leads to further adventures or encounters which are related in other stories.

Throughout the many textual variations which followed, the main players of this story underwent a series of changes and became con-fused with other, similar characters from associated texts and stories. Thus the original, perhaps unnamed Goddess, as is the way with all such deities, became fragmented into several disparate personalities, including, among others, Morgain la Fée; while the original hero, also giving his attributes to several later and lesser figures, including Cuchulainn, Owein/Yvain, and Perceval, became, in the shape of Gawain, the *son* of the Goddess whose lover he had originally been.

This theme, as we shall see, is by no means limited to this particular cluster of stories. It is, indeed, a primary strand in a larger pattern in which Morgain, as mother, lover and tester, will feature again and again, as Gawain, metamorphosing from son to lover to champion, follows his destiny.

⟦ornament⟧

FROM FAIR UNKNOWN TO CHAMPION OF ROME

In the late medieval text of the *Brut Tysilio*,[112] which like the chron-icles of Wace and Layamon derives ultimately from Geoffrey of Mon-mouth's *Historia Regum Brittaniae*, we find a startling statement. The passage reads: 'And Arthur gave the earldom of Lindsey to Llew ap Cynfarch, since he was his brother-in-law, and to Gwyar the mother of Gwalchmai the Emperor.'[112]

Is there anything to support this astonishing claim? We know of at least one already, the *Perlesvaus* in which Gawain does indeed rise to a position where he is offered the imperial diadem. And, although this seems a very long way from the hero of Arthur's warband, Gwalchmai the Golden Tongued, who never failed to return successfully from any quest he undertook, there is a consistent tradition which does indeed associate Gawain with not only Rome but with no lesser figure than the Supreme Pontiff himself — a strange companion for one whose roots were certainly not Christian. However, the tradition exists and cannot be ignored. We must look more closely at it if we are to understand its part in Gawain's career.

Scholarship is divided as to whether Geoffrey of Monmouth or the author of *De Ortu Waluuanii* was the first among the medieval writers to tell of the birth and deeds of the youthful hero. It seems likely however, on internal evidence, that Geoffrey may have drawn upon the *De Ortu* when he was writing his own book — or that he at any rate knew of, or shared, a common source. What that source was we may hazard a guess, but first let us continue the narrative of Gawain's early life, as told in the *De Ortu* from the point at which we broke off (see p42).

The merchants to whom Anna had entrusted her child came to land not far from the city of Narbonne, and leaving the ship and the baby in charge of a cabin boy hurried into the city to enjoy themselves. A fisherman named Viamundus (Way of the World?) happened to be passing and on the spur of the moment investigated the empty ship. Seeing the child, wrapped in rich clothing, and the many goods belonging to the merchants, the fisherman helped himself to both. They, returning, were devastated but despite a search found nothing. Viamundus meanwhile carried the child home to his wife and the couple, being childless, decided to bring him up as their own. After many years Viamundus finally thought it safe to begin making use of the riches he had stolen. The whole family therefore moved to Rome where they set up house in some splendour. There they soon came to the attention of the newly crowned Emperor, to whom Viamundus represented himself as a nobleman from Gaul. He soon rose high in Imperial favour, but when his adopted son was still only 12 years old Viamundus fell gravely ill, and anticipating his death sent for the Emperor and Pope Sulplicius to grant him one last interview. To them he finally confessed all, and produced the papers which proved that the boy was in fact nephew to King Arthur. The adopted son, who was still called Boy-Without-A-Name, as thus entrusted to the Emperor's care.

With the death of his foster-father, and still in ignorance of his true identity, the youth rose swiftly to a place of honour and trust in the Emperor's household. After he displayed great courage in the annual games he requested and was granted the position of Champion to the Emperor. The youth, now called 'The Knight of the Surcoat', achieved many adventures, including one in which he led a secret raid upon an island ruled over by a pirate king named Milocrates. Penetrating this villain's fortress the youth met a captive Queen who fell in love with

him on sight and awarded him magical weaponry. Gawain later rescued her, killing the pirate king in single combat. After this, and many
more adventures, he crossed the Alps to Gaul and then to Britain, carrying letters to King Arthur from the Emperor. These included a full
account of the youth's true parentage, which delighted Arthur and
caused him to summon Anna and Loth (now King of Norway) to confirm the truth of the matter.

The youth was to have several more adventures before his identity
was at last revealed, at which time all men hailed him as 'Gawain,
nephew of Arthur.'[39]

Both Mildred Leake Day (the work's editor) and Roger Sherman Loomis
have pointed out the similarities between the episode of Gawain's adventures with the pirates and those of the later *Gawain and the Green
Knight*. Both see the pirate king, Milocrates, as a kind of Curoi figure,
as is Bercilak; while the queen, who awards Gawain with magical
armour and weapons, has, like Lady Bercilak, been manoeuvred by
others into a position where she is bound to offer amorous advances
to the hero. Just as in *Gawain and the Green Knight*, Gawain courteously avoids these, attending instead to the matter of the coming battle
rather than the lady's sighs! Loomis notes also[105] that the whole episode is very like that of Curoi's abduction of Blathnat, which we have
already seen to be part of the important theme of the stealing of the
Flower Bride. *De Ortu* thus offers valuable evidence for an understanding of Gawain's true role in the matter of the Besieged Lady.

This part of the text, though differing in some respects from the rest,
is connected to a group of works which deal with the theme of the Fair
Unknown. These include the French *Le Bel Inconnu* of Renaude de
Beajeau,[3] the English *Libeus Desconus* attributed to Thomas of Ches-
tre,[28] the German *Wigalois* of Wirnt von Grafenberg[62] and the Italian
Carduino.[6] Each of these, with certain variations, tells the same story
— from which we may judge the universality of the theme. The following summary, which derives in part from all of these, deals only with
the main themes of what is often a prolix story.

Arthur is holding court at Caerleon when a young knight appears and
craves a boon. He will not give a name, so Arthur calls him *Li Biaus
Desconeus* (the Beautiful Unknown). A maiden now appears who asks
for a knight to rescue her lady. The hero claims the right to pursue
this quest and sets out. He overcomes many knights on the way but
finally arrives at the Castle of the Isle d'Or (The Golden Isle) whose
mistress La Pucele aux Blanches Mains (Girl with White Hands) is a
great enchantress. The castle is glorious but has an avenue leading to

it which is decorated with the heads of 143 knights who had failed the tests which await within. However the hero overcomes the resident knight Malgiers li Gris and the whole court is overjoyed with his coming. The lady of the castle offers the hero her love but he declares that he must finish his original quest. He arrives next at the Waste City and encounters ghostly figures whom he overcomes. He then submits to the test of the *fier baiser* (The Bold Kiss) from a dreadful serpent and a voice tells him that he is Guinglain, Gawain's son by a fairy woman. He falls asleep and on awakening finds a lovely woman, Blonde Esmerée, at his side. She tells him he has freed her from enchantment through braving the kiss and that she had been enchanted by the magician Mabon. She offers marriage to Guinglain who agrees, but his thoughts are still with the lady of the Isle d'Or, and on the way back to Arthur's court he manages to slip away. The lady meets him and takes him to her bed, but not before he has undergone several frightening tests, including entering her room only to find himself apparently walking along a narrow plank over a deep drop, or seeing the roof falling upon him. Both times these prove to be dreams, and at last the lady gives him her favours. He remains with her for a time until he hears of a great tournament at the Castle of Maidens, and though at first the lady of Isle d'Or resists, in the end she knows that to prevent his going is useless and he awakes one morning in the middle of a wood, alone. Journeying to the Castle of Maidens he vanquishes all-comers and is reunited with Blonde Esmerée whom he now marries amid general rejoicing.[137]

The importance of this story to our argument will at once be apparent. In virtually all the Fair Unknown romances the hero is connected in some way with Gawain, either by blood or through like roles. In each case, among his many adventures, he meets or rescues a woman who turns out to be of otherworldly origin. In order to win her he undertakes a series of dreadful ordeals, including battles with demons, the terrible kiss of the serpent, and the evil dreams inflicted upon him by the lady of the Isle d'Or.

There is little doubt that the putative heroines of the romance, Blonde Esmerée and La Pucele aux Blanches Mains, are aspects of the same otherworldly woman, and that the latter appears to the Fair Unknown in the form of the serpent in order to test him further. (It will be seen, in Chapters 3 and 4, that this theme of test and trial by an otherworldly mistress is central to Gawain's story.)

Finally we are once again confronted by the theme of the Besieged Lady and are thus not surprised to find that the great tournament which draws the hero back to this world is held at the Castle of Maidens.

Indeed, this whole story, with all its complexities, is crucial to our reassessment of Gawain, for it will be seen that in this, as in other texts yet to be discussed, he retains the same relationship towards the goddess of his choice — that of son, lover and champion.

It remains for us, in the present chapter, to show by what route Gawain moved from this position to one where he is offered either the throne of empire, or the papal crown.

We saw in Chapter 1 how Gawain derives to some degree from the Celtic hero-figure Gwri Gwallt Euryn. An episode in the *Perlesvaus*, of which the hero is actually Perceval, offers further evidence for this identification and points to a possible origin for the connection of Gawain with the history of Pope Gregory. The episode may be summarized as follows.

Perceval finds himself at an island where dwells a poverty-stricken widow (who turns out to be his aunt) and her two daughters. Perceval learns that her son, Galobrun, son of Galobrutus, has been imprisoned by Gohas del Chastiel de la Baleine (Belinus?). Perceval sets out to rescue him, and coming to another island finds there a cave at the top of the cliffs 'round and narrow and secure like as it were a little house'. Inside is Galobrun, chained at neck and feet to a ring in the rock. He has been there for a long time, kept alive only by the ministrations of the Daughter of the Wounded Knight, and can only be released with a certain key kept by Gohas himself. Perceval departs, fights and kills a dragon who had swallowed the key, rescues the Daughter of the Wounded Knight, who is besieged by Gohas, and forces the evil king to return with him to the island and set Galobrun free. Gohas is then himself chained in turn and left to die as he had wished Galobrun to die. Perceval and the rescued king return to the first island and all the people swear allegiance to him.[23]

There are a number of key points to interest us here. In the first place the name of the imprisoned king, Galobrun, (and of his father, Galobrutus) can, as Professor Loomis has shown,[104] be derived from the name of Gwri Gwallt Euryn who was himself, as we have seen, also chained up on a distant island. There is also a striking similarity between the names of Galobrun and Gawain le Brun in the *Enfances Gauvain*. To this we may add also the Besieged Lady theme, discussed above, which is here represented by Perceval's release of the Daughter of the Wounded Knight, who has cared for Galobrun during his own captivity. Perceval is also Galobrun's cousin.

The similarities between the above story and the apocryphal history of the historic Pope Gregory (c.540-604) are so marked as to be clearly connected, though opinions differ as to which influenced the other.

In the *Gesta Romanorum*[137] we find 'The Tale of the Wonderful Dispensations of Providence and the Rise of Pope Gregory' which tells the following story:

The Emperor Marcus has a son and a daughter, who after his death rule jointly, 'sitting in the same chair' and sharing the same room at night. Despite the girl's pleas the boy violates her and she becomes pregnant. Horrified by this she confesses her sin to an old knight who advises the Emperor to go on crusade at once while he sees to the needs of the Empress. Only the knight's wife and he know the secret.

When he is born the child is placed in a cask and cast into the sea. Soon after news comes of the Emperor's death in battle, and the Duke of Burgundy at once seeks the hand of the Empress, who refuses him and flees to a strong city and shuts herself up.

Meanwhile the child, having been washed ashore, is cared for by some monks and baptized with the name Gregory (Gregorious). One day while playing with some other children, a quarrel breaks out and a boy accuses Gregory of his doubtful birth. Disturbed by this Gregory sets forth from his home and in his wandering comes to a city where his mother (unknowingly) is besieged. He single-handedly defeats her enemies and marries her. Later his true identity is discovered and the double sin disclosed.

Gregory, discovering that he is the child of incest and the unwitting partner of incest, adopts pilgrim's garb and requests a fisherman to take him to a huge rock in the middle of the sea and there to chain him with chains that can only be opened by a certain key. The fisherman, having done as requested, throws the key into the sea and returns home. Gregory remains there for seventeen years, until the current Pope having died, a voice from heaven announces that the next pontiff shall be named Gregory. A search is begun, the fisherman found and, the key having miraculously been discovered inside a fish, the prisoner is set free, taken to Rome and there made Pope.[80]

Once again the similarities are striking. Like Galobrun, and before that Gwri, Gregory is imprisoned by being chained to a rock in the sea. His history is like that of Gawain in the *Enfances*, *De Ortu* and *Perlesvaus*. The key which holds him prisoner is discovered in *Perlesvaus* in the belly of a dragon and in the *Gesta Romanorum* inside a fish (A theme, incidentally, well known in Celtic tradition.) The name Gregory is itself derived from Gwri Gwallt Euryn, via the Latinized name Walwanius (Gawain). The theme of incest may also account for the temporary desertion of the hero from the service of the Goddess, as discussed above.

It has long been recognized that this story either influenced the author of *De Ortu Waluuanii* or was, in turn, influenced by him. The likelihood is that the story of the Fair Unknown, which was circulating widely at the time, influenced *both* versions. There seems, anyway, to be small doubt that it is from this confusion of stories that the notion of Gawain's connection with Rome originates.

The fact that Gregory is a child of incest adds one more strand to our argument. We have already seen the similarities between the stories of Gawain and Medraut, the product of an incestuous union between Morgause (Morgain) and Arthur. The subsequent history of his birth, as told by Sir Thomas Malory in *Le Morte d'Arthur*, is interesting.

> Mordred is begotten in ignorance (on the part of his father) of the relationship of the parents, but when Arthur does learn he sends for 'all the children born on May-day, begotten of lords and born of ladies. For Merlin told King Arthur that he [who] should destroy him should be born on May-day, wherefore he sent for them all . . . and all were put in a ship to the sea. . . And so by fortune the ship drove unto a castle, and was all to-riven, and destroyed the most part, save that Mordred was cast up and a good many found him, and housed him til he was fourteen year old, and then brought him to court. (Bk 1, Ch. 10)

The *Huth Merlin*[34] further adds that the infant Mordrec (Mordred) was discovered by a fisherman and that his name was revealed by a paper in the cradle and his status by the rich clothing in which he was wrapped.

This story, as we can see, is ultimately the same as that of Gawain *and* of Pope Gregory, who is also the product of incest. It further bears out our supposition that Gawain himself may once have been described as the son of Arthur and Morgain, which would better account for his mother's fear and her desire to hide his birth in *Enfances Gawain* and *De Ortu Waluuanii*. In the *Mabinogion* tale of Gwri we may remember that his mother, Rhiannon, was also accused of a crime (though of infanticide rather than incest) and that he is discovered by Teyrnon Trf Lliant, wrapped in a rich robe, also on May Day.

All of this leads one to believe that the Gregory legend, originally of oriental origin, became attached to the Gawain complex by an author who saw the similarities between the legends as an opportunity to bring a pious element into a rather pagan story. Modred, who begins life as a hero in the lists of Arthur's warriors,[121] also descends, once he has become Arthur's incestuous child (as well as his prophesied slayer), to the dark and evil figure of the later tales. The pattern is one that we shall see applied to his brother Gawain again and again throughout this book.

The inference to be made from the story found in both *De Ortu* and the *Gesta Romanorum* is that Gawain was brought up by a priestly, if not otherwise, personage, as was Lancelot by the Lady of the Lake in the *Vulgate cycle*. A lingering memory of this may well be seen in the fact that the *Historia Regum Brittannia* associates Gawain with Norway, and that in the Welsh *Brut Tysillo* he is said to take service with the Bishop of Ryfain, also in Norway, while elsewhere he is said to be the grandson of King Sichelm.

The significance of this is not hard to find, for the medieval name for Norway is often given as *Lochlann*, a name also attributed, again and again, to the Otherworld. The reason for this seems to be that the Celtic word *Llychlyn* originally described an aspect of the Otherworld which was a land beneath the lakes or waves of the sea, and that about the time when Arthur was said to be conquering Scandinavia (as related both by Geoffrey of Monmouth and various other chroniclers) the name was transferred to the fiords and inlets of Norway. Presumably this reflects the idea then current that if Arthur was conquering any land over the seas it must be the Otherworld, as in the famous early Welsh poem *Preiddeu Annwyn*.[120]

Thus all the references to Gawain's education and training by Romans, or the curious idea of his being knighted by the pope, can be explained and traced back to the confusion of the Gregory story with that of the Fair Unknown.

A final episode, which completes this picture of Gawain's early life, is found in both the *Conte del Graal* of Chrétien de Troyes,[10] the *Parzival* of Wolfram von Eschenbach,[63] and *Perlesvaus*.[23] It will be dealt with more fully in Chapter 5, but it requires our attention here for the light it throws upon Gawain's relationship with the Besieged Lady. In this incident Gawain arrives at the mysterious Castle of Marvels, where three women, Igrain, the mother of Arthur, Morgain, and Gawain's own sister, are besieged by a nameless knight. Gawain rescues them, but is unaware of the identity of the three women, one of whom is, of course, his own mother. He does not, in fact, discover his true identity until much later.

The importance of the three women, as we shall see, lies in the fact that they form a perfect image of the triple-aspected Goddess, in which guise they also appear in Malory (see pp99-103). The inference from this incident is that Gawain sets free the Besieged Lady (or in this case Ladies) and receives as his reward the favours of at least one of them. The possibility that this was Morgain is not to be ruled out, since the weight of evidence so far gathered suggests that just such an intimate relationship existed between Morgain-as-Goddess and her champion-son.

If we now refer back to the tangle of incidents surrounding Gawain's birth and childhood, and add to this the new evidence of the Gregory story and the *Enfances* of Modred, and the episode at the Castle of Marvels, we are at last enabled to offer a reconstruction of the first part of Gawain's story as it must once have been:

Gawain is born to the Goddess Morgain and her brother or half-brother the demi-god Arthur. When it is discovered that her child is the product of incest and that he will be the destruction of his father, he is cast adrift on the sea in an open boat. There he is found by a servant of the Lady of the Lake and taken into her realm, where he is educated and taught the manly arts which will equip him for a great task. He is to be the Champion of the Goddess — but before this can happen he must undergo a series of tests. The first of these is the rescue of his own mother, whom he does not remember and who is besieged in a castle. He successfully overcomes enormous odds and is rewarded by becoming her lover. He subsequently discovers the true relationship and is driven mad by the knowledge, having now rejected the Goddess.

After a time he is discovered wandering in the Wastes and restored to health by one of Morgain's agents, who also causes him to forget all that had driven him mad. Thus prepared, he sets forth again and arrives in due course at Arthur's court, where is is recognized as the king's nephew (but not as his son) and is welcomed. He now prepares for the next test he must undergo, that of the Beheading Game...

In conclusion of this brief overview of the rise of Gawain we may observe that in all of the pseudo-historical texts examined so far Gawain's character is generally consistent. He is brave, fearless and a little hot-headed. There is something strongly reminiscent of the old Celtic heroes about his behaviour at the meeting between Arthur and the Emperor Lucius (in the *Historia Regum Brittaniae*) where is is so enraged at some slighting remarks made by the emperor's nephew that he races forward, cuts off the man's head with one blow and returns triumphantly to his own side.

The theme of Gawain's courtesy, of his noble behaviour, emerges more in Layamon where, before the beginning of the Roman wars, Duke Cador exposes a very typical attitude towards war — that it is a good thing because it encourages bravery etc, while idleness brings about nothing but evil works. Gawain's reply is astonishing for the time:

Cador, you are a powerful man: [but] your advice is not good... Peace makes a good man perform good works; for all the men are better and the land is merrier. (Trans. Markman).

This does not sound like the words of someone brought up in Rome in the papal household. It is perhaps the only sign of an attempt to present Gawain with Christian characteristics rather than with pagan (and therefore evil) ones. But this was a direction which few subsequent writers chose to follow. Gawain's earlier, half-forgotten origins continued to follow him throughout his literary career, so that in Geoffrey of Monmouth we already see the beginning of a decline when we read how when Gawain was chosen to be one of the three messengers sent to the camp of the Romans, the retinue of young men who attended him were delighted, and urged him to find occasion for a quarrel!

We will leave the last word (for the moment) to Layamon, who says (vv 2325-58, Trans. Markman):

> It was a splendid thing that Gawain was born to be a man, for he was
> exceptionally noble-minded, he excelled in each virtue. He was liberal
> and peer of the best of the knights.

Not until the anonymous Gawain-poet, in c. 1400, do we again see the hero's qualities so generously expressed. It is to his remarkable testimony that we turn next.

Chapter 3.

The Green Gome: Otherworldly Chivalry and the Round Table

A CHRISTMAS GAME AT CAMELOT

Far and away the most famous adventure of Gawain's career is contained in the great alliterative poem *Sir Gawain and the Green Knight*,[49] composed by an unknown author somewhere in the Midlands of Britain round about 1400. More attention has been lavished on this single text than on any other in the entire Arthurian corpus — justifiably since it is a remarkable work of genius which tells an astonishing story with pace, colour and unforgettable imagery. For the purposes of our present argument it is crucial, containing many vital clues to Gawain's original role.

At Camelot, as the court is preparing to celebrate the feast of Christmas, a huge and terrible figure crashes into the hall. Riding a green horse and dressed in green clothing, even his skin is green. He carries a huge axe and a bough of holly to show that he comes in peace. He offers to play a 'Christmas game' with anyone there, and taunts the assembled knights and their ladies when no-one comes forward immediately. The object of the game is an exchange of blows, the first to be delivered with the Green Knight's own axe, upon himself, the second to be returned in a year's time. When no one appears willing Arthur himself is about to accept the challenge — then Gawain steps forward and requests that he be allowed to play the game. Hefting the huge axe he strikes off the Green Knight's head, only to see it picked up and placed back upon its owner's shoulders. The terrible figure departs, reminding Gawain to seek him out in a year at the 'Green Chapel' for the return blow.

The year passes all too quickly for Gawain, who watches the seasons pass in trepidation. Finally he sets out in search of the Green Chapel, and wanders for many weeks in the 'wilderness of Wirrell' until he comes to the castle of Sir Bercilak, who welcomes him warmly and tells him that the place he is seeking lies only a few hours distant. At supper that night Gawain sees his host's beautiful wife, and an ancient, ugly woman who seems to be her companion, but who yet is treated with great courtesy.

Next day Bercilak prepares to set out hunting, and invites Gawain to join him. Gawain, however, prefers to remain behind, resting after his long and arduous search. Lady Bercilak enters his chamber and attempts to seduce him, though Gawain refuses to accept more from her than a single kiss. When Bercilak returns with the spoils of the hunt, which he offers to exchange for anything Gawain has won that day, the hero has only the kiss to offer. The same procedure is followed on the two successive days, with Bercilak bringing more and more spoils and Gawain gathering first two and finally three kisses from the amorous Lady Bercilak. He retains his chivalrous attitude however, only on the third day agreeing to accept a gift of another kind — a baldric of green lace which he is told will preserve him from all harm.

Next day Bercilak sends him forth with a guide to take him to the Green Chapel. Resisting the guide's offer to lead him to safety, Gawain reaches a strange place and hears the sounds of an axe being whetted against a stone. The Green Knight appears and Gawain prepares to take the fatal blow. Twice the Green Knight feints, mocking Gawain for flinching; on the third stroke he nicks the hero's neck and Gawain springs up declaring that he has taken his blow in accordance with the agreement. The Green Knight now explains that he is indeed Sir Bercilak, and that he has been enchanted into this shape by the old woman at the castle, who is really Morgan the Goddess. She it was who forced him to test the Arthurian court with the Beheading Game. Gawain has passed the test with only one failure, that he accepted the Green Girdle from Lady Bercilak, who had also been constrained by Morgan to seduce Gawain.

Chastened by his adventure Gawain returns to Camelot and tells all that has occurred. The knights all agree to wear a green baldric in token of Gawain's honourable and chivalrous behaviour.

As long ago as 1888 it was noticed that certain aspects of this complex plot were to be found within various ancient Irish stories.[134] In particular the Beheading Game, which also appears in no less than eight other Arthurian texts, was seen to have originated with a story from the Cuchulainn saga called *Fled Bricriu* or Bricriu's Feast. We have already met this story in Chapter 1: the following summary makes it clear just how much the story of *Gawain and the Green Knight* owes to the Irish original:

Once, when the men of Ulster were at Emain Macha, the capital of King Conchobar mac Nessa, they saw a huge and terrible churl coming towards them. (The word is *Bachlach* in Irish; the Gawain-Poet uses *Gome*.) In one hand he held a great block and in the other an axe so huge it would have required six oxen to move it. He challenges the heroes to find one among them who will submit to having their head cut off in return for a chance to perform the same feat upon him the next night. The heroes discuss the matter and finally one Munremar mac Gerrcind agrees that if the churl allows *him* to strike the first blow he will accept the challenge.

The churl agrees but of course picks up his head and departs promising to return. Next night however Munremar is nowhere to be found. Scornfully the churl renews his challenge and this time it is taken up by the hero Loegair, who also fails to reappear the next night. Finally Cuchulainn, who had been absent on the two earlier occasions, returns and accepts the challenge. He alone has the courage to face the churl who, when he strikes his blow, only grazes the hero's neck with the blunt edge of the axe. He then declares Cuchulainn the bravest man in Ireland and says: 'The sovereignty of the warriors of Ireland to you from this hour, and the champion's portion without dispute, and to your wife precedence over the women of Ulster forever...' He then departs and it is later revealed that he was Curoi in disguise, testing the courage of the heroes and the worthiness of Cuchulainn in particular.

The similarities between the two texts are obvious. R.S. Loomis[104] and Alice Buchanan[78] noted a total of 32 distinct features, among the most notable of which are the similarities between the descriptive epithet attached to the giant herdsman in *Fled Bricriu* — bachlach (pronounced bachelach) the name of the Green Knight, Bercilak, and the word for grey (*liath*) the colour of the cloak worn by the Irish giant, and the word for green (*glas*) which are close enough to have given rise to confusion between the two (although if so the confusion was a happy one, as we shall see). We therefore have two immediate points of similarity which suggest the identification of the bachlach with the Green Knight: the description of a colour and the name. And since the *bachlach* is really Curoi, an even greater degree of coincidence attends, since we have already seen in Chapter 1 that there is a considerable overlap between the figures of Gawain, Cuchulainn, and Curoi. In this instance we have an unusual situation where Cuchulainn/Gawain faces Curoi/Bercilak, while in fact *all four* derive from the same primal figure!

Strange though this may seem, it is by no means uncommon in mythical structures to find a single character split into several aspects. Thus the figure of Bendigeid Vran (Bran the Blessed) appears in various Arthurian texts in at least 10 different guises[126] all of which relate back to the original. In the same way, although the figures of Cuchulainn, Gawain, Curoi and Bercilak seem to be opposing pairs, at a deeper level these variables disappear, leaving us with a single figure — the Champion of the Goddess.

To discover how this came about we need to look at the other texts in which variants of the Green Knight's challenge are featured. This will not only enable us to understand certain puzzling features of Gawain's great adventure, but will also add to our overall argument, in which we shall see how successive champions came to occupy a single archetypal role.

The first of the texts at which we need to look is the thirteenth-century French poem *Hunbaut*,[42] in which a number of points help to flesh out the part once played by Gawain.

Gawain is sent by Arthur to collect the overdue tribute of the King of the Isles (possibly Gawain's own father, Loth). He takes with him his sister. Hunbaut, a senior knight of the Round Table, notes that this may not be a good idea and also points out that Gawain is not always the most tactful or diplomatic of emissaries. He persuades Arthur to let him follow. On overtaking brother and sister Hunbaut persuades Gawain to leave the girl behind. They leave her at the nearest crossroad to be taken back to court by the first passing knight (!) Unfortunately this happens to be a man with a grudge against Gawain, who therefore carries her off.

The two knights spend their first night together with a friendly and pleasant host (cf Bercilak) and continue on their way. Hunbaut warns Gawain that their next host is very different, hot tempered and with a beautiful daughter of whom he is the most jealous guardian. Hunbaut's advice is that Gawain should pay no attention to her and that he should eat abundantly since the next day will find them entering the Waste Lands.

Everything falls out as Hunbaut has said, except that Gawain falls in love with the daughter and talks to her all through supper — until their host notices and is enraged when the girl offers Gawain four kisses. Hunbaut pacifies the host and all retire for the night, during which the girl finds her way to Gawain's chamber and remains there until morning.

The two knights continue on their way, and Hunbaut reproves Gawain for taking advantage of the girl. Gawain responds that he is not made of wood, and regrets not eating more. Later they see a camp-fire and Gawain asks the knight to whom it belongs if they can share his meal. When he is refused Gawain furiously drives away the knight and eats a full meal. Hunbaut shares this, but again reproves Gawain for his actions. He subsequently effects a reconciliation with the knight (whom he apparently knows) and the two travellers go to his castle, which guards the port from which they must take ship for the lands of the King of the Isles.

Arriving at an island they are met by a knight who challenges them. Gawain wants to fight but Hunbaut again seems to know the man and persuades him to wait. They proceed towards the castle of the King of the Isles and encounter a man with a wooden leg who challenges their crossing of a narrow plank bridge. Gawain knocks this man into the water and then at the gate of the castle they are met by a *villein* who offers them a game: that one of them should behead him, on condition that he be allowed to return the blow. Gawain agrees, chops off the man's head and then restrains him from picking it up again by holding onto his clothes, thus causing him to remain dead and the 'enchantments' to end.

On their way further into the castle they meet a dwarf who challenges Gawain to an exchange of insults, but Gawain loses his temper and kills the dwarf. Confronting the king they demand Arthur's dues, but get no reply since the king seems to be in a kind of trance. They decide to leave, but when the king realizes what they had said to him and learns what Gawain has done, he is angered and pursues them through the castle and beyond.

The two knights escape and cross to the mainland, where they meet a maiden whose father and lover have been kidnapped. Gawain and Hunbaut separate and the story turns to Gawain first. He meets a knight who boasts of having won the favour of his lady by promising to marry her and to bring the famous Gawain to their home. He now intends to fulfil neither promise, but Gawain forces him to honour at least the promise of marriage.

Gawain meets another knight travelling to Arthur's court. He will not disclose his name but tries to get Gawain to name the best and bravest knight of the Round Table. He is dissatisfied with every answer and the reason is only disclosed after the two have fought and beaten off a band of ruffians and the young knight reveals himself as Gawain's own brother Gaheries, who waited only to hear Gawain himself named as Arthur's best knight.

The brothers now meet a friendly knight who tells them that neither Hunbaut or Gawain's sister have reached the court and the three separate, the brothers to look for their sister and the knight to return to Arthur and tell of the events that have taken place.

When Arthur hears of Gawain's adventures he vows to set out at once in search of the missing girl accompanied by 10 other knights. They encounter Gawain at a ford, where a faery boat is the only means of crossing. It will however only carry odd numbers and since the party now numbers 12 Gawain crosses first and alone, continuing on his way and leaving the rest to follow later.

That evening they reach the castle of Gant Destroit, whose lady is so much in love with Gawain that she has a life-size statue of him next to her bed. Kay and Griflet see this and think that Gawain is really present. They report to Arthur that he is hiding with his lover but the truth is revealed. Hunbaut arrives and explains how he and Gawain came to separate.

The story now turns to Gawain himself, who comes upon his sister in the company of Gorvain Cardaus of Castle Pantelion, the knight who had kidnapped her. Gawain defeats him and learns that he had killed one of the man's relatives. Reconciliation is achieved and Gawain sends the knight to Arthur along with the girl and word that he will return soon.

The poem breaks off here, leaving us to assume that the remainder of the story would have, in all probability, concluded with gaining of the fealty of the King of the Isles and possibly the wedding of Gawain's sister to Hunbaut who is, after all, the real hero of the poem.

And a very interesting hero he makes, acting in a most unusual manner for an Arthurian knight — refusing to give battle, effecting reconciliation between Gawain and various people and generally behaving in a way that leads one to suppose that he knows more than he is letting on. At every junction along the way he knows the nature and history of the people the two heroes meet, and though Gawain is the prime mover in virtually every adventure, Hunbaut is there in the background, advising, cajoling and more than once censuring his companion.

He thus becomes a foil to the character of Gawain, who suffers greatly from the comparison, acting in a manner which is better suited to other, corrupt characterizations. However, even here we may notice two important details: firstly that from the moment he leaves his sister at a crossroads, things begin to go wrong for him and second that whenever Hunbaut is not present Gawain reverts to his former chivalrous character. It would not be wise to press these points too far, but we have already seen that the deserting of the woman at the crossroads is the equivalent of deserting the Goddess herself, and that the mysterious Hunbaut (who appears in no other existing text) may really be under enchantment, acting out a fragmented version of the Green Knight's role.

There are certainly a number of echoes of *Gawain and the Green Knight*, including the exchange of kisses, the temptation theme (to which, in this case, Gawain succumbs). Even the castle of Gant Des-

troit reads like a variation of Bercilak's castle of Haut Desert, while
the name of the knight who carries off Gawain's sister, Gorvain Cardus,
is a curious conflation of Gawain's own name with that of Carados.
This knight features in an episode of the *Vulgate cycle*[60] in which he
undertakes to play the Beheading Game, and in the Modena archivault
story, where he is ranged against Gawain as the captor of Winlogee
and defender of the otherworld castle.

In all, *Hunbaut* reads at times like a parody of *Gawain and the Green
Knight* with some interesting variations which point to the deeper mean-
ing behind both works, as well as others in which the story of the Green
Knight appears.

The next of these at which we must look are *Le Chevalier à L'Epée*
(The Knight with the Sword)[57] and *La Mule Sans Frein* (The Mule
without a Bridle).[57]

The two romances were probably written by the same person — who
calls himself Paien de Maisires — and may be intended as continua-
tions of the Gawain episodes of Chrétien de Troyes' *Conte del Graal*.[10]
When the two stories are combined — as has been done by Dr D.D.R.
Owen[57] — they tell substantially the same story as *Gawain and the
Green Knight*.

Le Chevalier may be summarized as follows.

Gawain loses his way in a forest and strikes up an acquaintance with
a mysterious knight, who offers him shelter. That night the host offers
his daughter (to whom Gawain is strongly attracted) for the night. But
there is a mechanical or enchanted sword in her room which falls upon
anyone who attempts to touch her. Fortunately Gawain, though
tempted, resists and in the morning, amazed to find him still alive,
Gawain's host calls him the best of all men and offers the girl's hand
in marriage. They set out for Arthur's court and on the way encounter
another knight whom the girl really wishes to go off with. Gawain and
the newcomer fight over the latter's dogs and Gawain kills him. He
leaves the faithless girl to her fate and returns to the court alone.

This clearly relates to the scene in *Hunbaut* where Gawain is tempted
by his host's daughter (but does *not* resist) and to the temptation episode in *Gawain and the Green Knight*, with which the whole poem
shares so many details. The quarrel over the dogs, which initiates the
fight between Gawain and the knight in the forest, is significant also,
as we shall see. It is a theme familiar from more than one Celtic story
and adds another clue to the Green Knight's probable identity. It is
worth noting also that as Gawain struggles with his desire for the host's
beautiful daughter, the sword actually descends far enough to strike

him a blow on the neck (with the flat of the blade only) — another analogy of the Beheading Game and the chastity test which precedes it. *La Mule Sans Frein* adds a further dimension:

A maiden comes to Arthur's court asking for a knight to recover the lost bridle from her mule — the animal itself will guide whoever takes up the quest. Kay tries first and passes through a wilderness and a haunted forest where monsters bow to the mule and leave Kay alone. But he quails before a kind of sword bridge and returns empty handed to court. Gawain now sets out and following the same route successfully reaches a revolving castle surrounded by a fence of stakes on which are ranged human heads. At the castle he is called upon to suffer the Beheading Game at the hands of a huge *villein* who emerges from a cellar and encounters serpents and lions. He is however successful and receives from the Lady of the Castle (sister to she who sought help) the bridle. The inhabitants of the castle are joyful at Gawain's success. He returns to Arthur's court and returns the bridle to the damsel, who 'dare not stay' but departs at once.

Once again the story offers parallels with *Gawain and the Green Knight*, and when conflated with *Le Chevalier à L'Epée* makes a close approximation to the whole of the Green Knight's story.

The episode in which the mule leads Gawain to his destination forms an important parallel with a later Grail text (the *First Continuation* of Chrétien's poem) in which Gawain sets out on an adventure which will lead him to the Grail castle, riding a horse which, though not without a bridle, he has been instructed to give its head. When he leaves the castle at the end of his adventure, the people express their joy at being set free in very much the same way as the inhabitants of the Grail castle in the same text, who have been freed from the effects of an even greater spell by his efforts.

The object of the elaborate charade in which Gawain takes part in *La Mule* is specifically designed to test him. His greeting by the churl and the dwarf, after he has crossed the Perilous Bridge, the fence with the frieze of human heads, the revolving castle, are all aspects of the otherworldly scenario of the test — which Gawain passes with flying colours, setting free not only the people of the castle but also its master. This is clearly reflected in the Middle High German *Diu Crône*, by Heinrich von dem Turlin,[22] which adds further significant details to our argument.

The King of Serre (Sear, Withered?) leaves his kingdom to twin daughters and with it a bridle which has the talismanic virtue of preserving the kingdom for its possessor. The elder daughter, Amurfina, seizes both bridal and kingdom, and to forestall any request for aid from Arthur, lures Gawain to her castle and makes him her lover. But Gawain does not stay long and returns to court in time for the coming of the younger daughter, Sgoidamur, who asks for help. . .

The story then follows the version found in *La Mule Sans Frein* with the following exceptions:

The churl who offers to play the Beheading Game is first handsome, then hideous. He is called Gansguoter and is the uncle of the two sisters. The third test Gawain undergoes is a fight with the knight who had placed the heads on their stakes; when Gawain first encounters him he is wounded, but at once springs up healed and fights until noon when Gawain slays him. At the end Sgoidamur offers love to Gawain, but as he is already pledged to her sister he declines and instead arranges a marriage with Gansguoter.

These additional details not only make far more sense of an otherwise strange and rather motiveless story, they add significantly to the portrait of the churl, who in each of the texts discussed can be seen to derive from the same source as the villain Bermaltus of the *Modena archivault*.

For the meaning of the mule itself, Professor Loomis points to another text, *Le Chevalier de Papagau* (The Knight of the Parrot),[25] in which the hero (who in this instance is Arthur) follows a strange, composite beast which turns into a white-haired and venerable man who is really the ghost of King Behain of the Realm of Damsels. Loomis suggests[104] that the beast to which the animals do homage in *La Mule* may be a disguised form of the castle's real master, Gansguoter, who is probably also the giant churl who submits Gawain to the Beheading Game.

This allows us to consider the bridle as a means of returning the enspelled person to his true shape. In the text this has fallen out of the story to be replaced by the adventure of Gawain. But traces still remain within the subtext of his role. It is worth noting further that the bridle appears to confer sovereignty over the castle and its lands — which, as we shall see in the next chapter, included marriage to the Lady of the Castle (i.e. the Goddess herself). Other evidence suggests that it is the *wife* of the shape-shifting churl who is behind the whole manipulation of events, allowing us to speculate further that the Chatelaine of the Castle in *La Mule*, and she who seeks aid at Arthur's court, were originally not merely sisters but almost certainly aspects of a single character, split into two to further the outlines of the story.

The apparently wounded knight in *Diu Crône*, who is restored in order to do battle with Gawain is clearly another aspect of the otherworldly champion, while the much sought after bridle becomes a token of power, the owner of which is preserved from harm and whose kingdom flourishes.

The test of the Beheading Game appears in four other distinct versions: Two medieval English poems, *The Carl of Carlisle*[21] and *The Turk and Gawain*;[21] the French *Perlesvaus*[23] and the Vulgate cycle *Lancelot*.[60] In the first of these we find yet another version of the story:

Gawain, Kay and the Bishop Baldwin, while out hunting, take refuge in the castle of the Carl of Carlisle. He is a giant, terrible to see. By the fire in his hall lie four beasts: a bull, a boar, a lion and a bear. They are fierce and dangerous until the Carl bids them lie under the table. He calls for wine, complaining when it is brought in four-gallon cups — until the butler brings in a great golden cup which holds nine gallons. At supper Gawain sits next to the Carl's wife, who is of human size and beautiful. After dinner the Carl asks Gawain to play a game, throwing a spear at his head. The Carl ducks and the spear shatters. That night the Carl bids Gawain to go to bed with his wife and kiss her while he looks on. But when Gawain begins to caress her he grows angry and cries stop! He then rewards Gawain by giving him his daughter instead. Next day the Carl shows Gawain 10 cartloads of bones — all victims of his animals; and that evening, when they have eaten, asks Gawain to cut off his head. When Gawain finally does so the Carl rises up a normal man and thanks him for releasing him from enchantment, Gawain marries the Carl's daughter and Arthur makes the restored man a knight of the Round Table.

There are so many analogies here to the Green Knight's story as well as to the story of *Briciu's Feast* that there can be little doubt that the author of the *Carl* knew a version of the Irish tale. Loomis lists five key points of similarity.[105]
1. The description of the two churls
2. Their beautiful wives
3. A visit to the castle at nightfall by three heroes
4. Curoi and the Carl are both shapeshifters
5. The nine-gallon bowl in *The Carl*; a silver *kiever* (bowl) in *Fled Bricriu*
  Loomis also believes that the underlying theme of the text is a) that of the young god overcoming the old god — a well-attested mythological scenario — or b) that the young god, having passed the test set for him, *restores* the old god to health and youth. This is in part suggested

by the version found in *Perlesvaus* which we shall consider in a moment. There is also a third possibility, not put forward by Loomis, that the real nub of the action lies with the mysterious female personality, whether she is 'Morgane the Goddess' as in *Gawain and the Green Knight* or simply the wife or daughter of the Hospitable Host in both *The Carl of Carlisle* and the other texts under discussion. More importantly perhaps is the fact that once again the outcome of the tests and trials experienced by Gawain is the hand of a lady (see Fig 5). The word 'Carl' stems from the Old Norse *Karl* (Man) but has acquired the meaning of 'churl', and with it certain supernatural connotations for the medieval audiences. It is possible also that the same figure, with his attendant animals, is a reflection of the 'Lord of the Animals', found both in Chrétien de Troyes' *Yvain*[8] and its earlier Welsh variant *Owein*.[31] Here the churl is described thus:

> [He is] no smaller than two men of this world. He has one foot, and one eye in the middle of his forehead, and he carries an iron spear which you can be certain would be a burden for any two men. Though ugly, he is not an unpleasant man. He is a keeper of the forest, and you will see a thousand wild animals grazing about him. (*Mabinogion* Trans. J. Gantz.)

In this version we can see elements of both the Green Knight and of the Carl. Yet another example comes from *Perlesvaus*, where the protagonist is Lancelot.

He arrives at the Waste City and finds it crumbling and apparently deserted. Yet he hears voices lamenting his own approaching demise. He sees a handsome young knight dressed in white and gold and with a chaplet on his head descending the stairs with a great axe in his hands. He demands that Lancelot either cut off his head or submit to being decapitated himself. If the former, he must return in a year to submit to a return blow. Reluctantly Lancelot agrees and does the deed. As he departs he looks back but cannot see the body.

A year passes and Lancelot finds himself again at the Waste Castle. The young man with the axe, apparently restored, approaches. It transpires that he is the brother of the knight whom Lancelot beheaded. Lancelot submits himself to the axe, but flinches. Before a second blow can be struck two women appear one of whom intercedes because she recognizes Lancelot. At once the knight throws down his axe and demands Lancelot's forgiveness. All are then restored, both lands and women, to their former state.

Loomis thinks that this preserves the earliest version of the story, in particular because of the implied restoration of the land when the

Text	Hero	Challenger	Wife/Daughter/Otherworldly Woman
Bricriu's Feast	Chuchulainn	Curoi	
Gawain and the Green Knight	Gawain	Green Knight	Lady Bercilak/Morgane the Goddess
Modena archivault	Gawain	Bermalt	Winlogee
Hunbaut	Gawain	Villain	Daughter of Hospitable Host
The Carl of Carlisle	Gawain	Carl	Carl's wife
Perlesvaus	Lancelot	Young Knight	Two women
Le Chevalier à l'Epée	Gawain	Hospitable Host	Daughter
La Mule Sans Frein	Gawain	Villain	Lady of the Castle
Diu Crône	Gawain	Gansguoter	Amurfina

Figure 5: *The Beheading Game: Its Players and its Heroes.*

challenge is worked out. This, together with the fact that apparently a different person is sacrificed every year, points again to the well-attested theme of annual kingship, traces of which are to be found both in Mediterranean traditions as well as those of the British Isles and Ireland. In each of these countries, during prehistoric times, kings were elected for the duration of a year, at the end of which time they were ritually slain, generally by a challenger who was not permitted to fail.

The shape of the champion's role is circular and is best described by the following diagram, which shows the successive nature of his rise and fall as it appears in the texts.

Figure 6: *The Succession of the Champions.*

In the way of things, the ravages of time bring her champion to near decrepitude (at the place of winter), ready for toppling by the young hero (at the place of spring) on whom she has had her eye for some time and whom she tempts into her enclosure in order to effect a challenge. When he has grown to full manhood, the Hero (at the place of summer) is ready to make his challenge. He successfully overcomes the old champion and summer and winter change places (see Fig 7).

Summer   Winter

New Champion◄───►The Goddess◄───►Old Champion

Figure 7: *The Exchange of the Champions.*

The challenge takes place at the winter solstice, the day 'out of time' in the sacred sense, when the shortest day shows winter at its strongest. The day after the solstice shows the lengthening of the light and the restoration of normal time in token of the Hero's victory.

The new champion then has a whole cycle to run before he need fear the incursions of a new challenger and thus it is ensured that the Goddess has a virile and vigorous champion at all times.

In one of the Grail texts, *The Didot Perceval*,[43] a combat takes place which makes the original nature of the challenge unequivocable. Though the participant is not Gawain this need not deter us from viewing it as a basic element of the original scenario.

Perceval encounters a knight at a ford who will not allow him to water his horse until he has fought — which Perceval does, soon overthrowing his adversary, who then begs for mercy. Perceval offers it on condition that he is told the reason for the man's behaviour. The knight, who is named Urban, tells how he was overtaken by a furious storm and that as he rode to escape it he met a damsel riding on a mule who led him to a most beautiful castle and there offered him her love. Urban was glad enough to accept but wondered how he would be able to pursue his knightly calling. The damsel replied that he should pitch his pavilion at the ford, and that no one would be able to see the castle except he, and that he should offer combat to any knight who passed that way — thus continuing to enjoy her love while indulging in manly pursuits. This he had done for almost a year, and had Perceval not defeated him, in just eight more days he would have been declared the best knight in the world.

On hearing this Perceval grants Urban mercy on the condition that he cease the custom of fighting with every man who comes that way. At this

> there was heard so great a tumult that it seemed that the whole forest crashed into an abyss. And from this noise. . . there issued a smoke and a shadow so huge that one could not see another person if he were a half league away. And from this shadow a voice issued that was very strong and dolorous and it said: "Perceval le Galois, accursed may you be by whatever we women can contrive, for you have caused us greater sorrow today than we could ever have. . . (Trans. D. Skeels)

Next moment Perceval finds himself surrounded by a cloud of black birds, who threaten to tear him to pieces. He fights them off, finally wounding one which falls to the ground. At once it becomes a beautiful woman whom the rest of the birds, ceasing to attack Perceval, carry upwards into the air. Astonished, Perceval demands that Urban explain all of this and is told that the birds were the Lady of the Castle and her sisters, who had transformed themselves into birds to try and kill Perceval. He adds that the one who was wounded will even now be 'in Avalon', where she will be healed, and begs Perceval to let him go. When the Grail knight does so, Urban runs off at speed, not even waiting to mount his horse. Perceval's last view of him is seeing him carried off by 'one who bore him away with the greatest joy in the world' (ibid).

This fascinating episode tells us a great deal about the original nature of both the challenger and the champion. Urban has been encountering knights at the ford for almost a year and clearly would have received some prize at the end of that time had Perceval not overcome him. The fact that the Lady of the Castle (whose identity we do not have to look far to establish) curses Perceval for his interference makes it clear that in eight days time Urban would have been released from his year-long stint as champion — either my meeting his death at the hands of the next contender, or by being set free to remain with the Lady thereafter — perhaps in Avalon itself, that otherworldly realm where all Arthurian heroes once went.

But Perceval has spoiled all this, broken the pattern, and he is attacked for it by otherworldly women in the shape of black birds. We have only to know that both Morgan le Fay and the Morrigan possessed the ability to shape change, and that both took the form of the crow (sacred to the Morrigan as Goddess of War) and we have as clear an indication as we could wish that this is once again the Goddess that we are encountering, and that Urban is at this stage her champion. This pattern of events is reflected twofold in the Gawain myths — in the story as we have it in its most developed state, in *Gawain and the Green Knight*, and in the successive reappearance of the interrelated figures of the challenger and the champion. Here the ritual element attendant upon the kingship has been suppressed in favour of a story more acceptable to medieval audiences. But vestiges of the original scenario are still to be seen in the encounter of the young hero with the otherworldly challenger, the mock-death or transformation of one or the other, and the presence of a mysterious female figure in the background. This is such a primal element in the original story of Gawain that we need to look more closely at the whole nature of the exchange of blows (and its attendant theme of the exchange of winnings which may, however, be of later origin) as well as at the identity of the challenger, in order to better understand the relationship of all three protagonists.

THE CHALLENGER AND THE CHALLENGE

The first point we need to consider is the location in which the Beheading Game takes place. This may seem an obvious question, since in *Gawain and the Green Knight* at least, the locale is clearly indicated with geographical precision (see Appendix 3). However it is important to establish that in almost every instance the challenge takes place in what is clearly an otherworld locale. We have only to look at the description of the Green Chapel to see this and there is another text, which we have so far ignored, which tells us even more.

The Turk and Gawain[21] is another of the series of English Gawain poems — all dating from between 1300 and 1500 — which, including Gawain and the Green Knight, form a loose-knit cycle. The story it tells is remarkable for the way in which it has preserved certain primitive elements missing from the other texts relating to the Beheading Game.

A monstrous man comes to Arthur's court 'huge and broad like a Turk'. He challenges all there to an exchange of buffets and Gawain gives him a powerful one — the return to be delivered elsewhere. Gawain and the Turk leave together and ride North. When Gawain complains of hunger the Turk leads him into the side of a hill which closes behind them with the sound of thunder, flashes of lightning and a deluge of rain. They reach the Turk's castle where Gawain is first forbidden to eat then encouraged. They leave the castle and cross a sea to the palace of the King of Man. The Turk warns Gawain there will be giants there but promises to help. They enter the palace and the king insults Arthur by name and then produces a brass 'tennis ball'. Nine giants enter and prepare to attack. There is then a gap in the text in which we can assume that Gawain and the Turk defeat their adversaries. Presumably with the aid of the brass ball. A trial of strength follows involving a giant cauldron. At Gawain's bidding the Turk (who is apparently invisible, and clad in grey) easily lifts it. The King of Man then shows Gawain another cauldron full of boiling lead, whereupon the Turk throws both the remaining giants and the king, into it. There is another gap in which apparently Gawain receives the return blow from the Turk, who then gives Gawain his sword and bids him strike off his head. Gawain does so and a fair knight leaps up whole. His name is Gomer. They release the prisoners from the palace and return together to Arthur's court where Gomer is made the new King of Man.

There are a number of remarkable aspects to this poem. To begin with, the 'Turk' — so called from a period when this word was synonymous with monsters — is clearly an otherworldly character. Not only does he know the way into the 'Hollow Hills', but he possesses superhuman abilities and cannot be killed. Inside the hill Gawain is first prevented from eating — a fact which reflects the usual prohibition against all mortals from eating the food of the Otherworld. He is then permitted to eat, presumably of normal food, and immediately after crosses the sea to the Land of Man. This is probably the Isle of Man, which despite its physical existence was frequently identified with the Otherworld.

There Gawain encounters giants, cauldrons and other wonders and ends by releasing the Turk from enchantment and (through Arthur) bestowing upon him the crown of Man.

The importance of this story cannot be overstated. Here we find Gawain involved in an adventure in which he passes into the Otherworld, is helped by one of its guardians and after various tests is able to award the sovereignty of the otherworld island to his guide. It is clear that at one time there must have been a girl — either the daughter or wife of the Turk — who also offered help. Possibly the initial prohibition against eating followed by its rescinding also echoes the theme of the host offering his wife or daughter to the hero after previously warning him against touching her. The other versions of the story examined so far confirm this hypothesis, and suggest that at one time the motive for the various confrontations between the challenger and the champion may have been very different.

We begin to see this more clearly by looking at a text which may seem at first only vaguely related to the story of the Green Knight, but which deals not only with a form of the Chastity Test, but also with the reason for the challenge.

The first branch of *The Mabinogion* concerns the hero Pwyll, who undergoes a series of adventures which strongly echo those of Gawain:

Pwyll, Prince of Dyfed, was out hunting when he encountered a strange pack of white, red-eared hounds, which set upon his quarry and brought it down. Driving off the other hounds Pwyll set his own pack onto the quarry. Then the rival huntsman appeared, dressed in grey, and threatened Pwyll. He was Arawn, King of the Otherworld kingdom of Annwn. The only way that Pwyll might save himself was by agreeing to change places with Arawn for a year, at the end of which time he must fight his enemy Hafgan, giving him but a single blow.

During the year which followed Pwyll lay every night beside Arawn's wife but never touched her once, despite her blandishments. At the end of the period he successfully fought with Hafgan, whose name means 'summer song', refusing to trade a second blow when he had struck him once. He then received the homage of the people of Annwn in Arawn's name and returned to his own place. Arawn found his kingdom well governed and his wife untouched and honoured Pwyll as the most honourable of men.[31]

Apart from the obvious parallels between this story and that of *Gawain and the Green Knight*, it also introduces a theme which is well-attested by numerous other texts as well as in the heritage of folklore and tradition. This is the struggle for the Flower Bride (or the Spring Maiden) by the champions of summer and winter. In Wales as late as the nineteenth century a yearly conflict took place on *Calan Mai*, 1 May (also, we may remember the birthday of Gawain). The captain of the summer forces rode on a horse, wore white and was crowned with flowers. Winter, also mounted, was dressed in firs and carried a blackthorn stick. A mock battle was fought in which summer always won, the season being recognized as beginning from that day.[108]

This reflects both the battle fought by Pwyll and perhaps those in the Green Knight texts. In most traditional instances of the story, summer carries a green branch, which has been transformed into a holly bough in the case of Bercilak or a blackthorn stave in the Welsh battle of the seasons. If this is applied to the story of *Gawain and the Green Knight* we may be justified in seeing Gawain as the representative of spring — a role in keeping with his solar attributes — and Bercilak as winter. Also we may note that, in the poem, the seasons are actually described as 'wrestling' and 'battling' with each other, a clear enough reference to the physical battle which takes place between their outward representatives — Gawain, and the Green Knight himself.

This is also appropriate since despite doubts cast upon the origin of the Green Knight's original colour, this is still the most appropriate with all the other seasonal indications contained in the poem (i.e. references to thunder and lightning, the holly bough and his overall bearing) which confirm his identity as the champion of winter (the old champion in Fig.5).

It is also worth noting that in *Gawain and the Green Knight* Gawain 'knows' how to reach the Green Chapel, not because he is told, but perhaps, as John Speirs suggests[139] because this was an area long associated with the cult of the Green Man and the Battle for Spring. We should also note that according to Western tradition, ritual combat was oriented from North (defender) to South (challenger), rather than East-West, as in the tournaments and jousts so popular in the Middle Ages. In the instance of the battle for the spring Flower Maiden we may assume that the same rule was followed. Certainly in *Gawain and the Green Knight* Bercilak comes from the North, the realm of winter, while Gawain journeys there from the South, the realm of summer.[3]

The same elements are found in the 'Creiddelad' story from *Culhwch and Olwen* and in the abduction of Guinevere in the *Vitae Gildae*, where the struggle is represented as being for a real woman. In the latter text Arthur is the rescuer, which points both to the original story being similar to that told in the *Modena archivault* and shows us that the versions of the story found in *Pwyll* and *Diu Crône* also represent a genuine tradition.

When Chrétien de Troyes comes to tell the story in his *Chevalier de la Charette*[8] he makes certain changes which, despite courtly trappings, nevertheless embodied a more primitive structure. The actual opening of *Chevalier de la Charette* is interesting:

Arthur is afraid to let Keu (Kay) accompany Guinevere and to defend her against King Bagdemagu of Gorre. If Keu wins, some of Arthur's knights, at present held captive, will be released; if he loses, then Guinevere will be taken hostage into Gorre. We find Guinevere chiding Arthur with this decision, as well she may, for it is likely that he knew of Gorre as an entrance to the Otherworld, and that once Guinevere was within, it would be difficult to enact a rescue.

We have already seen that in the story of the abduction of the Flower Bride, in each case an otherworld element was present. Bagdemagu (the suffix *magu* or *magus* cannot be coincidental) is an otherworldly king and, as such, once Guinevere has entered his realm, she is bound to remain there until rescued. This constitutes a reversal of the champion theme. As we have seen, at one time Gawain himself was probably her rescuer, at which time he would also have become her champion and lover.

It seems not unlikely that the choice of Lancelot for this role, in *Chevalier de la Charette* and elsewhere, influenced the course of his career, since he begins as the greatest knight in the world and is demoted because of his love for the queen — a sequence of events not unlike that which befell Gawain. From the moment that word comes of the queen's abduction, Chrétien begins to compare Gawain and Lancelot, who *both* set out in search of her. Gawain on the whole, though not the obvious hero, comes off better. He is thoughtful, plans ahead, and acts out of selflessness, rather than the secret passion of Lancelot.

Just as Hunbaut seemed to know more about the perils of the Otherworld than his companion, so Gawain, in Chrétien's story seems to know more about Gorre than Lancelot, a detail which would certainly not be inconsistent with his otherworldly status. Certainly he is met with recognition on several occasions on the way there, and with general admiration and acclaim by almost everyone in the poem.

The relationship between the two heroes is expressed with some subtlety in *La Chevalier de la Charette*. Gawain and Lancelot are constantly backing each other up in one tight corner after another; constantly rescuing each other, or making reference to their respective abilities. After the rescue of Guinevere has been successfully accomplished by Lancelot, who is captured and imprisoned shortly after, Gawain offers to fight Meleagraunce in his stead — though this proves unnecessary in the event, since Lancelot gets free and returns in the nick of time.

Even then Gawain tries to persuade his friend to let him continue the combat and although he refuses the offer Lancelot does wear Gawain's armour — a totally unexplained action *unless Gawain was the original hero*...

Douglas Kelly, commenting on the way in which Chrétien compares the two heroes throughout his poem, remarks:

> Lancelot takes the more difficult route to rescue Guenièvre yet arrives before Gauvain, virtually defeats Meleagant twice in combat, and is then instrumental in saving Gauvain from drowning at the Underwater Bridge. And it is Lancelot who, replacing Gauvain, fights and kills Meleagant at the end of the poem, thus definitely saving Guenièvre from captivity. Yet Lancelot's superiority stems from his love for Guenièvre, not from inherent knightly virtues that would have existed in spite of that love.[99]

We might add that in Gawain's case it is his love and devotion to the Goddess which fuels him and makes him such an outstanding hero and lover! In all, Lancelot fights three indecisive combats with Meleagant, Guinevere's abductor, who then demands a fourth *in a year's time* — yet another reminder of the pattern of the yearly challenge which is so much a part of the abduction of the Flower Bride theme.

In *Pwyll*, where the encounter is with Arawn, King of Annwn, who takes the role of the Hospitable Host in this instance, and who once again offers his wife (together, in this instance, with the kingdom) for the period of a year, Pwyll, like Gawain, accepts the challenge but is faithful and does not take advantage of Arawn's wife.

This story makes sense of an episode in *Diu Crône* which we shall examine in a moment, where Arthur fights an adversary for what is really the hand of Guinevere. When we notice that Arthur is said in later times to lead the Wild Hunt, which was also Arawn's responsibility, and that Arawn wore grey, which is believed, rightly or wrongly, to have been the origin of the Green Knight's colouring, and when we also recall Gawain's quarrel with the unnamed knight in *Hunbaut* over his dogs, we begin to see the extraordinary links between these stories.

If we turn again for a moment to the text of *Diu Crône*, which we have already found to preserve several more primitive elements of the original story, we find an episode in which the following events take place:

Queen Ginover gave a protective girdle to Gasozin, a knight whom she favoured. Near a ford in the neighbourhood of Arthur's court he overthrew three Round Table knights but was less successful against Arthur himself. Learning the king's identity Gasozin declared that Ginover has loved him and had been his captive and that Arthur had taken her away against his will. He showed the magic girdle as proof and proposed to fight Arthur there and then. Arthur refused but said they should meet again in a year. When Gasozin appears Ginover denies any claim upon her and he departs crestfallen. Later he abducts the queen who is then rescued by Gawain.

What are we to make of this version, in which we find Arthur fighting a type of the challenger (who has been given a protective girdle by Guinevere) at a ford? The fact that they also prepare to fight again at the end of a year, as in *Gawain and the Green Knight*, may well lead us to suppose that in the changing pattern of roles which accompanied the genesis of the story, it must originally have been Gawain and *Arthur* who fought for the hand of the Spring Maiden, here disguised as Guinevere.

Gasozin himself is described thus: 'he rides all night, summer and winter, in nothing but a white shirt . . . his horse is ermine white, his shield white, his banner white on a red lance; and he haunted the Ford of Noirespine (the Black Thorn).'[150] (Trans. K.G.T. Webster.) He thus combines elements of both the Green Knight and the Lord of Summer. Both have a single colour, are associated with a season, and both possess a girdle with magical properties, in the case of Gasozin given him by Guinevere. Gasozin fights at the 'Black Thorn', while a blackthorn stick is carried by the Lord of Winter. If we are correct in supposing that Arthur was once the hero of a test of this kind and remember as well that Guinevere instigated the quest for the understanding of women in *The Wife of Bath's Tale*,[7] we see another link in the chain — where Guinevere gives her magic girdle to the winner of that quest, just as Lady Bercilak gives hers to Gawain when he has successfully passed the test at her hands.

Her own role, as we may see from the thirteenth-century romance *Yder*,[44] may once have been seen more clearly as conforming to this role.

Yder is born to a noble lady who has been abandoned by her lover. He is brought up by his grandmother until at the age of 20 he sets off to find his father. On the way he comes to the court of Queen Guenloie and they fall in love. Not wishing him to be too confident she sends him away to prove himself. Yder meets a knight in the forest and kills two knights who attack him. The stranger turns out to be Arthur who invites Yder to return with him to the court. The two fall out however and Yder leaves, to undergo many more adventures. When Yder is later wounded by Sir Kay, Arthur and Guinevere go to visit him. Arthur is strangely jealous of Guinevere's interest in the young knight, whose own mind is only on Guenloie. Meanwhile in an effort to draw Yder, whose whereabouts she knows, back to her, Guenloie lays siege to the castle of one of Arthur's vassals, certain that Arthur will come and that Yder will be with him. More adventures follow, in which Arthur, Kay and Gawain all feature. Yder discovers his father, Nuc, at last and finally they meet Guenloie in a forest and she offers to marry the man who can bring her a knife belonging to a giant who is terrorizing the neighbourhood. Despite some treacherous behaviour from Kay, Yder succeeds and when all the parties are reunited there is general celebration, in which Yder's father marries his mother and Yder and Guenloie are joined in matrimony also.

The poem's editor, Alison Adams, suggests that the story only makes proper sense if the queen, Guenloie, was once identified with Guinevere and Yder with Gawain/Lancelot — as indeed they seem to be in the Modena archivault story, where the Besieged Lady is Winlogee, one of her rescuers Yder and the giant defender with the *baston cornu* Bermaltus, which, as we have seen, is a variant of the name Bercilak.

The Celtic scholar Rachel Bromwich[71] has successfully shown that the transmission of incidents from Irish myth to Arthurian romances happened in part because the Irish heroes were already known in Wales at the time (a number of Irish heroes are named in the Hero List contained in the *Mabinogion* story *Culhwch and Olwen*, and the Welsh bard Taliesin wrote a Death Song for Curoi). Thus the original Beheading Game probably started out at the court of Conchobar mac Nessa, then was translated to Wales and the Arthurian court of the romances, where it was first attributed to Caradoc Vreichvras (once equal in fame to any of the Round Table knights) then Gawain and finally to Lancelot.

The very fact that Lancelot in all probability descends from the Irish god of storm and sun, Lugh Loinennbemnach, made it inevitable that he should undergo the Beheading Game which his alter egos Cuchulainn and Gawain endured. Indeed, as far back as the Modena archivault where Gawain takes the role usually attributed to Lancelot as rescuer of Guinevere, we can perceive a blurring of the two characters. This is borne out further in the story of Yder, where we find at least three characters from the basic scenario appearing in the same text, with the figure of the queen taking a primary role.

We are thus able to suggest an as yet tentative identification of the Besieged Lady (see Chapter 2) with the host's wife, and to posit a possible version of the story in which Guinevere was besieged (possibly by giants) and in which the hero rescued her. This has been carried over into *Yder* in the episode of the giant's knife, where the hero's own story identifies him with a type of Gawain figure. (His father, Nuc, I take to be a kind of Lot; both rule over Pictish kingdoms, both are kings, both abandon their offspring — though Yder is brought up by his mother and grandmother.)

The original story is there still, but has changed with the climate of the times so that Gawain has become a secondary figure and Yder has replaced him, while the original relationship of Guinevere and Gawain has been lost entirely, except in Arthur's otherwise motiveless jealousy, and the clues provided by the episode in *Diu Crône*.

Two major themes have thus emerged and require further study. These are the relationship of the hero and the host and the motivation of the host's wife with regard to the hero. In examining these we shall finally be able to identify the key figure of the old woman in *Gawain and the Green Knight* and through her the original role of the hero in the primal story of the challenge and the Beheading Game.

THE GODDESS AND THE FAIRY BRIDE

In the second part of Lancelot's adventure as the Waste City it is notable that he is saved from death by the intervention of a woman who recognizes him.[60] In *Gawain and the Green Knight* and its various close analogues, Gawain is saved by the gift of a magical token which protects its wearer from harm. In *La Mule Sans Frein* this has become the magical bridle which gives to the person who possesses it dominion over a country and probable invulnerability. This is also given to Gawain by a woman. Are they acting simply out of love for the hero, or is there a deeper reason?

The least understood aspect in *Gawain and the Green Knight* is undoubtedly the role of Morgan. At present we have the rather curious and unsatisfactory statement of *Gawain and the Green Knight* that the motivation for sending Bercilak to Camelot in his fearsome guise was to frighten Guinevere, whom Morgan hated even more than she hated Arthur.

Two theories have been forward to explain this enmity, neither of which is really satisfactory. According to one, Morgan's enmity towards Arthur and Guinevere, which continues throughout the Arthurian cycle, is aroused by Guinevere's interference in an affair with either Accolon of Gaul (in Malory) or Guiomar (in *Livre d'Artus*), after which she built a chapel in a valley from which none could escape who had been untrue

in love. There she tested the fidelity of every knight who came that way
— hence, perhaps, the Green Chapel. However, it is not so much the
fidelity of those she tests towards a single woman which is the issue,
but rather that towards the Goddess herself, in whatever aspect she
chooses to appear.

The second theory was put forward originally by Richard Griffith[94]
and is reaffirmed more recently by Dr Helmut Nickel.[129] Both have
attempted to identify the Lord and Lady of Hautdesert in *Gawain and
the Green Knight* with Sir Bercilak le Rouge and his wife, who is the
false Guinevere of the *Vulgate cycle*.

Guinevere's father, Leodegran, begets the real Guinevere on his queen,
and the false on his Seneschal's wife. They are so alike that they can
only be told apart by the crown-shaped birthmark which appears on
the real daughter's loins. The false Guinevere arranges her half-sister's
abduction, substituting herself for the real Guinevere after her wedding to Arthur. He is at first deceived, but eventually recognizes the
truth and the false Guinevere is banished along with her husband.

Caitlín Matthews, in her book *Arthur and the Sovereignty of Britain*[113]
suggests that this duplication came about because the author of the
Vulgate *Lancelot* felt that the reputation of Arthur's queen would not
bear association with the Flower Bride theme, and that he therefore
invented a second Guinevere to disguise the original intent of the story.
The fact that both the false Guinevere and Bercilak are exiled at the
end of the incident and could be supposed to be found later, disguised,
living in an isolated castle and filled with hatred of Arthur and the real
Guinevere, seems a natural sequel to this story.

However, there are several facts which make this, admittedly fascinating, theory untenable. In the first place, despite an attempt to persuade
us that the change in colour from Bercilak 'the Red' to Bercilak 'the
Green' is the outcome of a translator's accident, there is still something inimicable about the Green Knight's greenness, which is the
colour of Faery, of the Irish *Sidhe*, of the Otherworld and of the
dead.[102] Further, the very nature of both the Green Knight and his
alter ego is such as to be wholly in line with the overall picture of the
Midwinter King and his Christmas Game, while Bercilak's hearty,
boisterous character in *Gawain and the Green Knight* make him an
unlikely surrogate for the banished Bercilak le Rouge. More important
is the way that this theory ignores the importance of Morgan, who is
relegated to an even more minor role.

Fascinating though they may be, neither theory seems to offer sufficient reason for the complex Winter Game. Clearly a deeper mean-

ing lies behind the challenge.

It is the present author's belief that this inadequate motivation arises from a confusion between two essentially different characters — namely Morgain and Guinevere. These two are, in effect, rather like the so-called dark and light aspects of the Goddess, primal archetypes well-attested in myth cycles from almost every corner of the world. Thus, as it was believed that the existence of one inevitably called for the existence of the other, it has frequently been the case that qualities relating to these two aspects were apportioned to more than one character, who though they may have begun life in harmony, became estranged, forced apart by the very archetypal roles they now fulfilled. This, it appears, is what happened to Morgain and Guinevere and it is this which has given rise to so much confusion and misunderstanding of the roles of the two women.

Guinevere, as we have seen, was at one time recognized as representing the Flower Bride in the contest fought over her by the champions of summer and winter, making her consequent with the idea of the Goddesses' 'light' aspect. Morgain, as sorceress, shape-shifter and implacable enemy of Arthur and the Round Table Fellowship, clearly represents her 'dark' side. This, more than anything, gave rise to the rivalry between the two, which is attested to in several of the texts we have been discussing.

Between these two poles Gawain, the hero, swings like a veritable pendulum, becoming as a result much maligned, among other things, for his so-called libertine attitude to women.

It is partly for this reason too that although several times married, Gawain never remains with one woman for any length of time. Indeed, his role became more that of consort to the otherworldly queen than simply that of her champion — a fact to which all the evidence so far gathered has pointed from the start. And this, of course, relates in turn to the whole nature of annual kingship and thus to the original reasons behind the challenge and the Beheading Game. It is, however, the nature of the *winnings* derived from this encounter which takes our argument a stage further.

Focusing on the episode of the magic girdle, both the Gasozin episode in *Diu Crône*, episodes from *De Ortu Waluuanii, La Mule Sans Frein* and another text, *Wigalois*[62] written in Middle High German around the year 1230, confirm that the power of the magical talisman given to Gawain by Lady Bercilak, is in fact the same token by which the Green Knight was able to avoid death. That it may also, like the magic bridle in *La Mule*, confer sovereignty over the land and is an outward symbol of the power of the Goddess, we shall hope to prove hereafter.

In *Diu Crône* the girdle is given to Gasozin by Ginover (Guinevere).
It had originally been worked by the Fée Giramphiel for her husband
King Fimbeus, who had in turn offered it to Ginover as a gift. When
she refused it he left it behind anyway and it gave her great beauty
and empowerment. Later on, after the Gasozin episode, it had been
reclaimed by Fimbeus, and Ginover finally persuaded Gawain to fight
him for it. During the fight Fimbeus wore the girdle and as for a time
invulnerable — then the jewel which had the real power fell out and
Gawain, picking it up, won the conflict and gave the girdle back to
Ginover.

In *Wigalois* the girdle is again given to Guinevere, this time by Joram,
a mysterious otherworldly king. When she refuses it he challenges the
knights of the Round Table to joist for it, beating them all, including
Gawain, whom he carries into captivity in his beautiful realm hidden
behind impenetrable mountains. There he offers the hero his daughter Florie as his wife, an offer which Gawain happily accepts. But after
six months he becomes restless and slips away to visit the court, leaving Florie with the magic belt for protection and instructions that it
should be given to their son.

When, after a short while with his companions of the Round Table,
Gawain tries to get back, he finds his way barred. The way back through
the mountains is hidden. After a year of fruitless searching he returns
sadly to Cardoil.

Wigalois is born and educated by a mysterious queen (who has not
appeared before) until he is 20, at which time he sets out for Arthur's
court to find Gawain. At the Round Table he sits in the Siège Perilous
(Perilous Seat) and refuses to admit his true identity, wearing the belt
concealed until Gawain acknowledges him.

This seems to offer some powerful parallels with two other figures,
also father and son. In the *Vulgate cycle*, as in Malory's redaction,
Lancelot begets a child on the Grail princess after being tricked into
believing that she is Guinevere. Once he discovers the trick he leaves
her and rides away. Galahad is born and brought up by a princess, (his
mother) and on arriving at Camelot, sits in the Siège Perilous, but keeps
his identity hidden until Lancelot can knight him in secret.

The parallels are obvious. Lancelot, like Gawain, and their sons, were
all brought up by mysterious women; while Irish parallels further show
that the mother of the child was in each case almost certainly herself
a goddess or at least a queen of the Otherworld). The fact that Gawain
cannot get back into the country behind the mountains in *Wigalois* indicates once again that this is an otherworldly place, and Joram's daughter
a type of otherworldly queen or maiden.

From the foregoing we may put together another part of Gawain's lost story, in which he encounters an otherworldly queen and engenders a child upon her who is brought up in secret after Gawain has departed. Later, grown to manhood, this child arrives at Arthur's court and proves himself by passing the test of the Perilous Seat.

There is now enough evidence to suggest that at one time Guinevere took the role later played by the Green Knight's wife (or the temptresses of the various other texts) and that Gawain was her champion. Taking this a step further we may suppose that behind the figure of Arthur's queen, lies that of a Goddess whose champion Gawain was, and who presents him both with a talismanic object which makes him invulnerable, and later with a son.

Traces of this story are still to be found within the *De Ortu Waluuanii*, where Guinevere (here called Guendoloena), who is said to have been initiated into sorcery and to be able to read the future, told Arthur of the imminent approach of a young knight who was possessed of such strength that none could overcome him. This is, of course, Gawain, though he does not, as yet, even know his own name. Arthur, his curiosity (and perhaps his jealousy) aroused, leaves the palace in secret and encounters Gawain at a ford, where they fight and where Arthur is soundly beaten.

There are a number of important details in this story. To begin with there is Guinevere's 'sorcery', her ability to foretell the future. Neither of these are attributes generally ascribed to the queen; however they *are* frequent aspects of Morgain's character. Guinevere also has an obvious interest in Gawain. Then there is the fact that Gawain defeats Arthur, the only person, apart from Lancelot, who is allowed to do so. (Presumably because he is wearing the golden, impenetrable armour given him by the Pirate Queen — in parallel to Gasozin's magic girdle given to him by Guinevere.) Finally there is the place of their encounter, the ford, which is inevitably reminiscent of the place where the champions of Summer and Winter met to do battle for the maiden of spring.

All this points even more strongly to Guinevere having been, at some point, either the wife or daughter of the Hospitable Host, and those who fought for her originally Gawain and Arthur. We may remember Arthur's unreasonable jealousy in *Yder*, and also perhaps that in certain old Welsh texts Guinevere's father was said to have been a giant.

Much of the confusion in the later stories arises from the fact that in the original, lost version, it must have been the Goddess herself who gave the token to her champion; the only version which still retains this is *Gawain and the Green Knight*, where Morgan and Lady Bercilak are clearly one and the same, so that it is she who gives her champion the magical token. Later, the motivation for this became confused or suppressed, as did the original roles and characters of Morgain and Guinevere.

The conclusions to be reached from all this complex of evidence only add to the idea of Gawain as the rightful Champion of the Goddess (be she Morgain or Guinevere,) and that he becomes so through winning the test of the Beheading Game. That he is already marked out for this role is indicated by the fact that the Goddess herself, through her earthly representative (Lady Bercilak or Guinevere) awarded a token which, worn with faith, protected its wearer from harm and possibly also conveyed sovereignty. (See Chapter 4 for a fuller discussion of this.)

This outcome had always been intended from the point when Gawain first rescued the Besieged Lady (see Chapter 2) or even earlier, possibly during his childhood in the Castle of Maidens. In *Gawain and the Green Knight* it is finally made clear — though in a confused and only partially understood fashion, where the story of the Test, the Temptation and the Green Girdle is told, but with less importance given to the real prime mover in the game, Morgane the Goddess, whose consort Gawain was to become.

It is evident, from all the romances in which the Beheading Game appears, that the proper outcome involved the marriage of the Lady and the Hero. In *La Mule*, Gawain clearly does win her; in *Gawain and the Green Knight*, where the ending has been changed, he should by rights have won the favours of Lady Bercilak as the beautiful 'aspect' of the Goddess.

However, once he has achieved the test of the Beheading Game and proved his faithfulness to the queen of all women, Gawain is firmly established as the Champion of the Goddess. As such we will recognize him throughout his adventures, despite every effort on the part of the later (Christian) writers to make him a murderer and a libertine. He has but one more test to undergo, before beginning his greatest adventure — that of his wedding to the earthly representative of the Goddess. It is at this episode that we must look in the next chapter.

Chapter 4.

A Knight Adventurous: Gawain and Women

THE KNIGHT WHO LOVED TOO MUCH

Gawain's prowess, as both warrior and lover, far outstrips that of any other character in the entire Arthurian cycle — including both Lancelot and Tristan, who though more renowned in the lovers' gallery, loved one woman only. Gawain, on the other hand, loved many — or at least, it would be fairer to say that he was himself loved by many: wherever he went he caused hearts to flutter, breasts to heave. Women fainted when he approached, or like the Lady of Gant Destroit, who kept a life-size sculpture of Gawain by her bed, seemed almost to worship him. Lancelot, it must be admitted, drew his own share of this kind of adulation, but he remained true to Guinevere and never succumbed to the wiles of the various lovely women (usually sorceresses) who came his way, whereas Gawain seemed always to find it difficult to refuse the generous offers of numerous ladies — either because he did not wish to hurt their feelings, or perhaps, as seems more likely in the light of what we know of his character and role, because he saw in each woman an earthly representative of the Goddess whom he served. Jessie Weston[152] pointed out as long ago as 1898 that tradition regarding Gawain's many mistresses was 'vague and incomplete'. However it will be clear from the evidence presented here that there is far less inconsistency than at first appears to be the case. Indeed, it will be seen that if we list the best known of Gawain's loves, that each has an aspect of the otherworldly about her — and in some cases, of the divine.

Taking first of all those already mentioned in the texts we have been examining so far, we find:

Guinevere: Although not usually connected with Gawain, we have already seen that in earlier versions of the story he seems to have assumed the role later attributed to Lancelot. The evidence of the Modena archivault, of *Yder* and of *De Ortu Waluuanii* supports this.

Morgain: We have seen the very considerable evidence which points to Gawain being the lover of this complex character, who is without doubt of the status of Goddess, which she is called in *Gawain and the*

Green Knight, Giraldus Cambrensis' *Speculum Ecclesiae* and the Vulgate *Lancelot*.

Levenet: The queen of the Meide Lant in *Diu Crône* though not specifically described as Gawain's mistress, gives him a vessel containing a mysterious substance which grants eternal life — surely both an indication of her feeling towards the knight as well as to her probable otherworldly status.

La Pucele aux Blanches Mains: Also known as the Lady of Isle d'Or, in the various texts of the Fair Unknown cycle this lady consistently plays the part of one who offers her love to Gawain or his representative. Described as a great sorceress, she is clearly much more than this, as her title alone indicates.

Blonde Esmerée: In the Fair Unknown cycle she is the mistress and later the wife of Gawain's son, whose role, as we have seen, is indistinguishable from that of his father. Like the Girl With White Hands she is an otherworldly woman.

The Daughter of the Unfriendly Host in *Hunbaut*: One of many such young ladies who offer themselves to Gawain. In this instance the lady first offers four kisses but ends by staying the night in Gawain's chamber.

The Lady of Gant Destroit: She who is so much in love with Gawain that she keeps a full-sized statue beside her bed and does her best to lure him into her castle.

The Daughter of the Friendly Host in *Le Chevalier à L'Epée*: In this instance the host himself offers his daughter to Gawain, who though strongly attracted to her, resists her presence and is thus saved from the mechanical sword which hangs above the bed. Perhaps because of this she later deserts him for another and proves generally faithless.

The Lady of the Bridle: Though there is no remaining evidence that this lady or her sister actually entertained amorous notions of the hero, the fact that the magical token is given to him indicates that the underlying story is the same as in *Gawain and the Green Knight*.

Lady Bercilak: This lady is clearly an aspect of the ancient crone-like Morgain, and not only offers a series of favours to be 'exchanged' for the spoils of the hunt, but also awards Gawain the baldric which will protect him from hurt.

The Daughter of the Carl of Carlisle: Another daughter of an otherworldly host, who offers her to Gawain after he has undergone various tests. In this case the hero ends by marrying her. (The same story was almost certainly once a part of *The Turk and Gawain*, see pp 79-80)

To these may be added the following:

Blancemal in *Le Bel Inconnu*. A typical example of the Fairy Bride who is the mother of Gawain's son, Guinglain.

Karmente, Gawain's fairy mistress in the thirteenth-century French romance *Saigremor*.[80]

Blanchemal le Fée: Mother of Gawain's son Guinglain in *Le Bel Inconnu*.[3] Her title makes it clear that she is once more of other-worldly origin.

Florée: Daughter of King Alain of Escavalon, she was certainly the mother of Gawain's son Guinglain and possibly of two other children. Florence and Lovell. She appears in Malory as the unnamed sister of Sir Brandiles. Her full story appears in the *Vulgate cycle*,[60] where after being rescued by Gawain, Florée comes to his bed rather as Lady Bercilak in *Gawain and the Green Knight*. In the *Pseudo Robert Trilogy*[70] she is later married to Meliant de Liz (Lis) whose name suggests he was a member of her family, possibly a cousin.

In the Middle High German poem *Rigomar* she appears as *Lorie*, in *Diu Crône* as *Flori* in *Wigalois* as *Florie*. These names all connect her with the Flower Bride, whose role she also adopts in the majority of these texts. While elsewhere in *Diu Crône* Heinrich makes *Amurfina*, Gansguoter's niece and Gawain's wife, originate in the *country* of Florie. This is clearly a memory of her original name, and as such she becomes one of the many flower brides to whom Gawain becomes wedded.

A momentary glance at some of the various names attributed to her father and brother give indication of Florée's otherworldly status. Alain is a name associated with the lineage of the Grail kings, Escavalon is clearly a corruption of Avalon; while Brandiles (Bran di Lis) is one of the many aliases under which the character of the Celtic god Bran finds his way into the Arthurian cycle.

It seems more than likely that we have here another piece of the missing story of Morgain, who was sent to Avalon to study magic, or who is, in other versions, a daughter of Avallach (Alain?). It would not do to pursue this too far, but there is sufficient coincidence in the material to suggest that the identity of the mother of Gawain's children may well have been Morgain in her role as Goddess, an idea not inconsistent with our argument so far.

These are only a few of the many women whom Gawain encounters during his career. To list them all would be tedious and only duplicate the evidence which they supply. All point quite clearly to one thing — Gawain's amours are all with otherworldly women, or goddesses, each of whom tests him in some way — either physically or morally, and who afterwards, as well as granting sexual favours, usually gift him with a token or talisman which will protect him from further harm, or which bestows sovereignty (see Appendix 5).

If we were in any doubt as to the importance of this strand in the story of Gawain, two further episodes not, so far, referred to, leave us in no possible doubt.

The first of these is another of the remarkable cycle of English Gawain poems, written between the twelfth and fourteenth centuries, and is perhaps, next to *Gawain and the Green Knight* the most important of the group.

Gawain and Ragnall was composed round about 1458 in the same part of the country as most of the cycle (i.e. the Midlands), and the story it tells, in two slightly differing versions, is as follows:

King Arthur is out hunting in the Forest of Inglewood near Carlisle and pursues a white hart, which runs so swiftly that it soon leads the king away from his men. He then encounters a 'quaint gome' who accuses him of wrongfully giving his lands to Gawain and promises to kill Arthur unless he can discover, in one year, what thing it is that women love best. The name of this churl is Gromer Somer Jour.

Arthur returns to Carlisle and places his problem before Gawain. Together the two set out in different directions in search of answers. They ask everywhere and as the year passes compile great books filled with answers. Then, on his last foray into the forest Arthur meets a monstrous old hag sitting beside the road. She gives her name as Ragnall and swears that she alone knows the correct answer to the question. But she will only give it on one condition, that she be given the hand of Gawain in marriage.

Shocked, Arthur returns to Carlisle and places the facts before Gawain, who loyally swears that he would marry the hag even though she were as ugly as Beelzebub. Arthur sets out to meet Gromer with the two books of answers and on the way meets Ragnall again. She gives Arthur the answer and promises to come soon to claim her husband. Arthur meets Gromer, and after trying all the answers he and Gawain had collected — to no avail — gives the answer of Ragnall. Gromer flies into a rage and says that only his sister could have given that answer, but he has to set Arthur free according to the bargain.

Arthur and Ragnall return to Carlisle and the hag is duly married to Gawain in a garish ceremony in which the table manners and general grossness of the bride shock and distress everyone, especially the women who love Gawain!

Next comes the wedding night and the hag demands a kiss of her husband. Gawain courteously obliges and to his amazement and delight Ragnall turns into a beautiful woman. But the enchantment which binds her is not yet broken — Gawain must decide whether he would have her fair by night or foul by day or vice versa. Unable to decide Gawain says that she alone has the right to choose, at which Ragnall gives a cry of joy and declares the enchantment broken. Gawain has given her the freedom of choice, sovereignty, which was also the answer to Gromer's question. The story ends in rejoicing, Gromer is forgiven and accepted into the court, and Ragnall remains with Gawain for five years, giving birth to his famous son Gyngolyn (Guinglainn).

This story, together with its variants, is an essential key to the whole saga of Gawain. It is a subtle and delightful parody of many of the greater romances, yet it contains sufficient depths to reward intensive study. Behind it lies a vast spectrum of lore and meaning, stretching back to prehistory. For Ragnall, gross and silly and appealing, is no less than the ancient Goddess of the Land, sovereignty herself, who alone can gift the king with the right to rule over his land. Her marriage to Gawain is an echo of the ancient rites where the king symbolically married the land itself, by mating with its representative in the form of a woman. In this instance, it is a different form of sovereignty which is conferred upon Gawain; through this he becomes the rightful Champion of the Goddess, destined to serve her until another shall come in time to take his place.

In much the same way the story confirms Gawain in his role of the supremely courteous knight. Not for a second does he hesitate when Arthur asks him if he will marry the hag. And, when the moment comes for him to choose whether he will remain the subject of laughter and pity by day (as the husband of a hideous wife) while having the joy of a beautiful woman in his bed at night, or the reverse, he sees that it is the right of Ragnall herself to choose, thereby breaking the 'spell' which binds her and freeing himself to enjoy her beauty all the time.

The moral and comic elements of this tale brought it to the attention of no lesser person than Geoffrey Chaucer who incorporated it into *The Canterbury Tales*[7] as 'The Wife of Bath's Tale'. There it is an unnamed knight who encounters the Loathly Lady, and who experiences the subsequent adventures directly — from which we may assume that at some stage in the transmission of this story Gawain (or a similar figure) was the central hero of the plot, and that it was only later, as the story became part of the Matter of Britain, that the more complex version, involving Arthur and his court, came into being.

Thus we see drawn together several of the different strands we have so far identified. We saw in the previous chapter that the outcome of the challenge and the Beheading Game included marriage or mating with the earthly representative of the Goddess, and that this resulted in the new hero becoming her champion. We saw also that various characters represented the single figure behind them all. Morgain and Guinevere were shown to represent the dark and light aspects of the Goddess.

Now, in *Gawain and Ragnall*, we see revealed the third aspect, that of the Loathly Lady whose perilous kiss confers sovereignty. These three aspects together make up the central figure of the Goddess, whom Gawain served. If we look even more closely at the elements which went into the creation of this story and its variants, and at another episode which reflects its inner meaning, we shall discover much more about the true nature of Gawain's original role.

THE LOATHLY LADY AND THE RESPONSIBLE KNIGHT

The figure of the Loathly Lady is, as stated above, of very ancient provenance. She appears in many of the Grail romances as the black or hideous damsel who chides and instructs the Grail knights upon their quest. In Wolfram von Eschenbach's *Parzival* she is Kundry, the accursed maiden of the Grail, who must free herself by aiding the innocent knight Parzival in his long search. It is interesting to note, that in the same romance, Gawain has a *sister* called Kundry *la Belle* (the Beautiful), which seems to suggest that at one time the story of the change from hideous to fair was told of her. If this is the case, then it is clearly no coincidence that the lady in question is associated with Gawain — though as sister rather than wife or mistress. As we shall see, this has an important bearing on Gawain's Grail adventures.

Behind this figure, as indeed behind all the Loathly Ladies of the Arthurian mythos, stands a far older, more primitive figure, that of the Goddess of Sovereignty herself. In Ireland, where her role is preserved more fully than anywhere else, we find many stories of her appearance, of which the following is one of the most typical.

The Adventures of the Sons of King Daire

> There was a prophecy that one of the sons of King Daire Doimtech would obtain the kingship of Ireland. As the name of this son was to be 'Lughaidh' each boy was given that name. One day King Daire asked a druid which son would be his successor. The druid replied that a golden fawn would appear and the son able to capture it would obtain the kingship. . . When the fawn appeared the princes chased it until that Lughaidh known as Mac Niad caught it.
>
> Then a great snow fell and one of the Lughaidhs was sent to seek shelter. He found a large house containing an inviting fire, food, ale, silver dishes,

couches of white bronze and a loathly hag: 'My boy, what seekest thou?'
says she.

'I am looking for a bed till morning.'

And she says: 'Thou shalt have one if thou wilt come and lie with me
tonight.' And the youth said that he would not do this, and he went to
his brothers.

'Thou has severed from thee sovranty and kingship', she saith.

Each of the others entered the house. . . Finally Mac Niad entered. The
hag asked what he had won during the day, and he answered that he had
caught the fawn and that he alone had eaten it. Thus he was given the
name Lughaidh Laidhe (the Fawn).

Lughaidh Laidhe then followed the hag to one of the couches of white
bronze. He made no objection to her advances; to his amazement, she
became a beautiful young girl. . . And after that he mingled in love with
her. 'Auspicious is thy journey,' quoth she. I am the sovranty, and the Kingship of Erin will be obtained by thee.'[1]

We can see immediately the analogies with the story of Gawain and
Ragnall. The hero must face a test which includes sleeping with a hideously ugly woman who, upon being kissed, immediately becomes beautiful and offers the youth a gift of great value. We have already seen
that several of Gawain's mistresses similarly give gifts, generally destined to preserve the life of the hero, or to bring him riches and fame.
In each case it is the inherent *courtesy* of the hero which causes a successful outcome.

The description of sovereignty in the text quoted above is also significant. To Lughaidh Laidhe '. . . it seemed. . . that the radiance of her
face was the sun rising in the month of May, and her fragrance was
likened by him to an odorous herb garden'. (Trans. Whitley Stokes.)
This is clearly a description of the Goddess and it seems more than
appropriate that the imagery reflects Gawain's title 'The Hawk of May',
and his solar attributes.

This is, once again, a far cry from the anti-image of Gawain as
represented, for instance, by the *De coniuge non ducenda* (1225-1250)
translated as *Gawain on Marriage*[8] a long anti-matrimonial satire written with the specific intent of dissuading men from the state of
matrimony. In this Gawain is advised by three angels, who persuade
him that marriage, and women in general, are not a good idea. Gawain
appears to agree, though it must be said that he has no real 'voice' of
his own, his compliance with the rather trite anti-feminist sentiments
of the poem being assumed rather than stated.

In the majority of the romances Gawain is shown as a lover of women
— not as profligate, as some writers would have us believe, but as someone who genuinely respects the wisdom of the feminine. This aspect
of his character would have been the first to come under suspicion by

the monkish writers who compiled the later Arthurian romances. Any suspicion of Gawain's 'pagan' affiliation would have called for one of two reactions; suppression or denigration. Hence the gradual change and decline of Gawain's literary career, which reflects the climate of the times. Only in cases where the references were not understood did the real story of the Knight of the Goddess remain untouched, but even here they were often deeply buried beneath layers of story and references to other characters in the shifting quicksand of medieval romance.

In *Gawain and Ragnall* the shape of the original shows through. The name of Arthur's adversary, Gromer Somer Jour, means Man of the Summer's Day, a clear enough reference to a character we have already encountered in the shape of Hafgan, 'Summer Song' in the *Mabinogion* story of Pwyll. He, we may recall, is a participant in the battle for the Flower Bride and lent so much to the formation of the Gawain saga.

Another Irish story, from *Cormac's Glossary*,[13] has the master poet Senchen journey to the Isle of Man in search of a lost poetess. They are accompanied by a hideously ugly youth and on arrival encounter an old woman on the shore. On hearing that the leader of the party is Senchan, she asks that he help her with the answer to a problem. When he agrees she speaks one half of a poem and demands that Senchan complete it. The ugly youth supplies the missing piece before anyone else can speak. The test is then repeated and Senchan recognizes the old woman as the lost poetess, clothes her in fine raiment and returns with her to Ireland. There they meet again the youth who had accompanied them, only now he is 'a young hero, kingly, radiant... fairer than the men of the world was he, both in form and dress.'

The youth is later revealed as the spirit of poetry, but it is clear from the nature of the story that at one time it must have been the old poetess herself who was first ugly and then beautiful, that her questions to Senchen, the poems he must complete, stood for the test that would transform her to her original form.

The third episode which adds to this gradually emerging picture is found in two versions: originally in the *Vulgate cycle*, it was retold by Malory in Book IV of *Le Morte d'Arthur*. Three knights, Gawain, Uwain and Marhaus ride together in search of adventure.

> They arrive at the forest of Arroy, where, says Marhaus 'came never knight since it was christened' but he found strange adventures; and so they rode, and came into a deep valley full of stones, and thereby they saw a fair stream of water; above thereby was the head of the stream a fair fountain, and three damosels sitting thereby. And then they rode to them, and either saluted other, and the eldest had a garland of gold about her head and she was three score winter of age or more, and her hair was white under the garland. The second damosel was of thirty winter of age, with a cir-

clet of gold about her head. The third damosel was but fifteen year of age, and a garland of flowers about her head. When these knights had so beheld them, they asked them the cause whereby they sat at that fountain? We be here, said the damosels, for this cause: if we may see any errant knights, to teach them unto strange adventures; and ye be three knights that seek adventures, and we be three damosels, and therefore each one of you must choose one of us... (Book IV, Ch.xix)

So the three knights each choose a damosel: Uwain, electing to take the oldest lady 'since I am the youngest and most weakest...and she hath seen much, and can best help me when I have need'. Marhaus chooses the middle-aged lady 'for she falleth best to me', leaving Gawain with the 15-year-old girl. They are each led by the bridle to a parting of the ways and each swears to meet again at the fountain in a year. Uwain goes West, Marhaus South and Gawain North.

So begin their adventures, at which we will look more closely in a moment. But what of the three damosels? The very fact that they are described thus, with a word used to imply young and unmarried women, is itself interesting, for it marks them out at once as unusual. But of course they are not of this world; their appearance by the fountain in the depths of the Forest of Adventure — the same forest in which Arthur met Ragnall — proclaims this at once. But even if we were in any doubt, their description only confirms it. Their exact ages: 60, 30, 15; their garlanded hair and general air of waiting, marks them out as the triple aspect of the Goddess, appearing in three separate forms at once, each one prepared to lead her chosen knight (for whatever the text may say, we may be sure it is they who choose and not the knights) into a path of adventure. In several later texts this same triplicity reappears in the guise of Igraine, Morgain and Gawain's sister Clarine.

Uwain, who is better known to us as Owain, from the *Mabinogion* story which bears his name, chooses the eldest lady in the belief that she must know more than the others. He is the child of Morgan le Fay and Uriens and as such may be seen as either a brother or more likely a variant of Gawain himself. Marhaus, the second knight, is to be identified with the Morholt, the legendary Irish hero with whom Tristan later does battle to the death. In many details he conforms to what we know of Cuchulainn, also a doublet of Gawain.

So that we may say that at a certain level both the older aspects of the Goddess choose an aspect of Gawain — who seems here almost to fulfil the role of triple-aspected hero! He himself chooses, or is chosen by, the youngest damosel, she of the 15 summers and the garland of flowers. We may see something familiar about her and find ourselves thinking of one of the Flower Maidens, Guinevere or Florée, whom we met earlier as partners of Gawain. There is only one way to read the imagery of this episode — as yet another story in which Gawain is chosen to follow an aspect of the Goddess into adventure. An adventure which, as we shall see, is itself not without significance.

Gawain accompanies the youngest damosel to the castle of an elderly knight, from whom they enquire of adventures. Next morning they linger by a crossroads, where all great knightly adventures are expected to begin, and there they witness the fight between a single knight and ten others, all of whom he defeats but then submits meekly to being pulled from his horse, bound and carried off. They then meet Sir Carados, with whom Gawain fights until they are cheerfully accorded. At this point the Damosel of Fifteen Summers, accuses Gawain of cowardice for not going to the assistance of the knight who fought ten men single-handed, and departs. From his new friend Gawain learns that the knight is named Sir Pelleas. It transpires that he loves a lady named Ettard, who does not, however, return his feelings. Therefore he remains always near her castle, and when, each day, she sends out fresh knights against him, he first of all defeats them but then allows them to take him prisoner in order that he may catch a glimpse of his love. Each day he is released, after ignominious treatment, and undergoes the same torment again.

Gawain marvels at this and decides to do what he can to help Pelleas. Next morning he enters the forest and waits for the knight, learning more of his story and swearing to help him. He then takes Pelleas' armour and rides to the castle of Ettard, where he tells her that he has killed Pelleas and taken his armour. Ettard is pleased and entertains Gawain warmly. Gawain then claims love for another and requests that Ettard do all she can to win his love. When she agrees he announces that it is herself that he loves, and the two become lovers in earnest.

A few days later, Pelleas decides to find out what is happening, and discovers where Gawain and the Lady have pitched their pavilion in the forest and are abed together. Heart-broken Pelleas at first wants to kill them both, but finally leaves his sword across their necks and rides away, declaring to his followers that he will give them all his goods because he intends to die. When Gawain and Ettard wake and discover the sword, Ettard realizes what has happened and curses Gawain for his falseness. He departs for the forest.

Enter, at this point, Nimue, the Damosel of the Lake. Learning of the story she first of all enchants Ettard into loving Pelleas desperately, and then Pelleas (who needs little encouragement) into hating her. His affections are now transferred to the Lady of the Lake herself and the two go off together. Ettard dies of grief, while Gawain wanders on his way to further adventures.[32]

This episode is often quoted as an example of Gawain's unchivalrous behaviour. However, a variant version is provided by the fragmentary *Adventure of Yvain, Gawain and Morold*[60] which gives a 'cleaned up' version in which Gawain appears in a better light. Here the woman whom Pelleas loves is called Arcade. She is far more interested in Gawain and in fact seduces him (the implication being that he in fact loses his virginity at this point). On waking they find the evidence of Pelleas having been there, and Gawain remorsefully persuades Arcade to marry him. She does so, rather reluctantly, and all ends happily without the intervention of the Lady of the Lake.

Though rationalized, the story is interesting for the way it tidies up Gawain's otherwise tarnished reputation. Again, when we look more closely at its constituents, in the light of evidence already gathered, we may see it differently.

The elderly knight with whom Gawain and the Damosel of Fifteen Summers stay may be seen as a shadowy memory of the Hospitable Host who offers his daughter to the seeker, and indeed the name of the knight with whom Gawain fights, but who then invites him to stay, seems to confirm this, since we have seen that Carados is frequently associated with Gawain in this role, as far back as the Modena version.

Then there is the fact that the damosel, whom we have already identified as an aspect of the Goddess, suddenly departs from her chosen knight — returning, we may suspect, in the guise of Nimue, the Damosel of the Lake, whose actions give us the clue to the real meaning of the story.

Gawain is, once again, being tested. The fact that he takes Pelleas' armour indicates that at some stage he probably fought and overcame him, thus earning the right to call himself Ettard's champion. Her subsequent behaviour, and the reappearance of Pelleas (who is really behaving contrary to an accepted code of practice, in which, as the defeated champion, he should retire gracefully) requires the intervention of the Goddess's representative to set matters right.

Gawain is thus playing his role as required, recognizing in Ettard another aspect of the Goddess he serves, to whose love he is thereby entitled. The author of the *Vulgate cycle*, on whom Malory based his version, clearly saw this as an unprecedented act of betrayal in the name of lust. Malory, with his novelist's eye for characterization, could not resist adding details of his own, which make a powerful episode but further disguise the original intent of the unknown story-teller who first devised the tale of Gawain's service to the Goddess.

We thus see in these episodes further evidence as to Gawain's original role as Champion of the Goddess. (Even Malory's statement that Pelleas chose Ettard to be his 'sovereign' lady adds to our case.) The original scenario, in which the knight was challenged by the retiring champion, overcame him either by simple prowess or with the assistance of the Goddess herself, who then became his mistress and rewarded him with a gift of life or strength or riches, thus becomes clearer.

The specific nature of the gift, in the case of both Lughaidh in *The Adventures of the Sons of King Daire* and of Gawain, in *Gawain and Ragnall* and *Le Morte d'Arthur*, as well as in the majority of Irish stories in which the hag appears, concerns sovereignty. Gawain himself does not become King of Britain (though, as we have seen, his claims to the throne were far from negligible); and interestingly, in another version of Lughaidhe's story, neither does he obtain the throne. It seems that another kind of sovereignty is being offered, one which is very appropriate to the role of Gawain.

Gawain and Ragnall and its variant *The Marriage of Sir Gawain*[53] were both written in the fifteenth century. Yet the story they contain is far earlier than this, dating back to the heroic period of the Celts and only latterly associated with Gawain. His choice for the hero of both texts is significant, since it implies an *already established* tradition in which he was associated with the Goddess. One has only to imagine for a moment the effect of transposing Lancelot to this role to see how rightly Gawain fits the part and how unlikely a hero Lancelot would have proved.

The difference between the use of the word 'sovereignty' in *Gawain and Ragnall* and in the Irish texts is one of kind. In the former sovereignty means 'mastery over a man or men', and in the latter 'mastery over the land'. By bringing in Gawain, the anonymous authors of the Gawain poems assured that while one meaning was understood, the second, deeper meaning, was also present. This re-emphasizes our point of Gawain's prior association with the thematic material.

Sigmund Eisner makes an important point when he suggests that the quest must once have been initiated by a woman — as it is in *The Wife of Bath's Tale*, the *Tale of Florent*,[89] *The Ballad of King Arthur and King Cornwall*,[53] and the Combat at the Ford episode in *Diu Crône* — all of which are variants of the Gawain and Ragnall story. In the context of our argument, it is clearly significant that the woman whom we may presume to have originated the quest and posed the all-important question is herself a queen (Guinevere), and that the test which follows is the work of a goddess (Morgain).

This only serves to strengthen our contention: that at some juncture the whole story was part of an initiation test which involved the hero becoming the new Champion of the Goddess, and through her, gaining sovereignty — not over the land, as in Arthur's case, but over all women, who are seen as her earthly representatives.

In *Gawain and Ragnall* the presence of Gromer Somer Jour, the retiring champion, complicates matters, since the test which should have followed, and featured him in the role of Bercilak — the Beheading Game — is missing from the Ragnall texts.

There are in fact two quite distinct test stories involving Gawain: a) The Riddle Test (*Gawain and Ragnall*) and b) The Beheading Game (*Gawain and the Green Knight* etc), which at one time formed part of the same story. In the versions still extant they have become separated into two distinct stories, the significance of which only becomes clear when they are reunited.

Even the reason for Gromer's seeking revenge has to do with his rights to *lands* (i.e. sovereignty) which had been given by Arthur to Gawain. Is this not a clear reference to the idea that Gawain had to *win* the rights to them, and did so through his marriage to Ragnall? Even this subtle re-working of the story does not exclude its greater significance, in which the 'lands' in question were those of the Goddess of Sovereignty herself.

If this is accepted we may posit another version of the story in which Arthur rather than Gawain was the hero, and won his lands by sleeping with the Goddess — as is perhaps the case when Arthur sleeps with Morgain/Morgause and begets Mordred. Arthur and Gawain thus exchange places exactly as do Pwyll and Arawn in the *Mabinogion*. In both cases their adventure is followed by a test involving a combat at a ford (see Chapter 3), and a test of fidelity. That Gawain was the original hero of both stories seems implicit, the later incursion of Arthur being part of the general assumption of material into the Arthurian corpus.

Sigmund Eisner, who has studied the sources of *Gawain and Ragnall*[89] thinks that there must once have been a combat at the ford in the original version of *Gawain and the Green Knight*, and notes that in one text (*The Adventures of Arthur at Tarn Watheling*) the challenge takes place at a site notorious for adventure and otherworldliness in Arthurian legend.

If this is correct, and there seems no reason to reject the idea, then we may propose a sequence of events as follows:

1. Gawain/Arthur encounters an otherworldly knight at a ford.
2. The Riddle Test.
3. The Beheading Game.
4. Marriage of Gawain/Arthur to otherworldly woman/Goddess.
5. Birth of a son to the Hero and the Goddess.

This pattern successfully makes use of all the elements which are to

be found in the various versions we have examined so far. It shows
Gawain's role clearly, and that he may have at some point exchanged
places with Arthur. The full significance of this leads us to a further
startling realization — that Gawain, as Arthur's closest relative, his sister's son, (a relationship long recognized among the Celts as sacred)
is *standing in for Arthur himself as the champion of Britain's
sovereignty!*[113]

In the light of this and if, as was suggested in Chapter 1, Gawain was
himself at one time known as the child of Morgain and Arthur, another
piece of the original story now falls into place:

Arthur, as the new king, encounters the Sovereignty of Britain (in her
guise as Morgain) and begets upon her a wondrous child (Gawain) who,
when he finally reaches manhood, undergoes a series of tests set by
his mother, which equip him to fulfil his father's role.

Events prove otherwise in the later romances, where Mordred has been
substituted for Gawain, but where the fact that this should not have
happened, that it was indeed Gawain who should have ascended the
throne after Arthur, still remains embedded in the story, though for
a different reason. We may see something of this in the stories of
Gawain's son Guinglainn — or indeed in the several 'Fair Unknowns',
who are each children of the Goddess and the champion. (It also
explains why Mordred plays the role of abductor and ravisher of the
queen in the later romances. He was simply fulfilling Gawain's original functions.)

Gawain's relationship to the Goddess of the Island is thus established.
He has passed the test which assures him the role of sovereignty's champion, the Knight of the Goddess, by acknowledging the inner beauty
of the hag and her right to choose her own destiny. Ahead lie many
new adventures, leading at last to the Grail Quest and Gawain's unique
role in it.

⚜

SEEKING THE NOBLE PATH: GAWAIN IN THE WORLD OF CHIVALRY

Before we begin our examination of Gawain's involvement in the great
Quest for the Holy Grail, we need to pause for a moment to look at
what we may call his 'worldly' adventures — though these are by no
means notable for their exclusion of the alignments of magic and

wonder. An image of Gawain — not inconsistent with what we have seen so far — emerges; the image of a man often at a loss to understand his place in the scheme of things, but who yet, through his faith in certain guiding principles, manages to make a name for himself which will be long remembered.

What appears to be Gawain's first quest is to be found in the *Suite du Merlin*[34] which is followed fairly closely by Malory in his account.[32]

At the first gathering of the Round Table after the wedding of Arthur and Guinevere, Gawain is knighted. That same day begins the Quest for the White Hart, which enters the hall at Camelot, pursued by a brachet (a small hunting dog of the kind kept by ladies) and 30 couple of black hounds. The Hart leaps over the Table, knocking over a knight who is sitting nearby. He then seizes the brachet and departs hurriedly. Next comes a lady who complains loudly about the theft of the dog and is herself then carried off by a knight who rides fully armed through the hall. Merlin declares that this is the first important quest of the Round Table, and advises Arthur to send Gawain after the White Hart, Tor after the brachet, and his father, King Pellinore, after the lady and the knight.

Gawain's story is told first. Following the trail of the Hart he pursues it into the courtyard of a castle where his own dogs pull it down. The owner of the castle — and of the Hart — runs out and kills Gawain's dogs. Attacking him furiously Gawain beats him to the ground, and despite his pleas for mercy is about to kill him when the knight's love appears and throws herself across his body. Unable to arrest his sword, Gawain beheads her.

Contrite, he sends the wounded knight back to Arthur, while he himself is attacked by a large group of knights, wounded by a poisoned arrow, and is on the point of being killed when four ladies rescue him. On learning his identity one of the women appears to know all about the recent events and chides him severely for his discourtesy. She then instructs him to return to Camelot, bearing the dead woman's head slung round his neck by its tresses, and there to accept whatever judgement is put upon him by the queen and her ladies.

Sorrowfully Gawain returns to the court and confesses all that occurred. Arthur and Guinevere are displeased and the queen passes the following judgement (the words are Malory's):

> And there by ordinance of the Queen there was set a quest of ladies on Sir Gawain, and they judged him forever while he lived to be with all ladies, and to fight for their quarrels; and that he ever should be courteous, and never to refuse mercy to him that asketh mercy.' (Bk 3, Chap.8)

This is very interesting. Gawain is sworn to 'be with all ladies, and to fight for their quarrels' — a stricture which it could fairly be said he obeys throughout his career. The author of the *Suite du Merlin*, and Malory after him, seems to preserve something of Gawain's original role in this passage. A 'quest' of ladies give judgement upon him that he shall be concerned with women throughout his life — for one who was to become the Knight of the Goddess surely a clear enough prediction.

But there are strange elements about all of this early adventure of the Round Table fellowship. Those of Pellinore and his illegitimate son Tor both bear the hallmarks of otherworldly origin.

Tor's adventure concerns a lady who, coming across him as he is about to offer mercy to a knight he has defeated, demands, as a favour, his head. Tor must obey, as he has given his word before he knew what the request would be, but he does so reluctantly.

Pellinore's adventure also features a headless damsel. In his haste to go about his part of the quest he refuses to help a girl who asks it of him, and she forthwith dies, hoping he may one day be refused in a similar manner. On his way back to Camelot, having succeeded in his task, he discovers the remains of the girl's body, which had been consumed by wild beasts except for the head. Remorseful now of his earlier actions he decides to take the head with him back to the court and there discovers from Merlin that the girl was his own daughter.

This rather tangled set of stories is extremely suggestive in the light of our investigations. The fascination with severed heads was peculiarly Celtic and there does seem to be a kind of relationship between the three deaths:

1. That of the woman Gawain beheads.
2. That of the knight Tor beheads.
3. That of the girl whose head Pellinore discovers.

It may even be that somewhere in this story lies the real beginning of the animosity which existed throughout most of the Arthurian cycle between the families of Pellinore and Lot, and which ended in darker deeds (see Chapter 7).

The whole episode is ringed about with otherworldly trappings and seems linked with the mysterious beginnings of the Arthurian Grail Quest. The lady whom Pellinore is sent to fetch back is Nimue, one of the Ladies of the Lake and the eventual nemesis of Merlin, who seems to know all about the adventure on which he advises Arthur to send the three knights. The strange dark matter of the Dolorous Blow, struck by the knight Balin in the Castle of the Grail, which causes the unhealing wound of the Fisher King, occurs shortly after this, and there is a similarity of tone and style which suggests that the two episodes are alike — part of the dawning enchantments of the Grail.

Gawain's role remains unclear at this stage. He is just 18 and still finding his way in the world. This first adventure is strangely prophetic of his dealings with women, a mixture of violence and gentleness, courtesy and uncouth behaviour, which colours his many relationships. Perhaps too, we may see the first signs of the otherworldliness which was to be such a strong feature of his career from then onward, and which was to culminate in the tests and trials which established him as the Knight of the Goddess.

Certainly it is not without significance that Gawain's next great adventure is also a tripartite one, in which three women, who together form an almost unique portrait of the Goddess, appear. This adventure, as we have already seen (pp 99-101) leads to Gawain's ambiguous role in the story of Pelleas and Ettard, wherein once again his behaviour towards women is shown to be less than ideal. We may perhaps see these early adventures, along with Gawain's more warlike exploits, as narrated in Geoffrey's *Historia or De Ortu Waluuanii*, as dating from before the time of his initiation test at the hands of the Green Knight, and of his marriage to Ragnall.

Many texts relate Gawain's subsequent career, not all of them adding significantly to the portrait which has begun to emerge. Among the most important are without doubt the Grail texts and these will be dealt with in the next chapter. However, a small group remains, some European, others English, which contain episodes that help extend our understanding of Gawain's primary role.

Certainly among the most interesting of these are two lengthy romances, both attributed to Raoul de Houdenc, and written within the first two decades of the thirteenth century. The first of these, *Meraugis de la Portlesquez*,[80] tells a curious tale of friendship and love, with undertones of comedy rare in Arthurian romance. Its contents, briefly summarized, are as follows:

Meraugis and Gorvain Cadrut seek to win the love of Lidoine, who has just decided in favour of the former when a dwarf arrives who reminds Arthur that his court is incomplete without the presence of Gawain. At once Meraugis declares that he will set out to find his friend, and taking Lidoine with him sets out in search of the 'Esplumoir Merlin'[141] where he is sure to find news of Gawain. Arriving first at the 'City Without a Name' he is told of an adventure which all who come there must attempt. On a nearby island is a great knight, whom Meraugis must fight — his reward for successfully beating the reigning champion being the hand of the Lady of the Castle. Apparently forgetting Lidoine, Meraugis crosses to the island and does battle mightily with the knight. Towards midday, when Meraugis thinks he is beginning to wear down his opponent, his strength suddenly waxes and in astonishment Meraugis asks his name. It is, of course, Gawain, and the two greet each other happily. Then Gawain explains painfully that the custom of the island is that whoever wins the combat must remain there until he himself is defeated.

This interesting state of affairs of course simply bears out the idea of annual kingship, discussed in Chapter 3. The fact that Gawain already occupies this position is important, as is Meraugis' expectation of being able to discover his whereabouts at the 'Esplumoir Merlin', a place associated with the entrance to the Otherworld. In a later continuation of Chrétien's *Conte del Graal* Gawain again faces such a prohibition upon his movements, but there chooses to ignore it (see p. 123).

Gawain and Meraugis now devise a plan. Since they do not wish to fight each other to the death, Meraugis will pretend to fall, Gawain will pretend to strike off his head, and under cover of darkness they will make their escape.

That they are able to do so is due entirely to Meraugis, who devises and carries out a remarkable plot. Tricking the Lady of the Castle and her people, who think him dead, into a tower, he locks them in, steals a dress and poses as the Lady herself to attract the ship which will carry them to the mainland. When it arrives, Meraugis introduces the sailors to their 'dame', which in this instance is his sword, and whose orders they are just as much bound to follow as if it were the Lady of the Castle herself!

The whole scene is handled in the best tradition of high comedy and is marked by Gawain's extreme passivity. Meraugis does all the thinking and the work, while Gawain simply follows his lead, apparently no longer bound to the ritual of the island.

Discovering that Lidoine has departed, mourning the supposed death of Meraugis, he at once sets out to find her, while Gawain goes his way in search of 'The Sword of the Strange Hangings', the quest upon which he had been engaged when he became the unwilling Champion of the Island.

When, much later, Gawain returns to the court, he finds that news has reached there that Lidoine and Meraugis, after being re-united, have been taken prisoner by Belchis le Lois, whose castle is now under siege by Gorvan Cardut, Lidoine's old suitor. Gawain at once begins to organize a relief force (paid for by Arthur) and leads an expedition by sea against Belchis. Meraugis, who had been believed dead, is found to be alive and well, and he now undertakes a desperate venture, offering to meet Gawain in single combat in exchange for his freedom. In fact, by a neat reversal of the earlier episode, Gawain this time feigns defeat (a considerable feat for someone of his innate pride and prowess), whereupon Belchis' men opt to follow Meraugis.

Meraugis and Lidoine are eventually released and the truth about Gawain's trick revealed — to his greater honour. All ends happily with Meraugis united with Lidoine and Gawain basking in glory. Despite moments of weakness, he is shown as a hero *par excellence*, equal in every way to Meraugis himself.

Complex questions regarding honour are asked throughout this romance, which despite its occasional moments of comic relief, has an underlying seriousness. Meraugis is by no means a typical hero, any more than the treatment of Gawain is typical for the time. One cannot, for example, imagine Gawain in any of the later texts offering to 'play dead' as he does here — especially not in front of a large assembly of hostile knights and ladies. That he does so adds to his stature and makes him, ultimately, a sympathetic figure.

The second romance attributed to Raoul de Houdenc is *La Vengeance Raguidel*.[38] The same element of satire is present, as are the elements of magic and adventure consistent with those romances in which Gawain features.

At the beginning of the story a barge arrives at Arthur's court bearing the body of a knight in which the tip of the murder weapon is still lodged. A letter is found demanding vengeance for the knight, which can, however, only be carried out by he who can remove the lance-point. In addition it is stated that a second person will be required who will be identified as the only one capable of removing the rings from the dead man's hand.

Gawain volunteers, as do several others, but he is the only one successful in removing the lance-point. While the forthcoming quest is still being discussed, word comes that a stranger knight named Yder has taken the rings. Gawain at once sets out in pursuit.

Arriving at an apparently deserted castle, Gawain sits down to a superb meal at times reminiscent of the Grail feast. While he is eating the castle's owner appears and challenges him. In another comic scene Gawain says that he will fight when he has finished three more mouthfuls — meanwhile putting on his helmet, and taking up shield and sword. Gawain is hard pressed by his adversary, the Chevalier Noir, but is eventually victorious. After asking for mercy, which Gawain grants, the knight explains that he once almost won the hand of 'La Pucele de Gant Destroit', only to be beaten at the last moment by Gawain. He has been seeking him ever since, but since Gawain is 'always off on some adventure or other' he is hard to find. Admitting that he is, indeed, Gawain, the hero demands the Chevalier Noir's fealty and sends him on his way to Arthur.

By a strange quirk of fate Gawain is next captured by the very same damsel whom the Black Knight loves. She has been hungering for Gawain ever since the contest in which he won her, and captures every knight who comes her way in the hope that one will turn out to be he. She already has Gawain's brother Gaheries in her dungeon, and keeps a servant-girl named Marot, who knows all the Round Table knights by sight, to identify each successive prisoner. But the girl herself has a fancy for Gawain and promises to help him, telling her mistress that he is Sir Kay.

Much is now made of Gawain's false identity, and Raoul pokes fun at his erstwhile hero at every juncture. Gawain is forced to reveal his name in the end, but makes his escape with Gaheriet to the Black Knight's castle. All three are besieged by an angry Pucele and her men.

Gawain suddenly realizes at this point that he has left the fragment of the lance-head, which was the cause of the whole adventure, behind, and resolves to try and break out to get it. He does so, along with Gaheriet and the Black Knight, and the three encounter a girl being threatened by two knights. Gawain at once offers combat and wins — the girl, whose name is Ydain, promising to love him forever for saving her.

They all return to the court together and shortly after a hunchbacked knight arrives, demanding of Arthur that he prove his legendary 'largesse' is all it is said to be. The king is reluctant, but Gawain urges him to acquiesce. He is made to regret this at once when the knight, whose name is Druidain, demands the girl whom Gawain had just recently saved. Angrily Gawain offers to fight and Druidain agrees, insisting, however, that the combat takes place at a place of his own choosing. Gawain agrees and the meeting is set for a month after at the castle of King Bagdemagu.

Gawain is thus once again distracted from his true purpose, but in obvious expectation of the outcome of the combat he takes the lance-point with him when he leaves the court a month later.

Since Ydain is the object of the contest she accompanies Gawain on the road, but they have not gone far before they encounter another knight who demands that the girl should go with him.

There then follows an important scene. Gawain strikes a bargain with the knight — that Ydain should choose whichever of them she likes the best, thus avoiding the need for combat. Perhaps he is simply trying to avoid the same situation happening again — after all he has still not fought the first man who asked for her — but for whatever reason he gives the girl freedom of choice in much the same way as in *Gawain and Ragnall* — except that here the result is very different.

Ydain is so angry at being treated as a bargaining token that she declares that Gawain cannot possibly really love her and promptly offers herself to the stranger. Gawain's reaction to this is concern that he will no longer be able to fulfil his promise to Druidain, since there is no point in their fighting if he no longer has Ydain. He therefore finds a fresh excuse to fight the knight and kills him anyway. Ydain then announces that she had engineered the whole thing in order to *test* Gawain! He is sufficiently put out by this to make Ydain ride in front of him all the way to Bagdemagu's castle. There, he defeats Druidain and sends him back to Arthur with Ydain, whom he has now totally repudiated.

This part of the romance is clearly intended to demonstrate Gawain's chivalrous conduct as well as his fatal charm to women. If, as Keith Busby thinks, Raoul's intention was to satirize Gawain, he is largely unsuccessful — though it must be admitted that Gawain does suffer some embarrassing moments.

The fact that he fights a knight named *Druid*ain at the castle of Bagdemagu (associated with the abduction of Guinevere) is of some note. As is the episode where he gives Ydain freedom of choice — a situation engineered by the lady herself in order to test Gawain's chivalry.

These adventures having been successfully concluded Gawain is now free to continue his original quest. Riding by the sea he catches sight of the same boat which had brought the body of Raguidel to Carlion, and after some hesitation he goes aboard. The boat at once departs of its own accord, landing eventually in Scotland, where the wild nature of the territory causes Gawain some concern.

However, he soon finds his way to a castle and there meets a dwarf and a curious lady riding backwards on a mule with her clothing on back to front. She invited Gawain to enter the castle and explains that she was the mistress of Raguidel, whose murderer, Guengasoain, is nearby. She had learned that the boat had reached Carlion with her lover's body, and that a knight named Yder had taken the rings from his hand. He, it transpires, loves Guengasoain's daughter and can only win her by slaying her father. She also knows that none other than the great Sir Gawain is on his way to avenge her lover, but does not, apparently, know that it is he to whom she is speaking.

Gawain sets out in search of the killer, who has apparently taken to travelling with a bear since hearing that Gawain is coming. (How all the characters seem to know what is happening from afar we may presume to be by some occult agency.)

Gawain does battle with Guengasoain, at first without success, then he gets out the lance-head and sees his adversary show signs of terror. Treacherously Guengasoain causes Gawain's horse to bolt and escapes, calling out that Raguidel remains unavenged.

Gawain gives chase on foot and Yder now appears. The bear attacks and kills Yder's horse before Yder kills it in turn. Gawain arrives and fights fiercely with Guengasoain, finally killing him with the lance-point as predicted. He then finds that he has 'won' the right to the dead man's exquisite daughter — which he accepts very willingly, much to Yder's dismay. Gawain pretends to be outraged when Yder begs him to release the girl, but after some rather comical exchanges relents and all ends happily.

The end of the romance shows Gawain in typical style, victorious over all his adversaries, magnanimous and gently amused by Yder's plight at the end. The episode of the mysterious ship is reminiscent of the Ship of Solomon in the Grail romances, an indication that Raoul de Houdenc may have been familiar with these.

Yder appears again as the hero of the romance which bears his name, where Gawain is presented in a largely sympathetic light, partly by contrasting him with Keu (Kay) who is painted very blackly indeed. The romance is summarized on pp84-5, where it is dealt with in the light of its contribution to Gawain's relationship with Guinevere.

Another of this group of romances (so called although they differ widely in quality and content) is *Gliglois*[20] probably written at about the same time as *Meraugis* and *Vengence Raguidel*.

Its hero is a youth whose father sends him to be educated in knightly pursuits by Gawain, who is clearly seen as the very best of men. Gliglois is made welcome, not only by Gawain, but by all the court, who recognize in him the qualities required of a Round Table knight.

Soon after his arrival a beautiful maiden arrives riding on a mule. Gawain falls extravagantly in love with her, but is (unusually) rebuffed. He sends Gliglois to wait on the girl (whose name, appropriately, is Beauté) and to plead his case. However, matters become complicated as Gliglois himself begins to fall in love with her.

A tournament at Chastel Orgueilleus is announced and Gawain, acting on the advice of Guinevere, determines to win Beauté's love by feats of arms. He is so smitten by this time that he even has a picture of his love painted inside his shield (a curious parody of the picture of the Virgin painted there in *Gawain and the Green Knight*).

Left behind by his master, Gliglois determines to follow Beauté on foot to the tournament. The girl accepts this form of declaration and though the day is hot, refuses to allow him to mount even when one of her ladies expresses concern for the young man.

Eventually, appearing to relent, she sends him with a letter to her sister, who receives him kindly. The letter reveals that in fact Beauté loves Gliglois deeply and instructs her sister to have him dubbed a knight.

At the tournament Gawain is much struck by the young, unknown knight, who carries all before him. Then comes the revelation of his identity and with it the fact that he and Beauté share a mutual passion. Dismayed, Gawain yet responds with generosity and love for his young protegée, willingly giving up any claim he may have had on the girl in favour of Gliglois.

The figure of the proud (*orgeleuse*) lady featured in this poem seems to be a further aspect of the Goddess. She makes an appearance in several other texts, particularly those where either Gawain or one of his family feature as heroes. In Malory's 'Tale of Sir Gareth' she appears in the guise of Linet, the waspish damsel who accompanies Gareth on his first quest, while elsewhere in *Le Morte d'Arthur* she reappears in what reads like a parody of the earlier tale, concerning the adventures of La Cote Mal Taille.

Again, in the majority of the Fair Unknown stories, she is to be found commanding the allegiance of Gawain's son. This seems to suggest that the whole of the Orkney clan were at one time acknowledged to belong to the household of the Goddess. Even Mordred, as one of the abductors of Guinevere, may be said to follow the archetype of the champion/challenger in this way.

Keith Busby describes the attitude in *Gliglois'* author as 'frivolous'[80] but in reality he presents Gawain quite seriously as a chivalrous and fine-spirited human being. It may well be that his confession of being merely infatuated with Beauté, at the end of the poem, strikes a false note, after his earlier, extravagant behaviour. But the crux of the work's motivation seems rather to be a satirical look at Courtly Love, in which Gawain is presented as rising above such sentiments. Certainly *Gligalois* is one of the most sympathetic portraits of Gawain to be written at this time, at least in France, where his reputation as someone light of love seems to have had more of an airing than in England.

There, where the group of texts including *Gawain and the Green Knight* and *Gawain and Ragnall* were composed over the period of the thirteenth and fourteenth centuries, a very different, more primitive idea of Gawain hold good. To complete this brief examination of some of the less central texts of Gawain's literary career, we need to look at these in more detail.

Including those already examined, the list of titles which make up the so-called English Gawain cycle are as follows:

Sir Gawain and the Green Knight
The Knightly Tale of Golagros and Gawain
The Adventures of Arthur at Tarn Watheling
Sir Gawain and the Carl of Carlisle
The Geste (Adventure) of Sir Gawain
The Green Knight
The Turk and Gawain
The Wedding of Sir Gawain and Dame Ragnall
The Avowing of King Arthur, Sir Gawain, Sir Kay and Baldwin of Britain
Of Arthour and Merlin

These 11 poems constitute the central complex of Gawain material in English, excluding Malory and later sixteenth-seventeenth-century retellings. Many share similar plots, borrowed alike from French romances and more primitive Celtic tales. They are frequently marked by a certain uncouthness or clumsiness of execution which does not, however, belie their energy and power. *Gawain and the Green Knight*, unlike the shortened version simply called *The Green Knight*, is a masterpiece of the highest order. Others, such as *The Wedding of Sir Gawain and Dame Ragnall* preserve a spirit of ancient magic often absent from European versions. Many contain elements and themes not found elsewhere, and certain of these add to our overall portrait of Gawain significantly. They were written and meant to be sung or recited by the minstrels of the day. As such they were open to change at almost any point in their lifespan, so that the texts we possess represent only a single version, caught by one writer, from a story still in the process of forming. The next day a completely different version may have been performed, which was never recorded. For this reason when we look at the tales we must not be afraid to separate incident from incident, circulating or remixing them as dictated by external evidence.

The Adventures of Arthur at Tarn Watheling is perhaps the only real ghost story in the whole Arthurian canon. In it Guinevere and Gawain,

sheltering from a storm near the Tarn (which is famed for its adventurous happenings) they witness the appearance of a terrifying appar-
ition which turns out to be the ghost of Guinevere's mother. The
description is worth quoting:

> The body of the thing was bare. Its only clothing was smoke, its dark
> bones visible but smeared hideously with clay. It wailed and groaned like
> a banshee, screeching madly... Its eyes were hollow pits, glowing like
> coals. Snakes circled around close by... (Trans. L.B. Hall)[21]

This horrific spectre proceeds to prophesy the downfall of the Round
Table, the death of Arthur and Gawain's own demise in graphic detail.
The purpose of all this is to deliver a kind of homily on the evils of
the flesh and a warning to Arthur against being too greedy for power
and lands. This theme is taken up again to good effect in the *Alliterative Morte Arthure*[24] where the failure of Arthur to practice sufficient
of the great medieval requirements of charity and largesse are noted
as reasons for his fall.

In *The Adventures of Arthur at Tarn Watheling* which might better
be called 'The Adventures of *Gawain*' the hero faces up to the ghost
without fear, protecting a terrified Guinevere. He is also specifically
said to wear green, which may or may not be seen as significant!

The second part of the poem, which is only vaguely connected to the
first, begins, as does *Gawain and the Green Knight*, with the arrival
of a large and ferocious knight who demands combat with one of
Arthur's knights as a means of recompense for his lands having been
given over to Gawain. He is Galeron of Galloway, and in the tremen-
dous fight which follows Gawain is often hard pressed to defend himself. At the start of the combat he is seen carocaling his horse about
the field, 'showing off' until Galeron strikes him a blow on the neck,
nicking his collar-bone in almost an exact echo of Bercilak's actions
in *Gawain and the Green Knight*. He then slays Gawain's valiant steed
Gringolet, and Gawain is so maddened that he screams aloud and
attacks with renewed ferocity, while Galeron rides about the field keeping out of the way of Gawain's furious sword-strokes. Finally he calms
down, Galeron dismounts and they continue the fight in earnest.

Gawain's life is feared for, so mighty are Galeron's blows, and Guinevere weeps openly. Then with a sudden mighty blow Gawain half crip-
ples his foe, and there the matter might have ended, but Galeron
manages to get in a last blow before collapsing, and this prompts Guinevere to beg Arthur to stop the fight. As Arthur hesitates Galeron begs
for mercy and acknowledges Gawain's claims on his lands as 'the most
powerful man upon earth, without peer.' Arthur at once orders peace.

The fact that Gawain more or less runs mad after the slaying of Gringolet, but then appears to regain his senses at around midday, suggests a reference to his legendary prowess waxing and waning at this time, and it is interesting to note that this appears to be the only reference to this ability in the independent English texts. The rest appear in Continental tales, where they presumably became lodged after the original stories had been taken over to the Continent in the general exodus from Britain at the end of the sixth century.

In *Sir Gawain and the Carl of Carlisle*, Gawain once again displays not only bravery but a deeper knowledge of the Otherworld than any of his friends. In this story Kay, Bishop Baldwin and Gawain become separated from their companions while out hunting. Daylight falls and a mist descends, and despite Gawain's suggestion that they should take shelter beneath some trees for the night, the others insist on approaching the haunted castle of the Carl, who, as we have seen, is a type both of the Green Knight and the Hospitable Host. The remainder of the story is summarized on p. 73, and we should here note that Gawain acquires yet another wife, whom he presumably deserts after a time. Both this and *The Turk and Gawain* combine elements found elsewhere in the twelfth-century *Pélérinage du Charlemagne* from the *Chansons du Geste* cycle.

The Geste (Adventure) of Sir Gawain[53] is a late fifteenth-century version of the 'Lady of Lys' episode found in the Second Continuation of Chrétien's *Conte del Graal* (see Chapter 5). But the author has radically altered the sense of the story by having Bran de Lys beat his sister black and blue for allowing Gawain to seduce her, and by making both Gawain and Bran unheroically express relief that they will never meet again!

In *The Avowing of King Arthur, Sir Gawain, Sir Kay and Baldwin of Britain* the setting is again the area of Tarn Watheling and Inglewood Forest, where so many of these adventures take place. As in *The Carl of Carlisle* the story begins with a hunting party. After an exchange of boasts each of the heroes elects to undertake a specific feat, Gawain's being to watch at the haunted Tarn throughout the night. In effect his adventure involves (as so often happens) the extrication of Kay from prison, after he has vowed to ride through the forest and kill anyone who tries to prevent him. He is, not surprisingly, defeated by the knight Sir Menealf, and it falls to Gawain to challenge and defeat him in turn, fighting him twice — once for the sake of Kay and secondly to save the damsel Menealf was carrying off when Kay first met him. Afterwards, when Kay mocks the fallen knight, Gawain is shown as acting magnanimously towards his defeated foe, who later becomes a knight of the Round Table.

In all of these varied tales we find Gawain portrayed in a remarkably unified fashion: as a brave, courteous, courageous knight, as the queen's champion, and as an honourable representative of Arthurian chivalry. This is a far cry from the kind of treatment he receives in the Continental romances, especially those involving the quest for the Grail, which we shall look at next. In the insular texts Gawain still retains something of his original role. As he became increasingly popular as the hero (or anti-hero) of the French *Romanciers* these fragmentary memories either vanished entirely or became subsumed in courtly fashion.

ADDENDUM

After I had completed work on the main argument of this book, a text called *La Pulzella Gaia* (The Merry Maiden), contained in the collection *Fiore di Leggende: Cantari Antichi*, edited by E. Levi, Bari, Laterza, 1914, came to my attention. *La Pulzella* is a later work, dated c.1350, but it contains some significant details for our argument.

The hero is Gawain (here Galvan), who goes in search of a 'deer of perfect whiteness' for Guinevere. In the forest he encounters a monstrous female serpent, with which he fights until noon but cannot overcome. Exhausted, Gawain prepares for death, but to his surprise the serpent does not attack further, but asks for 'courtesy and love of lady' if he is of the Round Table. When Gawain admits that he is, the serpent asks his name. He gives it as Lancelot, but the serpent answers that she has encountered Lancelot in arms and that Gawain is a far better man than he. Humbled, Gawain admits to his own name, at which the serpent with a cry of joy turns into a beautiful woman and embraces him. Gawain asks who she is and she tells him that she is called La Pulzella Gaia and that she is the daughter of Morgan le Fay. Gawain is happy until he remembers that he has still to bring a fair white deer to Guinevere. His new love gives him a ring that will fulfil his every wish, but counsels him not to reveal her name or identity for fear of losing her. She then turns back into a serpent again, and Gawain asks first for a fine charger, then for a hundred knights to serve as an escort and twelve wounded barons to take back to court as prisoners. Finally he demands a new game animal with horse's hooves behind and gryphon's feet in front, a fish's tail and peacock wings, a woman's face and one black eye and one white eye! He then returns to court and is welcomed by all. Guinevere displays the beast on a balcony and everyone marvels.

Later, to avoid the advances of Guinevere, Gawain discloses the existence of his new love and the ring at once loses its power. La Pulzella Gaia is imprisoned and Gawain has to rescue her. He does so in the end and they return to Camelot amid great rejoicing.

Such is the content of this remarkable tale. As stated, it is a late tale, and has qualities of the burlesque about it also. Gawain does not appear in a particularly good light — demanding the 'wounded prisoners' whom he has not actually fought, and pretending to be Lancelot. But there are significant details which seem to originate from a much earlier text. Gawain's quest for the white deer for Guinevere is a clear reference to the Sovereignty theme discussed in Chapter 2, and it is interesting that here, as in *Yder* and *Launfal*, Guinevere appears in the role of temptress. The theme of the loss of the otherworldly woman through giving away her existence is the same as that in *Launfal* and has the same effect — Gawain has to rescue the lady.

But what are we to make of the serpent who is really Morgan le Fay's daughter, and who becomes a beautiful woman when Gawain identifies himself? We have met the serpent before in the episode of the *Fier Baiser* in the Vulgate *Lancelot*. (Possibly this explains why Gawain is claiming to be the great knight). That the serpent becomes a beautiful woman and that she is related to Morgan le Fay is surely further evidence to Morgan's original role as temptress and initiatrix. It is notable that Gawain gives up his fight with her at noon, normally the time when his powers are at their height. For of course he cannot overcome the emanation of the Goddess who gave him the power in the first place!

In all *La Pulzella Gaia* is a fascinating, if somewhat muddled, text which reads like a story-teller's confused memories of several earlier tales. Possibly the author was trying to remember a text he had read or heard much earlier, and in so doing happened to enshrine some of the major themes from the original Gawain story.

Chapter 5.

The Fall From Grace: Gawain's Path to the Grail

RITES OF PASSAGE: GAWAIN AT THE CASTLE OF LADIES

The theme of the Grail Quest is of such central importance to the Matter of Britain that it really requires a book in itself, and there are, indeed, numerous studies which deal with the whole mystery in detail.[119] Strangely, however, few treat Gawain's role in any detail. Where he is discussed it is usually in the light of his *failure* to achieve the all-important Quest, which though less dramatic than Lancelot's, is nonetheless treated at some length by the medieval authors — as though, knowing the importance of Gawain as a character, they felt it was all the more important to show that compared with their new hero, Galahad, he was possessed of negligible capabilities (or anyway of insufficient grace to enable him to complete the Quest). Thus almost all the Grail texts which feature Gawain as a character agree that he was the first among Arthur's knights to pledge himself to the Quest, but that he was also a dismal failure.

The truth of the matter, when we examine the relevant texts in the light of what we now know of Gawain's true role, is very different. He appears, rather, as one of the foremost Quest knights, reaching heights far above most of his peers, and in the end aspiring to the very purest degree of intent required by the Grail winner himself.

This is not the place to go into the origins and development of the Grail myth in any detail. Suffice it to say that there are two distinct streams of knowledge relating to this most tantalizing symbol — the Christian and the pagan. Each has claimed more or less exclusive rights in the matter, but the truth, as is often the case, falls somewhere between. The Grail story as we have it today is the product of generations of story-tellers and mystics, who have each adapted, blatantly or subtly, the story to their own understanding.

Thus we have the complex, often uplifting and always fascinating story of the Sacred Cup of the Last Supper, used by Joseph of Arimathea to catch some of the blood of Christ after the Crucifixion, henceforward hallowed for all time. Or the more cosmic idea of the Grail as an emerald from the Crown of Lucifer which fell to earth during heavenly strife between the angels. Pagan versions of this tale revolve around the mighty Cauldron of Rebirth, possessed by various gods or goddesses of Celtic myth, which has the property of granting life or death, as well as meat for the hero (never the coward), and which is sought after by various heroic figures.

Out of this extraordinary mixture of half-remembered myths and legends emerged the story of the Grail — a symbol of the constant inclination in the human psyche towards a semi-unattainable, greatly to be desired goal, which only the very brave, the very foolish (in the sense of innocent) or those somehow chosen, stood any chance of getting near.

Versions of this story, probably widely differing, must have been in circulation for many hundreds of years before they began to be written down at all. The text which is generally believed to be the earliest we now possess is the *Conte del Graal* by Chrétien de Troyes, left unfinished by him in 1181. We have already encountered this text several times in our examination of Gawain's story — it is time that we looked at it in more detail for the light it throws on our hero.

Alongside this we shall place the twelfth-century German poem *Parzival*[63] by Wolfram von Eschenbach, which though it makes scathing remarks about the veracity of Chrétien's work, undoubtedly derives from the same, or similar, sources and which, furthermore, completes the story of Gawain in a more satisfactory manner than the several continuators who extended his original text to vast lengths.

In both poems the hero is ostensibly Perceval, the erstwhile Grail champion; but in both the actual space allotted to Gawain's adventures is far greater — a further indication of the importance and esteem in which the hero was held. In both poems also the first appearance of Gawain on the scene is after Perceval has visited the mysterious Grail castle, but has failed to ask the all-important question which will bring about the actual achievement of the Grail.

As he approaches Arthur's court, Perceval sees where a raven has killed its prey in the snow. The blackness of the bird's feathers, the redness of blood drops in the white snow, send him into a trance in which he remembers the black hair, red lips and white skin of his lady. Gawain, happening by, covers the image and thus breaks the trance.

The significance of this episode has not gone unnoticed. Several commentators have remarked upon it, noting that the colours, black, white and red, are those of the Goddess.[113] What more appropriate than that Gawain, her champion, should understand the mystery here expressed and break Perceval's reverie — which might otherwise have been extended indefinitely, by covering it with his cloak.

Thereafter the two knights continue to Arthur's court, and at the feast which follows the Loathly Damsel appears and upbraids Perceval with his failure to ask the question that would have ended the Grail mystery forever. In passing she also mentions the Château Merveil (Castle of Wonders) in which many ladies are held prisoner. Scarcely has she departed than Guingambresil (a kind of Bercilak figure) appears and, accusing Gawain of having murdered his lord, challenges him to single combat at Escavalon (i.e. Esc-'Water'-Avalon!)

Gawain sets out for the appointed meeting and on the way takes part in a tournament in which he fights on the side of an old knight who is being attacked by his elder daughter's rejected suitor. Gawain rides incognito as the champion of a younger daughter (an innocent maid) and wins the day.

Arriving at Escavalon he encounters a king who does not know him but who entrusts him to the care of his beautiful sister with whom Gawain at once falls in love and who seems to love him. Unfortunately, a passing knight recognizes Gawain and incites the people of the city to attack the lovers. They retire to a tower and defend themselves by throwing stone chess pieces at their attackers!

The King of Escavalon now returns with Guingambresil, who surprisingly brings about a reconciliation and also postpones the single combat for a year on condition that Gawain goes in search of the Grail Lance (Chrétien) or the Grail itself (Wolfram). This new quest leads to the great adventure of the Château Merveil but the details leading up to this are themselves highly significant — as indeed is the dénouement itself.

Gawain first encounters a beautiful woman sitting by a spring. She responds coldly to his advances but agrees to ride with him if he fetches her horse from a garden nearby. The inhabitants of the garden warn Gawain against the proud lady (l'Orgueilleuse de Logres in Chrétien; Orgeluse in Wolfram) but he ignores them and fetches her steed.

They set out, followed at a distance by a hideous dwarf who is apparently the lady's attendant. When Gawain encounters a wounded knight and stops to bind up his hurts, the dwarf steals his horse Gringolet, leaving Gawain his own broken-down nag in place. Continually mocked by the Lady of the Fountain, Gawain rides on until they reach the Château Merveil, where he is attacked by a knight riding Gringolet. The proud lady now deserts him, being ferried across a lake to the castle by a mysterious boatman.

Gawain defeats the unknown knight but the boatman returns and demands Gringolet as a toll. Gawain explains that it is his own horse and offers the defeated knight instead. The boatman accepts and having ferried Gawain across the lake entertains him courteously for the night.

Next morning Gawain sees a number of richly-dressed ladies at the windows of the castle and desires to enter. His host tries to dissuade him, warning of enchantments and dangers, but Gawain goes anyway and encounters the adventure of the 'lit merveil' (wonderful or enchanted bed) where he is assailed by stones and cross-bow bolts and by a furious lion as soon as he sits down.

With this the enchantments are ended, and the people of the castle claim Gawain as their lord. He is then introduced to three queens who reside there: an old white-haired lady, her daughter and her granddaughter. These turn out to be Gawain's grandmother (who is also Arthur's mother), his own mother and his sister.

This strikes an intriguing note of similarity with the episode from *Le Morte d'Arthur* discussed earlier, in which Gawain, Uwain and Marhaus encountered the three damosels at the well, and throws light also on the whole adventure of the Château Merveil, which was clearly engineered as a test to deem whether or not Gawain was worthy of serving the three women — who, despite their superficial identities, are clearly a glyph for the triple aspected Goddess. Indeed, from the moment that Gawain met the proud lady by the spring, and obtained for her the horse stabled in a garden in which many other people dwelled, he has been travelling in the Otherworld under the aegis of that very Goddess. The presence of the mysterious ferryman who takes Gawain across to the island also indicates that this crossing is really into the Otherworld. The conclusion of the episode clinches the matter:

Gawain is told by the boatman (himself a familiar otherworldly figure) that whoever achieved the adventure of the castle must remain there forever: because 'whoever became the protector of the house could, rightly or wrongly, never leave it again.'

In fact, nothing comes of this prohibition. Gawain is angered by it and departs without noticeable effect — however we may surmise that at an earlier stage in the transmission of the story, this would have been the proper ending, and that it provides us with a probable end to the story of Gawain. However, this must await it proper place as, in the story here related, other adventures are still to come.

Gawain's next task is to fight a new champion produced by the proud lady. Easily vanquishing this foe, Gawain then accompanies the still contemptuous lady on one further quest — to find and weave a garland of flowers (or pluck a branch) from a tree guarded by a knight named Guiromelans. This done, she now receives him pleasantly, apologizing for her earlier behaviour, which was intended to 'spur him on' to fight Guiromelans, who had killed her lover.

They return to the Château Merveil and Gawain sends a message to Arthur to come and witness the imminent, long-postponed combat. Here Chrétien's narrative ends suddenly. The story is completed by Wolfram.

Arthur and Guinevere eagerly promise to come. Gawain marries Orguelese and when the Arthurian court is seen to be approaching, leads the whole household of the Château Merveil to where they are encamped. The ladies of the castle, at Gawain's behest, form a circle around the king's tent.

Next day, as Gawain rides out to try his physical strength after the wounds he received at the castle, he encounters Parzival. Neither recognizes the other and they fight. Gawain is overthrown and might have been slain had not a passing squire called upon him by name. Hearing this Parzival flings away his sword and the two friends are reunited.

The combat between Gawain and Guiromelans is once again deferred and at length, through the efforts of Arthur and Guiromelans' uncle Brandeleidelein, a peaceful conclusion is reached, Guiromelans marrying Gawain's sister Clarisant, who had fallen in love with him during the siege of the castle.

It is sometimes assumed that this version, which generally tidies up the loose ends more effectively than any of Chrétien's continuators, was invented by Wolfram; however Jessie Weston guessed in her early book on Gawain,[152] that taken within the wider context of Gawain's career, it is more likely that Wolfram extracted material from several other sources then current, and that he probably did no more than re-work these into a connected narrative.

It should also be noted that in this version Gawain is left as the Lord of Château Merveil with its bevy of ladies, while it is left to Parzival to accomplish the mysteries of the Grail. Once again, as was to be increasingly the case, Gawain is used as a foil for Parzival, a direction far more attributable to the pen of Wolfram than the actual details of the narrative, which are, after all, rather clumsy.

The business of the combat that never happens between Gawain and Guiromelans remains something of a mystery. The fact that the latter guards a tree from which it is Gawain's task to weave a garland for the Proud Lady, as well as his general behaviour, mark him out clearly as an otherworldly character. One might indeed assume him to be the retiring Champion of the Goddess if it were not for the fact that he and Gawain do not fight. Possibly in the version of the story from which Chrétien was working, this was the outcome. Certainly the rest of the plot seems to call for it, despite the convenient fact of the marriage of Guiromelans to Gawain's sister at the end. The name of his uncle in Wolfram's text, is clearly derived from that of Bran the Blessed, a further indication of Guiromelans' otherworldly origins. In fact, although the two opponents, Guingambresil and Guiromelans, are distinct characters within the text, they perform the same function and virtually duplicate their roles, so that from the demands of the plot they are better served if they are seen as they almost certainly once were, as a single personality.

But what are we to make of Gawain's own marriage to the Lady Orguelese? This looks, on the face of it, very much in keeping with the rest of the story of Gawain as we have begun to perceive it. Tried and tested at every point along the way, mocked and reviled, he is eventually rewarded with the hand of the lady. He thus, by extension, automatically becomes the champion of *all* the ladies of the Château Merveil — hence earning himself the title 'Knight of the Maidens' or Maidens' Knight a title which later became, by a simple rationalization, the Maiden's — i.e. Mary's — Knight.

Weston points out that there are a number of tales in which Gawain crosses water to win an island ruled over by women, and draws parallels between this and various Celtic Isles of Women to which heroes such as Bran son of Febal were invited. Indeed, in the latter story a wondrous branch with silver bells, which when shaken caused enchanted sleep, may have provided the story-teller with the original version of Gawain's task of obtaining a branch from the tree guarded by Guiromelans.

Wolfram hints pretty clearly that the original master of the castle was a magician, and that Orguelese is closely connected with him — perhaps as his daughter — so that it is possible to see a connection with the Hospitable Host theme also. In fact the whole story, though in a rather garbled form in Chrétien and Wolfram, can be seen to conform fairly closely to the versions we have already examined. Indeed, as Weston points out, there are sufficient similarities between the Gawain story told by the two medieval poets and the old Irish tale of *The Wooing of Emer*[13] to suggest that this story, or a version of it, formed one of the original sources (see Chapter 1), in which the hero (in this case Cuchulainn), after overcoming insuperable odds, married a proud and otherworldly woman. Certainly the theme was carried on through numerous other versions. In the thirteenth-century romance *Saig-*

remor[80] Gawain is held captive on the island home of the Faery Karmente; in *Miraugis de la Portlesgues*[80] as we saw, he is imprisoned on
an island by its otherworldly owner and forced to take on all comers.
Details of his early adventures with the Proud Damsel are to be found
attributed to his younger brother Gareth, in Malory's 'Tale of Sir Gareth'.
All these texts and versions point to the original story telling how
Gawain, having passed all tests and trials with flying colours, is then
bound by the Lady of the Isle (in other words the Goddess) to remain
there until he in turn is overcome. This is, as we saw, a clear remem-
brance of the ancient theme of annual kingship, once disseminated
throughout much of the Western world. Hence also, perhaps, we may
see the reason why, in Malory, when Gawain's ghost appears to Arthur
in his tent, he is surrounded by women — a curious reminiscence to
the scene in Wolfram, where the women of the castle literally surround
Arthur's pavilion in a circle.

But does this indicate a satisfactory conclusion of Gawain's Grail
Quest? Clearly, it does not. But it does indicate the route we must follow to find a clearer picture. We need to look next at a whole group
of texts, in which Gawain's search for the Grail is continued in some
detail.

❧✸❧

THE SEARCH FOR THE INEFFABLE: GRAIL QUEST
AND CHAMPION

There are four distinct *Continuations* of Chrétien's *Conte del Graal*,
each of which advances Gawain's story in unique ways. The importance
of the first of these, written anonymously soon after Chrétien's death,
lies in the way it emphasizes the strength of the affection between Arthur
and his nephew — indeed the respect and adulation of the whole court
for the redoubtable hero. Guinevere 'loves' him, as do all her ladies.
Arthur actually lifts the messenger who brings news of Gawain's safety
bodily from his horse so delighted is he to learn that his nephew still
lives. However the continuator seems determined to show that Gawain's
failure in the Quest lies in his fatal attraction to the opposite sex. The
'Lady of Lys' episode is typical of the kind of adventure he has from
Chrétien onwards.

Discovering a splendid tent set up in a meadow, Gawain finds that
within reclines a lovely lady whose greeting is to the effect that whatever
the time, day or night, he should protect Messire Gawain and thus be

blessed! When Gawain admits that he is himself the object of these wishes, the girl at first refuses to believe him, then is so overjoyed that she cannot wait to offer him her love.

Next morning he departs, promising to return for her shortly. However he is soon overtaken by first her father and then her brother, both of whom challenge him with despoiling their family honour and with the earlier death of an uncle.

Gawain wounds the girl's father, Norre de Lys, and then has to face her brother, Bran, who demands vengeance for both father and sister. The whole question of Gawain's guilt is left unsettled. On the face of it, the girl willingly complied in their relationship, while the death of the uncle took place under the usual conditions of challenge and single combat.

Now, as he fights Bran de Lys, an old wound opens and Gawain is forced to strike a bargain with his adversary — that he will fight immediately with Bran wherever they happen to meet, and whether Gawain is armed or not at the time.

Gawain now retires to a nearby castle to recuperate for six months, and we are meanwhile informed that the Lady of Lys is with child.

Aside from the fact that the name of the lady's brother, Bran de Lys, marks yet another appearance of the Celtic god Bran, the whole episode reads like a conflation of both the Guingambresil and Guiromalans episodes in Chrétien. In all three Gawain is accused of killing a relative of his attacker. In the Guingambresil episode he has an amorous affair with a relative of the knight. And in all three the combat is interrupted and postponed — though for different reasons. As we saw in the previous chapter, a 'cleaned up' version of this story is told in the English *Geste of Sir Gawain*.[53]

Keith Busby, in his illuminating study *Gauvain in Old French Literature*,[80] points out that this is the earliest text in which Gawain is actually said to make physical love to a maiden (she is afterwards pregnant). Prior to this Gawain's amorous adventures seem to extend no further than dalliance; from here on, however, it is another story.

In due course the matter is resolved, though not without the dramatic intervention described below, as well as a rather demeaning scene in which Gawain, sitting at table, thinks he sees Bran de Lys approaching and spends the rest of the meal; sitting with helmet, shield and sword to hand!

The end of the Bran de Lys combat is interesting. When the combat is beginning to go against Gawain, a girl rushes in carrying a beautiful child of about five. The child actually enters the combat area and asks her uncle (Bran) not to kill her father (Gawain).

Bran kicks the child aside and only Arthur's intervention interrupts the combat long enough for Gawain to recover somewhat, so that he may fight back more strongly. Then the child is held up again by the girl and all the onlookers beg Arthur to stop the fight. Agreement is finally reached, with Gawain and Bran reconciled.

Gawain next takes part in a tournament against a knight who persuades him to fake losing the fight in order that he (the knight) may win the love of his lady. Gawain courteously agrees, is imprisoned and eventually freed. He then acts as Guinevere's champion after the queen has been insulted by a strange knight, who rides past without saluting her. Gawain follows him and requests that he return and apologize to Guinevere. The knight, (whose name is only revealed in one of the later continuations as Silimac) remarks upon the difficulty of his quest, which only he could possibly achieve (save perhaps for Gawain); then, while they are riding along together, the knight is struck down by an unseen assailant. Silimac begs Gawain to don his armour and to take his horse, allowing it to wander where it will until he reaches a place where all will be made plain. He expires with the mysterious words: 'God! Why has this happened to me? Surely I have done nothing wrong!'

Gawain takes the body back to court and donning the dead knight's armour rides off on his steed. He takes shelter from a storm in a chapel where a single candle burns. This is shortly extinguished by a hideous black hand, while a voice laments in a way that make both the chapel and Gawain tremble.

Fearfully he departs, preferring the elements to the terrors within. He continues through the night and all next day. Finally, towards midnight, he arrives at a castle where he is welcomed and hailed as a saviour. Only when he removes his armour is it discovered that he is not the expected knight (Silimac) and there is general sorrow and despair.

Left alone in the hall Gawain sees a corpse covered in a cloth of gold and with part of a sword blade laid upon its breast. A procession of mourners now enters and Gawain joins in their prayers until they vanish as mysteriously as they had come. The original inhabitants now return and all are fed from a mysterious vessel, called 'le rice Graal' (the rich Grail). This strange meal over, Gawain is once again left alone, and he now sees a lance bleeding though a golden pipe into an emerald conduit, through which the blood drains away.

The king now appears, bearing a sword from which the broken piece on the breast of the corpse had come. He begs Gawain to unite them, but the latter cannot and is told that had he done so great good would have come of it. He is then encouraged to ask questions of all that he has seen.

He asks concerning the lance, and is told that it is the one which was used to pierce the side of Christ as he hung on the cross, and that it has not ceased to bleed ever since. The sword is that which was used to strike a blow destructive to the Kingdom of Logres.

There follows a brief description of the bringing of the Grail to Britain by Joseph of Arimathea, a wealthy Jew who had become a secret Christian. While this is being told Gawain unfortunately falls asleep. He wakes next morning on the sea-shore, with horse and armour at hand. As he departs, castigating himself for failing to keep awake, those whom he passes bemoan his failure.

Much of this material is familiar from other Grail texts, including the hideous hand and the broken sword — which, as we shall see, forms an important part of Gawain's personal quest. We may also see some parallels with *Meraugis de la Portlesguez* (Chapter 4) where Gawain also feigns death and where there is a mysterious dead knight, in whose body is lodged the point of the spear which killed him.

But as Keith Busby points out[80] the points which characterize Gawain's attempt on the Grail are of helplessness; 'his quest is forced upon him, although he accepts it without question; he is sent he knows not where on a mission he knows nothing about; his method of location is not within his own control', while in the Hall of the Grail 'he stands by perplexed and indecisive.'

These characteristics are very much in accord with the portrait of Gawain contained in the *Conte del Graal*, where Gawain is presented as a well meaning but inadequate hero, striving to achieve the quest but failing because of his worldly status.

This seems to arise almost directly from the nature of the earlier Gawain figure, whose avowed pagan associations made him, in the eyes of the Grail romancers, such an unsuitable candidate for success. In the effort to reconcile the various versions available to them, Chrétien and his continuators set Perceval (as, later on, others set Galahad) against Gawain and found the latter wanting. Though even here, it will be noticed, Gawain at once resolves to improve himself in such a way that he is better equipped to undertake the quest again.

Indeed, the whole tendency of the characterization is to make Gawain appear generous, open-hearted, and eager to undertake all adventures. That he fails to reach the heights required of the Grail winner makes him all the more human; and indeed his reactions in the Hall of the Grail are no less puzzled and inadequate than those of Perceval on *his* first visit. The fact that Gawain does ask about the lance, even puts him some way ahead of Perceval, who had failed to ask any question at all when faced with the mysterious procession and the wondrous vessel in Chrétien's text.

The remainder of the *First Continuation*, which is also left unfinished, concerns the adventures of Gawain's son by the Lady of Lys, in which he performs in a manner so much like his father that it seems likely that the adventures once formed part of Gawain's own cycle, but were reattributed to his offspring in order to round off the story of Gawain's association with the family of Lys.

It still seems possible, even probable, that in one of the versions, possibly oral, which went into the making of both Chrétien's *Conte* and the *First Continuation*, Gawain was, indeed, the single hero, and that it was the bringing in of Perceval (also possibly from Celtic tradition) that forced him to be demoted to the role of unsuccessful candidate.

However, it is worth noting that there is evidence that Perceval himself may well have been related to Gawain — in fact that he may once possibly have been his son! Our reason for this belief is based on the similarity in the upbringing of the Fair Unknown, particularly in *Carduino*,[6] the Italian version of the story.

A comparison of the various Perceval texts with the Fair Unknown cycle, lead both Jessie Weston and W.H. Scofield[137] to the belief that Perceval was the original hero of both cycles; an oddly fitting idea since it would mean that like Galahad, who succeeded in the Grail Quest where his father could not, so Guingamore succeeded where Gawain (with one exception) also failed. Though this may seem to stretch a point, we may further note in passing that in the English *Syr Percevale* and the Welsh *Peredur*, Perceval is the son of Arthur's sister, thus making him Gawain's cousin; that in the *Conte del Graal* and *Parzival* he is introduced to the court by Gawain; and that again in *Syr Percevale* it is Gawain who helps the hero get the Red Knight out of his armour after Perceval has killed him.

All this may be no more than speculation, but as Jessie Weston notes, the traditions concerning Perceval's father are everywhere vague, and that he may have been Gawain's son is not only possible, it may even be probable.

If this is the case, can we proceed any further towards a reconstruction of Gawain's personal quest, in which the ending will be more satisfactory? I believe we can, though it is necessary to look at several more texts before we can arrive at a more accurate picture of Gawain's true role.

We find the next part of the story continued in fresh detail by Wauchier de Danaans in the *Second Continuation* of Chrétien's original.[12]

Here Gawain is once more unfavourably compared with Perceval, who single-mindedly continues his quest for the Grail while Gawain sets out on various smaller tasks, constantly returning to Arthur's court (whose chief representative he clearly remains at this point). However, he does finally set forth in search of the Grail king, referring back to the episode in the *First Continuation*, and to Perceval, who has been missing from court for some time.

Gawain features much less directly in this Continuation, although, as Keith Busby has noted[80] the author always brings him in with 'evident pleasure'. Each of the episodes, which need not be summarized in full here since they add little to Gawain's Grail search, are designed to emphasize his role as a lover. In one, he is specifically allowed to carry an enchanted shield which can only be born by a knight possessed of nobleness, generosity and sensibility — this despite his notable dalliance with yet another lady, who herself, in a long speech, characterizes Gawain as someone likely to have had several more women within a month of leaving her.

In all, the portrait of Gawain is ambiguous. On the one hand he is praised by all whom he encounters as a noble and powerful knight; on the other, his relationships with women imply a certain critical attitude on the part of Wauchier.

Finally, Gawain virtually gives up his search for the Grail king when he learns that Perceval will be returning to the court at Christmas and assumes that he will get further information from him — a clear indication that Perceval is still 'ahead on points' and is expected to have acquired more knowledge of the Grail and its mysteries.

The *Third and Fourth Continuations*, those, respectively, of Gerbert de Montreiul and of Mannassier, seem to have been written at more or less the same time (c.1225) and possibly in ignorance of each other, so that chronology with the earlier texts is difficult. Gerbert appears printed first in at least two of the extant manuscripts and I have followed Keith Busby in dealing with him first.

In the several minor episodes which lead up to Gawain's principle appearance in the text, we find him compared (unfavourably) to a newcomer on the scene: Tristan. The increasing popularity of this figure during the latter part of the thirteenth century has been noted by other commentators, so that it is perhaps not surprising to find him appearing in this light. Indeed, there seems to be a quite distinct 'pecking order' outlined by Gerbert, in which various knights are compared, either favourably or unfavourably, with each other. Tristan comes out generally on top, with Gawain second, Lancelot third and Perceval, at one time or another, defeating them all — once again emphasizing the superiority of the Grail knight over all-comers.

Shortly afterwards Gawain, together with several lesser knights, undertakes an adventure which only the best of them could achieve. He fails and has to be rescued, along with many other prisoners, by Perceval.

At this point there are several references to the close friendship between Perceval and Gawain, though once again they are compared, unfavourably in Gawain's case, whose own next adventure is yet another example of his somewhat libertine behaviour towards women.

Encountering a beautiful pavilion in the midst of a meadow, Gawain is welcomed and entertained by its owner's servants, who impress upon him the beauty of their lady before he has even met her. When she appears Gawain is not at all displeased and rather brazenly offers his 'services'. She, in turn, seems ready and willing to leap into bed with him, although she makes the unusual request that he wait until next morning to have his way with her.

Gawain begins to wish away the time, but as he lies in bed awaiting his paramour, discovers a knife hidden beneath the pillow, and suspecting treachery, repays the girl by raping her.

We now learn that Gawain had killed one of the girl's brothers and that as many as 20 other knights had been enticed and then slain in her bed. She now regrets her actions, so much so that she even goes so far as to warn Gawain of her two cousins who are about to attack him. He beats off both, killing one and wounding the other with only the girl's knife. She is apparently so impressed by this that she suddenly confesses her love for him.

While they are abed Gawain dreams that he is being attacked by two lions, and on waking is warned by the girl that her brothers are approaching. Arming himself, Gawain prepares to do battle, but now the girl herself tries to dissuade her brothers from the fight, announcing that Gawain has promised to marry her! Gawain surprisingly agrees that this is the case, though it had not been mentioned before, and even offers to exile himself for three years in recompense for the death of their sibling. He thus virtually confesses to murder according to the laws of the time, but the girl's brothers are not to be mollified and a general mêlée breaks out, during which Gawain bids farewell to the girl and makes good his escape.

However, the episode is not yet over. Gawain spends the night at a nearby castle, where custom requires that he tell his most recent adventure. Understandably perhaps he is reluctant to do so, and when finally prevailed upon discovers that his host, Urpin, is in fact the father of the girl he so recently abused.

At this juncture the girl herself arrives, together with the bodies of those whom Gawain has killed. Urpin threatens terrible revenge, but the girl persuades him to give Gawain into her hands first, so that she may personally extract revenge.

In fact the two spend the night in love-making, and in the morning the girl gives Gawain a sword and tells him to pretend to kill her. Urpin is unmoved however, until his wife begs that Gawain be permitted to meet him in single combat to save their daughter's life.

Gawain seems reluctant to do this, but eventually fights Urpin to his knees, forcing him to acknowledge Gawain's innocence in the matter, and agreeing to spare his accuser at the girl's request.

Gawain then departs, inviting the girl to follow him to court and promising that she will be his eternal love.

We next hear that Perceval has been successful in rescuing a maiden whom Gawain had promised so to do as far back as the original text of Chrétien. Gawain seems to regard this as an end to his quest for the moment, returning forthwith to the court, where he receives a rapturous welcome, despite all the rather unsavoury adventures in which he has been involved of late.

The character of Gawain in Gerbert's *Continuation* seems to take a turn for the worse at every opportunity. Though engaged ostensibly on the Grail Quest, all of his adventures are of an amorous nature, in which he loves and leaves women with casual promises of enduring faithfulness. (One wonders what would have happened if they had all appeared at court at the same time!) Yet despite this he never quite oversteps the laws of chivalry, is generous to his friends and a fierce adversary to his enemies exactly as one would expect.

There remains one further text to examine, completing this cycle of continuations in which Gawain's Grail Quest tries to get underway. This is the continuation ascribed to Manessier,[12] and which continues the story more or less independently of Gerbert.

Here we are taken back to the episode in which the unfortunate knight Silimac was slain while in Gawain's company, which event subsequently led him to his first real Grail adventure.

Manessier describes Gawain as wondering about these events, and determining to set out in search of the Grail king's house, presumably intending to discover the meaning of the events he had witnessed earlier on.

As he discusses his intention with the queen, a damsel appears and asks for him by name. Kay makes some scathing remark to the effect that one never finds Gawain anywhere for long, but admits he is present. The girl identifies herself as the sister of the dead Silimac and accuses Gawain of forgetting his promise to her brother. She adds that Gawain would *never* succeed in the quest for the Grail because of his sins.

The passage recalls an earlier one in *Conte del Graal* where a hermit addresses Perceval in similar terms after he has failed to ask the all-important question concerning the Grail. However, in that instance he offers encouragement to Perceval; while here there seems to be no possibility of Gawain's success at any time in the future.

Undaunted by this however, he agrees to undertake another adventure which Silimac would have achieved had he lived — thus atoning at least in part for his (Gawain's) faults. (Though in fact Gawain seems still unable to understand the reason for his failure.)

Proceeding on their way, Gawain's next adventure is the freeing of a girl about to be burned at the stake for murdering her brother. Her people aver that it is not she, but a Round Table knight called Dodinal le Sauvage, who is the real culprit.

Gawain, who clearly believes the innocence of the girl, defeats a knight who was intent on burning her, and is hailed as a saviour by the girl's vassals in almost Messianic terms: 'With your coming our joy increases.'

As a reward Gawain requests the freeing of Dodinal, who is being held against the girl's release, and although there are murmurs against this, it is done.

Returning now to his original course, Gawain arrives at the home of the dead knight's sister, who tells him of a prolonged war between her family and that of a powerful king, Margan. Deaths had occurred on both sides, but her brother would have brought matters to a successful conclusion had he lived. The girl then claims to know (by astronomy) the identity of his killer and names Kay. Gawain protests, and the matter remains for the moment unresolved.

Gawain undertakes to fight on the girl's side against Margan, who soon arrives, threatening dire reprisals. It does not take Gawain long to deal with him, however, and he is soon dispatched to turn himself in to Arthur for judgement.

The girl is grateful and there are hints (but no more) of a love interest between the two. Gawain leaves to return to the court, promising to investigate Kay's involvement in her brother's death and to avenge it if necessary. On his way home he encounters the niece of the dead knight, whose name is now revealed for the first time, as a member of the Grail family.[118] There is some misunderstanding over Gawain's role in the matter, but this is soon cleared up by Silimac's sister and Gawain is able to proceed on his way.

At the court he accuses Kay anonymously of the murder of Silimac and fights a duel with him in which the seneschal is wounded and placed at Gawain's mercy. He, however, is unable to bring himself to kill his irascible comrade and when Arthur is persuaded to intervene, shows every sign of relief.

This curious episode, in which Kay is presented as a murderer, seems aimed at making him suffer in order to reinstate Gawain as a premier hero. Indeed there is some evidence of a kind of internal struggle among the romancers of the period, who variously try to demote or reappraise Gawain's character according to their views of the matter. In *Perlesvaus*[23] Kay certainly does murder Arthur's son Lohot, and is himself killed in reprisal for this evil act. Elsewhere his character is treated as both mean-spirited and generally unpleasant, though he remained a popular figure in the Arthurian corpus. Indeed, as Linda Gowans has shown in a recent study,[92] a fate not unlike that reserved for Gawain himself, in which a once popular hero is consistently demoted, overtook the figure of Kay.

Certainly, his discomfiture is here intended to point to Gawain's generosity and nobility, which various characters declare at several points throughout the text. So that, while he remains unsuccessful in the matter of the Grail, his earthly endeavours generally succeed in ennobling his character in graphic terms.

In fact, one may suspect that the death of Silimac points in another direction altogether. It resembles the death of another knight in Malory's 'Tale of Balin and Balan'[32] where the culprit is Garlon 'the invisible knight', later slain by Balin. Garlon, along with several other anti-Grail figures, including King Amangons in the *Elucidation*[77] and Klingsor in *Parzival*,[63] may derive from a single anti-Grail king, of which Gawain's adversary in Manassier's tale, Margan, may also derive. It is possible therefore that at some point in the transmission of the tale, it was Margan himself who murdered Silimac (this would be in accordance with the story) and that the accusation against Kay was a later invention.

But we may go further. In an episode from Wauchier's *Continuation* Gawain meets 'La Pucele au Cor d'Ivoire' in the Adventurous Glade. When she blows her horn, 100 youths and maidens appear, but a felon-knight, Marcaron, steals it. Gawain gets it back and we learn that whoever possesses it suffers neither hunger nor thirst. This in turn reminds one of an episode from the Vulgate *Merlin*[60] in which Gawain and other Round Table knights rescue the Queen of Garlot (Morgaine) from a Saxon cup-bearer named Margon, Margoun or Margener, all of which takes place by a spring. In the *Lai du Cor*[27] King Mangonz, sends to Arthur a testing horn designed to establish the fidelity of women. All of this seems to relate to an ancient tale, now lost, in which a hero (Gawain) restored either a testing horn or a horn of plenty to Morgan La Fée (Morgaine) after it had been stolen by an evil lord (Margon, Magounz, Margan, Amangons, Klingsor). No such text exists in a simple form, but the many fragments listed here suggest there must once have been such a story current.

Whatever the truth of the matter, in *Perlesvaus* Gawain is shown in a better light than in any of the earlier Continuations, though he is still not, outwardly, seen as a likely candidate for the Grail Quest.

Two more texts, the *Didot Perceval*[43] and the *Perlesvaus*,[23] written during and after the period of the Continuations, remain to be examined, before we move on to the major Grail cycle, the so-called 'Vulgate' version, in which Gawain reaches new depths as well as heights.

❦

THE QUEST CONTINUES: GAWAIN AT THE TURNING OF THE WAYS

Gawain has now reached a turning point in his involvement with the Grail search. He has tried — and failed — several times, and each time Perceval outstrips him. In the texts to which we must turn next we find a variety of approaches to his continued efforts, both more, and less, sympathetic.

The *Didot Perceval*, written at the beginning of the thirteenth century, established Gawain's friendship with Perceval even more closely. Here, he becomes the champion of Gawain's sister Elainne (the only mention of this character by this name; in the Continuations she is called Clarisant), while it is at Gawain's behest that Perceval is permitted to try the test of the Siège Perilous, in which only the destined Grail knight may sit. A prophetic voice implies that although Perceval has braved this test too soon, he may well be the one destined to sit there. This does not prevent other knights, including Gawain, from vowing to take up the great Quest, each taking their own path towards their goal.

In due course Perceval is successful, while Gawain's career takes a turn into areas dealt with in texts — in this instance the source was probably the *Arthurian Chronicles* of Wace,[6] where Gawain's abilities as a soldier and ambassador are extolled at some length. His attempt on the Grail more or less fades out, partly no doubt due to the very compressed nature of the text, which in a brief and often original way, attempts to deal with the Grail Quest and the death of Arthur in such a way as to give unity to the story.

Gawain's death is reported also in the text, when he receives a mortal wound in the battle between Arthur and Modred (here referred to as Gawain's elder brother). The author describes the reactions of people to the death in graphic terms:

> When Gawain was killed the deepest sorrow was felt. Oh God, what a great loss of a worthy leader! He was a good knight and loyal and wise and was just in judgement and knew how to speak well. God, what great sorrow there was when his death befell. Then such great weeping could be heard. . . that the sound of it carried two leagues distance. (Trans. Dell Skeels)

This Gawain, we are made to feel, could easily have attained the heights required of the Grail winner. Here we find no reference to the decadent womanizer and libertine of Chrétien and his continuators. The fact that Perceval is the successful candidate seems due more to the requirements of plot than to the author's feelings.

The *Perlesvaus*,[23] a much longer and more detailed work, written sometime between 1191 and 1212, possibly at Glastonbury in Somerset, takes at all times a more uniquely original approach to the Grail story, adding many details not found elsewhere and generally integrating the Arthurian matter into the story of the Grail. Gawain's part in the quest is established from the start, he is already searching for the Grail king when we first hear of him, and is at once plunged into the thick of the mysteries.

The author makes it clear from the start that while certain knights, Gawain included, are 'good', the one destined to find the Grail must become *the* Good Knight, the implication being that Gawain has a chance in this direction itself.

Indeed when he successfully wins the Shield of Judas Maccabeus he is actually described as the Good Knight for whom many people have been waiting — though he is also upbraided for failing to ask a specific question which would have aided his search. (Arthur and the rest of the court also failed to do so, which makes Gawain at least no worse than they.)

Mindful of the task he has undertaken, Gawain asks a hermit how he may reach the Grail king's house, and is advised to pray to God.

He reaches a country ruled over by Perceval's mother, who at first thinks him her own son returned and faints when she discovers her mistake. However, Gawain is able to be of some service to her, overcoming in spectacular fashion two knights who had been besieging her. (The Besieged Lady theme again!)

His next adventure shows a reversal of the kind of role in which Gawain has been featured in recent texts. Arriving at the court of Marin the Jealous, who is absent, Gawain refuses to be tempted by his beautiful hostess (a reversal of the hospitable host theme) but thinks of his sacred quest. However, an evil dwarf goes in search of his master and tells him that Gawain is in bed with his lady, at which the jealous knight returns, beats and finally kills his wife, despite Gawain's attempts to intervene. Marin then departs, leaving a sorrowful Gawain to take the lady's body to a chapel to be buried.

He next meets a cowardly knight who refuses to offer any assistance when a challenger appears sent by Marin — though when Gawain has defeated the newcomer the cowardly knight offers him his sword, for which he has no further use.

There follows a lengthy comparison between Gawain, Lancelot and Perceval, who are said to be the three best knights in the world — although neither Gawain nor Lancelot will be admitted to the Grail country because of their fatal attraction for women.

Here Gawain has at last begun to be contrasted with Lancelot, who is destined to oust him in terms of popularity and valour — though, like Gawain himself, he possesses this fatal flaw.

The implication still remains that it is possible for Gawain to overcome the weighty imbalance, and he certainly tries to do so, arriving at the very edge of the Grail king's lands, only to be turned away until he can obtain the sword used to behead John the Baptist The acquisition of this will give him the right at least to see the Grail.

Gawain is so struck by this that he forgets to ask where he should look, but is told by a passing forester that the sword is in the possession of a certain pagan king named Gurgaran.

Gawain sets out at once, encountering on the way two damsels who try to seduce him. On this occasion they are unsuccessful and Gawain escapes unscathed, passing onward to other lands. He comes upon a fountain with a vessel of gold fastened to it by a chain of silver. A statue carved on one of the pillars speaks, foretelling that Gawain is not the one to be served by the vessel. He sees a priest approach, then three maidens in white come, one carrying bread on a dish of gold, one carrying wine in a vessel if ivory, the third bearing meat in a dish of silver. They leave their offerings at the fountain and depart. 'But as they went, it seemed to Sir Gawain that there was but one of them, and he wondered much at this miracle.' The priest tells him that the food and drink are being taken to a sick knight who lies at a hermitage nearby. Once again the implication appears to be that Gawain is to have no part of the richness of the Grail. Yet despite this he is successful in obtaining the sword from King Gurgaran, who agrees to become a Christian and is baptized, along with many of his followers, at Gawain's behest.

(Gawain then beheads those who refuse to be converted, a not unusual action in the story of the Grail.)

After this Gawain twice loses the sword and gets it back again, finally returning to the country of the Grail, which he is now permitted to enter, though warned of Perceval's earlier mistake and urged not to make the same one.

Arriving at last at the castle of the Grail king, Gawain is confronted by three bridges: one so narrow that it resembles a sword, a second of ice and a third guarded by a lion. He gets across all three, but only after being spurred on by a hermit who shames him into putting his faith in God. Yet he is still warned, by a whispering voice, that the final adventure may never befall him.

He enters the hall of the Grail castle, where he sees a wondrous chess board. He is taken to a room where the Grail king lies on a great bed, and when he hands over the sword is told that he could not have entered there without it, nor could he have won it if he were not a knight of great worth. He is also told that the light which now shines out all around him comes from God out of love for him — an indication that Gawain's achievement is indeed far from slight at this stage.

That night he is witness to the Grail procession, seeing first a chalice, the Bleeding Lance, and two angelic figures carrying candlesticks. Gawain is so overawed that he cannot speak.

Next he sees two maidens and with them three angels. In the heart of the Grail this time is a child. One of the knights at the table with Gawain cries out, but Gawain's attention has been caught by three drops of blood which have fallen on the table, and he still refrains from speech.

Finally the two maidens pass by once more before him, only this time Gawain thinks that he sees three, one of whom is carrying the Grail. Above it he sees a vision of a crowned and crucified man with a spear thrust into his side. This so fills him with sorrow that he once again remains silent, even though the knight who had cried out now urges him to speak before the chance is lost to him forever. But Gawain does not hear and the maidens vanish into a chapel with the Grail and the spear.

Gawain now finds himself left suddenly alone and tries to play a game with the chess pieces, which move against him automatically, checkmating him easily three times. He falls asleep in the hall and next morning finds his armour laid out beside him. The door to the Grail king's chamber is barred against him, though he can hear chanting coming from within.

A maiden tells him that he may not enter, but must leave at once — though she adds that his only real fault was in not asking about the wonders he saw. As he departs unhappily, the sun shines on all the countryside except where he rides, where a storm of rain and lightning batter him.

Disappointed, he returns briefly to court then sets out again in search of Perceval, but he is never to find his way again to the Grail castle, despite the fact that when Perceval reaches it again, he sees the sword which Gawain had obtained in the Grail procession.

A key episode here is that in which Gawain encounters the three women at the well. In almost every detail this prefigures the later Grail procession, however, although Gawain sees three maidens bring their offerings of bread, wine and meat, he only sees one depart. When, shortly after this, he arrives at the Castle of Enquiry, he asks of the hermit who dwells there the meaning of what he had seen, the priest answers unequivocally:

> Of that ... I will tell you no more than you have heard — and you should
> be thankful for that much — for no one should reveal the secrets of the
> Saviour.[23]

He might almost have said 'the secrets of the Goddess', for the implication that he has already told Gawain the answer is borne out by the explanation he had previously given to an earlier episode also concerning three damsels, whose appearance had helped instigate the quest. Here, the three maidens had arrived at the court on the 24 June, St John the Baptist's feast day. The first maiden was bald, rode a mule and carried her left arm in a sling. The second maiden carried a shield and a dog, both destined for the successful Grail knight. The third walked behind the others, whipping them on.

The hermit of the Castle of Enquiry explains the symbolism of this very fully and in Christian terms. However, the most interesting detail from the point of view of our argument, concerns the bald maiden whom the hermit specifically identifies as Fortune, and that her hair can only be restored when the destined knight has achieved the Grail. In the light of Gawain's visit to the Castle of Fortune in *Diu Crône* (see Chapter 6), this cannot fail to strike one as significant. Here, at a juncture where he comes closest to the Grail, Gawain once again encounters the Goddess, who appears, firstly in a triple form, then singly — showing that each of her aspects is contained within the other, and that together they form a single image.

The rest of the romance features Gawain in a number of adventures only tangentally connected with the Grail. In one at least he carries out a promise made during his quest, which indicates perhaps that he has learned from all that has occurred. Later, the episode in which his true parentage is revealed (see pp44-5) takes place, so that he is, as it were, rewarded in some senses for his efforts.

Generally, he is paired more often with Lancelot, the two representing a worldly vision of chivalry very different to that of Perceval, who
of course achieves the quest as he had always been meant to do. The
difference between Gawain and Perceval is emphasized by the way that
Gawain continually fails to recognize, or just misses his friend. His final
glimpse of Perceval is as he sails away in a magical boat towards the
lands of the Grail.

Gawain's quest is thus over. Despite his achievements in obtaining
the sword with which John the Baptist was beheaded (a notable choice
as we shall see), it has been a failure. He has been in the presence of
the Grail but has not asked the ritual question which will bring about
the conclusion of the great adventure.

Yet he has behaved at every turn in an exemplary fashion. It seems,
as Keith Busby suggests, that the author of *Perlesvaus* was counting
on a prior knowledge of Gawain's career in his audience, and that the
acts for which Gawain had been earlier condemned are what causes
him to fail.

It is a critical point in Gawain's literary career. This is the closest he
comes to the Grail (with the exception of *Diu Crône*, see pp148-151).
The Quest for the Sword, which is echoed elsewhere in the episode
where he acquires the Sword of Judas Maccabeus, and perhaps again
in shadowy form when he is offered a sword by the Cowardly Knight,
points to a story, of which we no longer possess a complete version,
where Gawain, having successfully passed this test, *does* achieve the
Grail.

As we come, finally, to the great *Vulgate cycle*, in which the Quest
for the Grail moves fully to the centre of the stage, and is seen to affect
the entire Arthurian mythos, we see Gawain carried even further from
any possibility of success. Malory, who followed the Vulgate *Quest del
Saint Graal*[37] closely, does nothing to redress the balance, but as we
shall see, continues the degradation of Gawain's character.

The *Vulgate cycle* consists of a number of loosely connected works
which were copied, probably in a Cistercian monastery, between 1212
and 1225. Three of them contain important references to Gawain and
in particular to his part in the Grail Quest.

In the first of these, the *Lancelot*, we find that hero firmly settled
as the major exemplar of Arthurian chivalry. Not only Gawain, but
just about everyone, takes second place to the great French knight,
whose prowess and his amorous liaison with Guinevere, occupy much
of the text. Lancelot's own failure in the quest is itself worth considering, since it closely resembles certain aspects of Gawain's own unsatisfactory performance — though with marked variations which are

themselves of interest for the light they throw on the medieval author's thinking.

From the start Gawain is closely involved in Lancelot's burgeoning career, supporting his early request for dangerous adventures and leading search parties when he is missing for a long time.

However, with Lancelot's ascendancy comes Gawain's loss of standing. He is frequently compared with Lancelot in unfavourable terms, sometimes ironically placed in the mouth of Gawain himself, when he praises Lancelot at his own expense.

Further tensions are added by the fact of Gawain's obvious affection for the younger knight, who in turn is slavishly worshipped by Galahaut the Haut Prince, an adversary of Arthur's who through Lancelot's efforts is constrained to make peace and to become Arthur's vassal.

Yet despite these tensions between the characters, Gawain's standing remains high in its own terms. In an episode which follows, his brother Agravain is discovered, lying sick with one arm and leg covered in sores which will not heal. The only cure for this is said to be blood from the two best knights in the world. Gawain of course offers his own, and at once Agravain's arm is healed. Later, Lancelot will complete the healing with some of his own blood but this indicates that Gawain is still ranked as equal to him — though just as much at fault, as we see in the next episode, where Gawain is found forcing his attentions on a damsel who has come to take him to her mistress, who is in need of help.

The middle section of the *Lancelot* stresses Gawain's closeness and loyalty to Arthur and the Round Table. During the episode of the false Guinevere, in which a double of the queen is produced and the real Guinevere impugned with unlawful and treasonous acts, Gawain stands by her even more noticeably than Lancelot at first. And, when Arthur is himself captured by the false Guinevere, and believed dead, Gawain is unanimously elected to take the crown after him — a detail which re-emphasizes Gawain's claims, through several links of blood, to be Arthur's successor.

As it happens Arthur is, of course, not dead; he sends a message containing references which only Gawain, with his intimate knowledge of his uncle's life, can detect. And subsequently, with the real queen's life at stake, although it is now Lancelot who defends her, renouncing his place at the Round Table to do so, it is Gawain who stands by them both, helping to arm Lancelot and even lending him Excalibur, which he happens to possess at the time (Arthur often lends Gawain his mighty weapon. An even clearer indication of their closeness, as well as the importance of the sword as an emblem of Gawain's power.)

When the truth about the false Guinevere becomes known, Gawain castigates Arthur for his failure to believe in the real queen's innocence, in a manner which, as Keith Busby noted, was more akin to the kind of remonstration usually put into the mouths of the hermit figures who throng the text, ever questioning, criticizing and directing the efforts of the Round Table knights.

The next part of the text deals with a reworking of the story told by Chrétien in *Le Chevalier de la Charette* (The Knight of the Cart),[9] in which Lancelot is forced ignominiously to ride in this vehicle — a mode of transport normally reserved for criminals — in order to save Guinevere from the clutches of Meleagraunce (see pp82-3). More important is an episode which follows this, later in the text, where Gawain repeats this act in order to rescue Lancelot — thus making an important parallel between the love of Lancelot for Guinevere and that of Gawain for Lancelot. Indeed, his affection for the great French knight, which is untrammelled by any taint of jealousy, is one of the finest features of Gawain's character, one which the author of the *Lancelot* is at pains to point out again and again — as in the frequent quests in which Gawain engages to rescue Lancelot when the latter is missing from court for long periods. The fact that it is usually Lancelot who then has to rescue Gawain, further indicates his superiority over the king's nephew.

Shortly after these events, the theme of the Broken Sword reappears, when Gawain and several other knights go to the assistance of Elyzer, the son of the Grail king Pelles. He had actually been searching for Gawain to request him to join the broken parts of the sword, even though this is apparently a task reserved for the Grail champion. We must presume that word of Gawain's better deeds had reached the Grail king and that he had seen in the king's nephew a possible Grail winner.

However, the fact that not only Gawain but also the other Round Table knights fail in this undertaking, is the first indication among many to come of the more general failure of the Arthurian order in the Quest for the Grail.

The first indication of Gawain's impatience or dissatisfaction with Lancelot's escalating abilities, occurs in an episode where Gawain is driven from a haunted graveyard and having been repulsed is told that Lancelot is destined to achieve the adventure. Gawain is so upset by this that he makes a second attempt, receiving serious wounds in the process.

Finally comes Gawain's second visit to the Grail castle, and with it his most ignominious defeat:

Viewing the procession of the sacred objects, his eye is drawn more to the physical beauty of the Grail maiden herself. Thus, when the Grail exhibits its miraculous property of feeding everyone present, Gawain alone receives nothing. He is then insulted by a dwarf and attacked by an invisible opponent who flings a blazing spear at him, wounding him in the shoulder.

Strange visions follow, during which Gawain is temporarily deprived of sight. As he regains it a knight advises him to sleep elsewhere, and Gawain attacks him in anger, despite the pain of his wound and the sacred place in which he finds himself.

Finally, both men faint and there is a violent storm which so bewilders Gawain when he recovers consciousness that he scarcely knows where he is. More cruel treatment follows, as Gawain lies paralysed and hears angelic voices speaking words that he cannot understand.

At last, as his faculties return, night falls, but Gawain is bound to the bed on which he has been lying all this while and is unceremoniously thrown out of the castle and the town.

Sorrowfully, he finds his way to a hermitage where he is given shelter and the recent events are explained to him in painful detail, each chastisement being shown as a failing on his part and a general indication of his inevitable failure on the Quest.

Even Gawain's great strength and courage is not left uncriticized, as the author crushingly remarks that he could have easily been overcome by other knights were it not for the fact of his waxing and waning strength — an otherworldly ability which gives him the edge over others, through no prowess of his own.

The effect of all this is to give a negative account of Gawain's character and it is customary to view this as due to the rise in popularity of Lancelot, a position brought about at the expense of Gawain. However, this seems a rather simplistic explanation, which fails to take into account Gawain's background and history previous to the Grail romances. These, as we have seen, draw heavily on pre-Christian symbolism, and despite a heavy overlay of theological exposition, cannot wholly disguise the origin of much of their background.

Gawain, as one of the earliest and most popular Arthurian heroes, occupies a unique position within the complex world of the Arthurian court. When he could not be ignored, therefore, he had to be shown in a less heroic and positive light, with the results that we have seen.

The succession of amorous adventures attributed to Gawain throughout the Continuations of *Conte del Graal*, as well as the *Lancelot*, is hard to explain unless Gawain was already associated with the idea of service to all women. The fact that he was, in certain circles, known as the Champion of the Goddess (or at very least of an otherworldly woman) seems to have spurred various authors who took him for a hero, to develop the theme by making him a lover of all women *literally* —

with the inevitable outcome that he attains the reputation of a rake
and a libertine. Significantly, perhaps, the texts where this takes place
are generally French, while those which continue the original Gawain
tradition most strongly are the English cycle of stories. Nevertheless,
while less obviously represented in the Continental works, there are
still a large number of references to these more primitive sagas dispersed
among the later elegance of Chrétien de Troyes and the theology of
the *Vulgate cycle*.

The final levelling of Gawain's character takes place in the major Grail
text of the cycle, *Le Queste del Saint Graal*[37] in which the didacticism
of the author increases and in which a new character, Galahad, appears
to challenge the status of *all* the Round Table knights.

It would not be stretching the point too far to suggest that the author
of the *Quest* set out systematically to degrade earthly in favour of
spiritual chivalry, and that he begins his attack with Gawain. Lancelot, too, suffers much the same fate. Only Perceval, and later Bors, Lancelot's cousin, are singled out to form part of the trio of successful Quest
knights.

The single, overwhelmingly powerful candidate is Galahad, child of
Lancelot and the Grail princess Elaine. He is destined from the beginning to achieve the Grail; indeed, it is his sole purpose for existing,
and all bow, sooner or later, to him.

Significantly, Gawain is the first among the knights to swear that he
will search for the Grail, though it must be obvious by now that he
has little real chance of succeeding. The rest of the court follows suite
and Arthur is distressed and angry with Gawain for what he sees (with
some truth as matters transpire) as the final breaking apart of the Round
Table order.

Now Gawain's continual searching for Lancelot, which dominated
so much of the action in the previous text, switches to a search for Galahad, whom Gawain seems instinctively to grasp as being the one to
follow. A hermit tells him that this would scarcely be a suitable com-
panionship, since the latter is so far above him. Later, when Gawain
encounters the hermit Nasciens, who is part of the Grail family, he
is told:

> Gawain, it is a long time since you became a knight, and little enough
> have you served your Creator since then. You are an old tree, bearing no
> longer either leaf or fruit. Now consider how Our Lord may have at least
> the pith and the bark, if nothing more, since the devil has had the flower
> and the fruit. (Trans. W.W. Comfort)

But Gawain uneasily retreats from any possible offer of forgiveness,
excusing himself and riding away. It seems that there is really no hope
for him.

From this point on indeed, Gawain finally abandons the Quest, which he now accepts is not for him — though he still seems unable to understand why. As one of the premier representatives of earthly chivalry he, like Lancelot, was never meant to achieve the Quest. That is left to Galahad, who in part redeems his father by his own sinless achievement.

In all, the *Quest* paints a bleak picture of Gawain and of all that he stands for. It is, with the single exception of the *Prose Tristan*[41] which we shall examine in the next chapter, the darkest of the medieval portraitures. Malory, following the *Quest* closely, if anything spares Gawain even less. His sympathies lie all with Lancelot, whose failure on the Quest becomes a magnificent human tragedy which cannot fail to move us even today.

Gawain's failure, too, is spectacular. In each of the texts we have looked at, where he attempts the path to the Grail, he achieves much before being finally, and it must be said in some instances, reluctantly, rejected. It is as though the romancers, knowing a little of Gawain's original role, felt constrained to bar him from the Grail mysteries, but were at the same time unwilling to make him seem wholly worthless.

Thus at every point, he achieves good and often great deeds, which emphasizes his loyalty to Arthur and his fellows of the Round Table, as well as his unfailing generosity and bravery. These were powerful assets for any knight in the Middle Ages, and it says much for the strength of feeling against those 'tainted' by associations with earlier, pagan times, that despite Gawain's popularity, he is still almost universally denied access to the Grail.

In part this was due to the monkish nature of the clerks and compilers of the later romances, especially the *Vulgate cycle* where the earthly splendour of the Round Table fellowship was openly criticized. In the next chapter we must look at the one text where this does not occur, and from there begin to trace another quest, a story which was once current, in which Gawain played a very different role. Traces of this are still to be found, even within the most anti-Gawain texts, and it is possible also that another, successful, hero may prove to owe much to Gawain. From this, it should be possible to construct that original quest and Gawain's part in it, thus transforming our view of him once and for all.

Chapter 6.

Mary's Knight: The Grail Champion Restored

GAWAIN AT THE CASTLE OF THE GRAIL

We are now in a position to begin piecing together the fragmentary references scattered throughout the various texts relating to the Grail which deal with Gawain's personal quest. We have seen how, beginning with Chrétien's *Conte del Graal*, and continuing through the various additions to his original text into the didactic world of the *Vulgate cycle*, Gawain's role as a Grail seeker was steadily undermined, leaving him, at the last, not only unsuccessful, but morally darkened in terms of his overall character.

This was a tendency which was to continue until, at the very end of his career, as we shall see in more detail in the next chapter, he experienced something of a renaissance, the very darkness of his character being transformed until, in Malory's *Le Morte d'Arthur*, it became a kind of triumph in which the closing pages of his life were decked with sombre splendour.

However, before we go on to examine this final change in Gawain's long career, we need to see what we can recover of his original role in the Quest for the Grail, beginning with the single text in which he appears as a successful candidate.

This is the *Diu Crône* of Heinrich von dem Turlin[22] which, as we have already seen, contains some markedly primitive aspects of Gawain's career, and in all probability represents a story which, though current at the time (c.1224) was subsequently lost, or suppressed for reasons already noted.

Diu Crône is an extremely prolix and at times ill-written work which contains an extraordinary rag-bag of stories drawn from the entire range of the Arthurian mythos. It is characterized by an unusual degree of autonomy in the author, who stamps every episode with his personal ideas at a time when such individuality was positively frowned upon. It's title, interestingly enough, comes from Heinrich's own statement, in which he compared the various stories he had chosen to retell as jewels in a crown made especially for the delectation of women everywhere — an idea which, in the light of his sympathetic treatment of Gawain, may itself be significant.

The episodes which interest us here are amongst the best in the poem and present a very different view of Gawain to the one we have seen so far. And although *Diu Crône* has been seen as an individual response to Wolfram's *Parzival*, it in all probability contains one of the earliest versions of the Grail story (though not written down until the thirteenth century) in which Gawain, still at the height of his fame, was permitted to achieve the Quest.

The relevant parts of the story are as follows, and are taken from the partial translation of Jessie L. Weston[51] and the summary of Professor J.D. Bruce.[77]

Gawain had been searching for the Grail for a long time, travelling through a land so rich in adventure that he had become exhausted. Yet his prowess stood him in good stead, and now at last he reached a fair and beauteous land 'so well tilled that naught was lacking of the fruits of the earth, corn and vines, and fair trees, all whereby man might live grew freely on either hand... it might well be held for an earthly paradise, since 'twas full of all delights that heart of man might desire' (Trans. Weston).

Scarcely entered into this realm of wonders, Gawain saw a dwelling the walls of which were as clear as glass; but the way was guarded by a great fiery sword, and it seemed deserted, so that he passed it by. Then, after riding 12 days through woodland, he discovered his companions of the Quest, Lancelot and Calogreant, sleeping under a tree, and the three greeted each other joyously and told of their separate adventures.

As night approached they were met on the road by a squire, who bade them accompany him to his lord's dwelling, where they would be made welcome and receive every comfort. The squire then rode ahead at full gallop, leaving the three knights to follow at an easy pace.

Arriving before the castle, they saw a goodly company of knights exercising their mounts and vying with each other in skills of horsemanship before the walls. When Gawain and his companions were seen, they at once left their sports and flocked eagerly to the roadside to greet their honoured guests.

Within, the castle was as fair a place as they had ever seen. In the great hall the floor was strewn with roses and the host, richly dressed in white and gold, reclined on a couch, while at his feet two noble youths played chess and made merry jests.

The old lord bade them welcome and seated Gawain beside him on a cushion of rose-coloured silk. There was much pleasant conversation, and as night came a host of fair people began to gather; knights and ladies, minstrels and chamberlains to serve them.

Their host kept his guests close by him, Gawain above and the others below him at the table, 'and when all were seated, and were fain to eat, then there came into the hall a wondrous fair youth, of noble bearing, and in his hand he held a sword, fair and broad, and laid it down before the host.' (Ibid.)

While Gawain wondered at the meaning of this, cupbearers entered with wine for all. But the host neither ate nor drank, and when he saw that neither did Gawain; but both Lancelot and Calogreant were so thirsty that they drank even though he bade them not to, and at once fell into a deep slumber.

Thereafter, though his host urged Gawain to drink, he would accept nothing, but was on his guard, 'lest he too fall asleep' — and it seemed at that moment that the hall became suddenly filled with a great host of people.

Then there came into the hall a wondrous procession.

> In the sight of all there paced into the hall two maidens fair and graceful, bearing two candlesticks; behind each maid there came a youth, and the twain held between them a sharp spear. After these came two other maidens, fair in form and richly clad, who bare a salver of gold and precious stones, upon a silken cloth; and behind them, treading soft and slow, paced the fairest being whom since the world began God had wrought in woman's wise, perfect was she in form and feature, and richly clad withal. Before her she held on a rich cloth of samite a jewel wrought of red gold, in form of a base, whereon there stood another, of gold and gems, fashioned even as a reliquary that standeth upon an altar. This maiden bare upon her head a crown of gold, and behind her came another, wondrous fair, who wept and made lament, but the others spake never a word, only drew nigh unto their host, and bowed them low before him.

Gawain looked with double astonishment upon this scene, for he found that he recognized the crowned maiden as one that he had seen before, and who had spoken to him concerning the Grail and told him that if ever he saw her again in the company of five maidens, he should be sure not to fail to ask concerning what they did there.

> As he mused thereon the four who bare spear and salver, the youths with the maidens, drew nigh and laid the spear upon the table, and the salver beneath it. Then before Gawain's eyes there befell a great marvel, for the spear shed three great drops of blood into the salver that was beneath, and the old man, the host, took them straightaway. Therewith came the maiden of whom I spake, and took the place of the other twain, and set the fair reliquary upon the table — that did Sir Gawain mark right well — he saw therein a bread, whereof the old man brake the third part, and ate.

At that Gawain could contain himself no longer, but asked his host 'for the sake of God and by His Majesty, that ye tell me what meaneth this great company, and these marvels I behold?'

At that every knight and lady in the hall sprang up with a great shout of joy, wakening Lancelot and Calogreant from their slumber. But when they saw the company around them, and the wondrous objects, they at once fell into an even more profound sleep which lasted for five hours.

Then the host bade the company be still and silent, and speaking to Gawain alone, told him the meaning of all he had seen:

> Sir Gawain, this marvel which is of God may not be known unto all, but shall be held secret, yet since ye have asked thereof, sweet kinsman and dear guest, I may not withhold the truth. 'Tis the Grail which ye now behold. Herein have ye won the world's praise, for manhood and courage alike have ye right well shown, in that ye have achieved this toilsome quest. Of the Grail may I say no more save that ye have seen it, and that great gladness hath come of this your question. For now are many set free from the sorrow they have long borne, and small hope had they of deliverance. Great confidence and trust had we all in Perceval, that he would learn the secret things of the Grail, yet hence did he depart even as a coward who ventured nought, and asked nought. Thus did his quest miscarry, and he learned not that which of surety he should have learned. So had he freed many a mother's son from sore travail, who live, and yet are dead. Through the strife of kinsmen did this woe befall, when one brother smote the other for his land: and for that treason was the wrath of God shown on him and on all his kin, that all were alike lost.
>
> That was a woeful chance, for the living they were driven out, but the dead must abide in the semblance of life, and suffer bitter woe withal. That must ye know — yet had they hope and comfort in God and His grace, that they should come even to the goal of their grief, in such fashions as I shall tell ye.
>
> Should there be a man of their race who should end this their sorrow, in that he should demand the truth of these marvels, that were the goal of their desire; so would their penance be fulfilled, and they should again enter into joy: alike they who lay dead and they who live, and now give thanks to God and to ye, for by ye are they now released. This spear and this food they nourish me and none other, for in that I was guiltless of the deed God condemned me not. Dead I am, though I bear not the semblance of death, and this my folk is dead with me. However this may be, yet though all knowledge be not yours, yet have we riches in plenty, and know no lack. But these maidens they be not dead, nor have they other penance save that they be even where I am. And this is by the command of God, that by this His mystery, which ye have here beheld, they shall nourish me once, and once alone, in the year. And know of a truth that the adventures ye have seen have came of the Grail, and now is the penance perfected, and forever done away, and your quest hath found its ending.

Saying which he gave Gawain the sword which lay before him, telling him that it would serve him well always and never break. And he said

that Gawain's quest was ended, and that as for the maidens:

> 'Twas through their unstained purity, and through no misdoing, that God had thus laid upon them the service of the Grail; but now was their task ended, and they were sad at heart, for they knew well that never more should the Grail be so openly beheld of men, since that Sir Gawain had learned its secrets, for 'twas of the grace of God alone that mortal eyes might behold it, and its mysteries henceforth no tongue might tell.

Therewith the day began to dawn and all the company faded from sight, save only for Gawain's two companions and the maidens who had born the Grail and the other wondrous objects.

> And Sir Gawain was somewhat sorry, when he saw his host no more, yet was he glad when the maiden spake, saying that his labour was now at an end, and he had in sooth done all that pertained unto the Quest of the Grail, for never else in any land, save in that Burg alone, might the Grail have been beheld. Yet had that land been waste, but God had hearkened to their prayer, and by his coming had folk and land alike been delivered, and for that were they joyful.

All the next day they remained in the castle, and were well fed. Gawain's companions mourned when they discovered what had transpired while they slept. And the maidens called down many blessings upon Gawain 'that he might live many years in bliss and honour. . . since he had set them free'.

I have given this summary in some detail and with lengthy quotations, because it is not easily obtained and because of its crucial importance to our theory of Gawain. For here, indeed, is a very different version of the events at the Grail castle to those related in the majority of texts we have examined so far.

From the start it is made clear that Gawain is entering an otherworldly realm, a fair garden where all good things required for the comfort of mankind are to be found. He also sees a building with glass walls — a sure sign of having entered the Otherworld. Then, having met with Lancelot and Calogreant (a minor knight who is nowhere else associated with the Grail) they arrive at the castle, to be greeted by the gentle, colourful knights and ladies of the court. They enter a scene which could have come from almost any Celtic tale, with the old lord, dressed in white and gold, with two youths playing chess before him. This may seem a far cry from the frail Wounded King of the majority of Grail texts, yet we are left in no doubt as to his identity in the events which follow: the procession of the sacred and mysterious objects, and the feeding of the lord with blood from the lance and bread from the plat-

ter — surely one of the clearest images of the Christian Eucharist in
the entire Grail corpus.

But there are other significant details, perhaps most astounding the
identity of the beautiful crowned maiden who carries the Grail, whom
Gawain recognizes as a mysterious figure he had met earlier on his way
to the Grail country. Miss Weston's translation avoids the specific appellation found in the text (11 28345 ff) where the maiden is referred to
as 'Vrau', which may be translated as 'lady' or 'goddess' — surely the
clearest indication we could wish for of Gawain's continuing links with
the otherworldly queen. Nor should we fail to notice that it is as a cause
of her earlier advice which prompts Gawain to ask the all-important
question; or that the host refers to Gawain as 'kinsman', implying a
possibly deeper relationship than is immediately apparent.

Then there is the mysterious lamenting maiden, whom Miss Weston
later derives from the weeping women of the Adonis cult, mourning
for their dead God.[15] Whether we accept this, or see her perhaps as
reflecting the generally Christian symbolism of Heinrich's work, as in
the story of the lamenting women at Christ's tomb, or whether we see
her, in the light of other evidence within the text, as one of several fragmentary references to the variety of Grail stories then circulating orally,
does not matter. She is, like the Grail maiden herself, part of the mystery.

The fact that the Grail king (for such he undoubtedly is) refers to
the cause of the situation at the castle as being 'the strife of kinsmen. . .
when one brother smote the other for his land' is also of considerable
interest. Heinrich makes no direct reference to the Dolorous Blow, which
in the majority of Grail texts becomes the point of origin for many of
the Grail mysteries, in which the king receives a wound that remains
unhealed until the coming of the destined champion, and which is followed thereafter by the fratricidal killing of one brother by another,
yet these references, together with the fact that we first see the lord
of the castle reclining on a couch, seem as though they are made with
an eye on an audience expected to be familiar with such details.

Heinrich is consistent with other versions in having the king preserved
in a state of suspended life until until the ritual question is asked, and
which here releases the entire court — the living maidens from their
service and the dead to their rightful state. Even the final reference to
the land being 'waste' had not God heard the prayers of the people
and sent Gawain to deliver both folk and land, is in keeping with the
most essential theme of the Grail romances — the Waste Land which
suffers because of the king's evil, and which is only healed when the
mysteries of the Grail are over.

Far from representing an independent, totally original variation on
the usual Grail themes, as some scholars have suggested, all or most

of the elements are indeed present, though in a somewhat jumbled, partially understood form.

Where the poem does differ from all other versions is in making Gawain unequivocally the Grail winner. Although both Lancelot and Calogreant are present, it is made clear from the start that they are secondary to Gawain. The author specifically states that their host gave Gawain the place nearest to him, and that at the feast, he was seated 'above' the lord (that is, in the higher position at the table) and the others 'below'

Neither Lancelot not Calogreant are able to resist drinking the wine which is offered to them, and which causes them to fall asleep. And when they do awaken briefly, in the presence of the Grail, they are at once cast into an even deeper sleep.

Perceval, too, is criticized for his failure to ask the question and 'hence did. . . depart even as a coward who ventured naught, and asked naught.'

Here we have, then, a powerful version of the Grail story, containing many of the elements traditionally associated with the story, in which Gawain is the successful candidate against others who are generally more successful than he. How much weight can we attach to its evidence and what light can we throw upon its sources?

The evidence it offers our assertion that Gawain at one time occupied the place of the Grail winner is extremely strong, as much because of the variations in the text as for unusual versions of events at the Grail castle. We may remember that this same text also contains the important episode of Guinevere's abduction by Gasozin and her subsequent rescue by Gawain (see pp83-4), as well as a close variant of the Magic Bridle theme found elsewhere in *La Mule Sans Frein* (see pp71-2). It also includes a visit by Gawain to the allegorical fortress of Dame Fortune, also a goddess, whose ring he is awarded after a number of trials. Even more astonishing is the description of Fortune herself, as seated upon a great wheel, which stops turning when Gawain enters the castle. The Goddess is one half fair and one half foul when the hero first sees her, yet in that moment she changes, becoming completely beautiful! The significance of this need hardly be over emphasized. Gawain has won his way to the home of a goddess who shares the aspects of the Loathly Lady and the Flower Bride *at one and the same moment*. His presence alone causes her to become transformed. Here, it seems, Ragnall stands revealed — not only is she the earthly aspect of the Goddess, she is Gawain's lady, whose champion he has finally become. After this his success in the Grail Quest is no longer surprising.

It is often stated that Heinrich had an almost unrivalled knowledge of Arthurian literature, but that his combination of numerous stories, together with his reattribution of many other heroes' deeds to Gawain, make him an unreliable source. But it seems clear that a writer who had access to such a wide variety of tales (the sources of which remain in some instances untraced) could, among others, very easily have known a story where Gawain successfully achieved the ultimate Arthur-ian adventure — that of the Grail. To assume that because no such text remains extant, Heinrich must therefore have invented the episodes of Gawain at the Grail castle, is without foundation. Even if he had done so, it is more than likely that he drew upon oral traditions still powerfully alive at the time he was writing.

Whatever view one finally accepts, there is no escaping the fact that *Diu Crône* places Gawain in the role he had always exemplified, and for which his previous career had fitted him — that of the supreme para-gon of chivalry, above both Lancelot and Perceval, and as a Grail knight *par excellence*. If we now look back at the texts already examined with this fresh evidence in mind, we will begin to glimpse the shadowy out-line of another story, whose trail we have followed from the Modena carvings to the Vulgate *Quest*.

⟡

THE HIDDEN ROAD TO THE GRAIL

What, then, was the shape of Gawain's original quest? We have seen many of the elements already, scattered throughout the Continuations of *Le Conte del Graal*, in the *Perlesvaus* and in the Vulgate *Lancelot* and *Quest del Saint Graal*. Here, though Gawain is generally presented as an unsuccessful candidate for the quest, he does, beyond question, achieve certain adventures in his own right.

References to various swords recur in all of the texts mentioned above, and in each case these are linked to the Grail. The most significant of these is the sword with which John the Baptist was beheaded, which Gawain successfully obtains, after a number of difficult trials, in the *Perlesvaus*. This directly precedes his visit to the Grail castle wherein, though he is unsuccessful at that time, he actually obtains a view of the sacred objects.

One is struck at once by the fact that this is a beheading sword, and that Gawain, as a successful winner of the Green Knight's game, is an obvious choice to go in search of this particular relic. Again, in the *Lancelot* King Pelleas actually sends his son Elyzar in search of Gawain with the broken sword, in the hope that he will be able to mend it. Thus indicating, beyond question, that at one time this particular task was closely linked with Gawain's name.

That this once formed part of a series of Grail tests is evident from a similar episode in the Welsh text of *Peredur*,[3] where the hero is first requested to cut through an iron staple, which when he does so reunites itself twice, only his third blow finally severing it. This is immediately followed by the appearance of a procession carrying a huge bloody spear and a head in a dish, the primitive elements of the Grail mystery which in this version — possibly a key source for Chrétien's *Conte del Graal* — has become a quest for vengeance rather than spiritual fulfilment. As we have seen, Gawain was also associated with another quest for vengeance in Raoul Houdanc's *La Vengence Raguidel*. According to Chrétien, Perceval is given a sword during his first, unsuccessful, visit to the Grail castle, which he is only later told will break at a crucial point. It can only be restored by taking it to a spring near the forge of the smith Trebuchet, the original maker of the sword, and dipping the pieces in.

All of these scattered references seem to refer to a lost story which at some point either became attached to Gawain or, more likely, was already part of his adventures in search of the Grail. It must have told how Gawain searched for and found a mighty magical sword, which later broke at a crucial moment (probably in the midst of combat) and which he later restored by dipping it in a magical spring or lake, and with which he subsequently performed further great deeds, including the cutting of an iron staple which presumably bound some prisoner or held the land enthralled until the coming of the prescribed hero.

All of which leads us back to the earliest Celtic elements of Gawain's story, where two of his other selves, Goreu and Gwri, respectively achieved quests for a magical sword and succeeded in freeing a prisoner (Arthur or Mabon) from bondage.

This is, of course, highly speculative, but the elements are certainly present, as we have seen, and the evidence points to their having once formed part of Gawain's original saga. Just as it may also be possible that the earliest Grail story, as we almost certainly find it in *Peredur*, centred around the theme of vengeance — which, as we shall see, also became associated with Gawain at a later stage of his career.

Among the other notable swords with which he is associated are Excalibur. Arthur's magical weapon which he several times lends to Gawain, and which may also be seen to break at a crucial moment during Arthur's combat with Accolon of Gaul (see Malory Bk IV, Chs 9-11); and the sword of Judas Maccabeus, which Gawain wins by rescuing a maiden, who rewards him by showing him an underground crypt where the sword is kept. This particular weapon appears again in the later romances as The Sword of the Strange Hangings, which is discovered in the mysterious Ship of Solomon, in which Galahad, Per-

ceval and Bors, together with Perceval's sister, voyage to the City of
the Grail. Here (in the Vulgate *Quest*) the sword is the destined weapon
of the Grail winner, and Perceval's virgin sister cuts off her own hair
to make a belt for it (hence the sword's new title), and afterwards Galahad bears it to the end of his quest.

All of this suggests that at one point the sword formed one of the
Hallows of the Grail — the four sacred objects which were to be discovered by the Quest knights, and that indeed there may once have
been four such successful candidates, Gawain being the fourth, though
later excluded from the overtly Christian versions of the story. Certainly
this is conversant with the symbolism of the Grail mystery generally,
and with the mystical vessel being associated with Galahad, the spear
with Perceval, the sword with Gawain, leaving the dish or platter to
Bors. That we no longer possess a story in which these elements occur
precisely in this way need not deter us. We have seen throughout this
study how widely separated the details of a single story can become.

It seems clear, then, that in the story of the Quest for the Sword we
have an important part of Gawain's original story, which at some point
during the making and remaking of the Grail story became fragmented
and dispersed among the more newly established heroes of that story.

The greatest of these heroes, and perhaps one of the most crucial
literary inventions of all time, is, of course Galahad, the sinless, virgin
knight, who in the Vulgate *Quest* comes nearest to the perfection
required of the Grail winner. He is, daringly, made the son of Lancelot
and the Grail princess, who tricks him into bed by her getting her maid-
servant to administer a potion which deludes him into thinking she
is Guinevere. Thus Galahad is conceived in sin (according to the theology of the time) but is enabled, because of his own purity, to win
the Grail, thus in a certain sense redeeming his great father, who had
it not been for his fatal love for Arthur's queen, might himself have
achieved the Quest.

With the character of Galahad, we seem to come further from Gawain
than ever before. But is this really so? We saw in Chapter 1 the great
variety of metamorphoses through which the name passed before it
became more or less standardized as Gawain or Gauvain. Among these
variants is the name Gwalcheved, and Professor Rhys argues persua-
sively for this as the origin of the name Galahad.[135] Gwalcheved is
listed together with Gawain (Gwalchmai) in the Hero List contained
in *Culhwch and Olwen* as the son of Gwyar. As we saw, this was one
of the earliest names applied to Gawain's mother, which would make
the two heroes brothers. Gwalcheved probably means 'Hawk of Summer', which makes him, as Professor Rhys puts it, Gawain's brighter
self. And he is indeed just that in the romances where Gawain has

become discredited, and where Galahad represents the spiritual dimension of chivalry, where Gawain represents its earthly aspect.

Another reason for supposing that there is more to Galahad than his seemingly Christian origins is found in Malory (Bk XVII, Ch. 18) where Galahad comes to a perilous forest 'where he found the well which boiled with great waves as the tale telleth tofore. And as soon as Galahad set his hand thereto it ceased, so that it boiled no more and the heat departed... and this was taken in the country as a miracle. And so ever after was it called Callahadys Well.'

This seems to offer a glimpse of an earlier Galahad, associated with a hot spring of the kind usually attributed to the guardianship of a local goddess. It would be unwise to pursue the idea too far, but one may certainly see in this episode, as in the probable derivation of the name, a deeper link between Gawain and Galahad than is usually acknowledged.

Galahad, of course, in common with both Lancelot and Elaine, is part of the Grail family, that ancient house, stretching back to Joseph of Arimathea, who were chosen to guard the Grail . If we accept for the moment the possibility of kinship between Galahad and Gawain, this would also explain the Grail king's reference to the latter as 'kinsman' in *Diu Crône*'. Though none of Gawain's usual family, except possibly Gareth, show any sign of being likely candidates for the Quest, this can be easily accounted for by their being established only later, after the original relationship of Gawain and Galahad had been forgotten.

It is perhaps worth noting also, by way of interest, that just as Galahad is the child of Lancelot and the Grail princess, so Gawain has a famous offspring, Guingamore, whose mother, in all probability, is an otherworldly aspect of the Goddess. Perceval, as we have seen, may also have been Gawain's son in an earlier version of the story.

Whether or not any of this can be proved, it is interesting to note that Lancelot is also said to have been baptized Galahad, but that this was changed either because of his fostering by the Lady of the Lake, or because (by implication) his son was to succeed where he had failed. The point being that, as we have seen. Gawain once occupied the place later given over to Lancelot, as the queen's champion (and possibly as her lover) — so that we have the interesting situation where two important characters, father and son, the latter a Grail winner, both owe something of their existence and subsequent roles to Gawain.

One further strand in the complex skein of Gawain's career remains to be examined: his devotion to the Virgin Mary and the appellation of the symbol of the pentangle on his shield in *Gawain and the Green Knight*.

We have already seen, in Chapter 4, the degree of traditional, pagan themes contained in this poem, which is actually a marvellous blend of the pagan and the Christian. The pentangle is itself a primary example of this.

The Gawain, poet gives over some 50 lines of text, interrupting the narrative at a crucial moment, to make what must be a very important point. The passage is worth quoting in full:

> When they showed him the shield of shining gules with pure golden hues, he brandished it by the belt, and about his neck he cast it, that he was seemly and fair to look upon. And I am intent to tell you, though I may weary you somewhat why that pentangle belonged to that noble prince. It is a symbol that Solomon set up some while for betokening of truth, as his name doth show. For it is a figure that hath five points, and each line overlaps, and is locked in the other, and everywhere it is endless, and the English call it, as I hear, the endless knot. Therefore was it befitting this knight and his clean armour. For Sir Gawain was known as a knight both good and true and faithful in five, and many times five, and pure as gold, and void of all villainy was he, and adorned with virtues
>
> in the mote,
>
> For the pentangle new
> He bears in shield and coat,
> And is a knight most true
> And gentle man, I wot.
>
> And first he was found faultless in his five wits. Then he failed not in his five fingers. And all his trust on earth was in the five wounds suffered by Christ on the cross, as the creeds do tell us, so that when the knight was placed in the mêlée, his thought was ever upon them above all other things. And so it was that all his strength he found in the five joys that the fair Queen of Heaven had in her child. And for this cause it was that the knight had made to be painted her image in comely fashion on the greater half of his shield, so that when he looked upon it his valour never failed him. Now the fifth five that this knight excelled in were frankness and fellowship above all others, his cleanness and courtesy never were crooked, and compassion, that surpasseth all else. These five pure virtues were fixed in this knight more firmly than in any other. And all five times were so joined in him that each one held to the other without any ending and fixed at five points, nor did they ever fail; for they were joined at no point nor sundered were they at all, nor could one find any end thereof at any corner when the games began or were gliding towards an ending. Therefore the knot was shaped on his strong shield, all with red gold upon red gules, called the pure pentangle among the people of love. (Kirtlan)[46]

Thus we see Gawain, that paragon of earthly chivalry, bearing a symbol which is said to represent the five wounds of Christ, the five joys of Mary and the five earthly virtues, and which is equated with Solomon's Seal, the endless knot, and as a symbol of Gawain's personal 'five kinds of faithfulness'.

In the above extract, we see that the intention of the poet was first and foremost to present Gawain as a most noble and splendid representative of the Fellowship of the Round Table knights, whom the Green Knight comes to mock and to test. He therefore selects every virtue he can that was considered important to a knight in the fourteenth century.

Spiritual, moral and social virtues are particularly emphasized in this passage where it refers to the relationship between these chivalric virtues and the series of the fivefold symbologies described by the Gawain poet. We may be sure that each aspect of Gawain's fealty was offered to the Goddess at some stage. The Gawain poet, as a Christian, interpreted them in Christian terms. Yet behind them still lies an evocation of the kinds of devotion required of the Knight of the Goddess: truth, trustworthiness, courage, courtesy, magnanimity and compassion.

His linking of them in the ancient symbol of the pentangle is a stroke of genius, for it not only unifies the elements of Gawain's exemplary character, it also links them, by inference, with his pagan origins. Whether the Gawain poet knew this or not, we cannot be certain, but wherever he learned of the pentangle there would almost certainly have been some reference to the mysterious history of the symbol. (See Appendix 2.) Its apposite use in the Gawain story can be inferred from various mystical traditions.

In the Gnostic system, Sophia, the divine emanation of the Godhead, would not permit anyone to enter her Realm of Light, unless they were in complete balance, and bore the sign of the pentangle upon them — a significant fact in our argument, since Gawain is indeed admitted to the inner realm of the Goddess, after he has undergone the necessary tests, during which he bears the pentangle.[47]

In English folk-tradition, the mummers whose ancient dances were a last flickering memory of more primitive rites, performed a sword dance, the climax of which was to link their swords into a star, and cry: 'A Nut, a Nut.' (i.e. a knot — the endless knot which was an ancient name for the pentangle.) They then placed the linked blades over the head of one of their number and pretended to *cut off his head*. This feature of the old mummers' plays is still retained by many groups of Morris dancers in England today.[97]

It hardly seems accidental that this should be connected, however obliquely, with Gawain whose most famous adventure involved the Beheading Game, and indeed we may see here a significant reference to a more ancient rite in which the participants worked themselves into a frenzy and ended by beheading the chosen victim.

With the passage of time, this would have become gradually more symbolic, though the beheading probably continued to be understood as opening a path to the Otherworld, whether or not it took place in a physical sense.

It may be of relevance to compare the Tibetan tantric practice of the Chöd, wherein the practitioner enters into an egoless state and visualizes his consciousness leaving through the top of his head, there to take on the appearance of a wrathful dakini (a meditational female deity). The dakini, with her hooked knife, is then visualized as beheading and chopping into pieces the practitioner's body, rendering his essential juices into his own skull-cap, which is then symbolically offered to all created beings as nourishment. The Beheading Game of British tradition obviously has more to do with agricultural and seasonal rites, but the concept of selfless sacrifice is a similar one. The wrathful dakini in the practice of the Chöd parallels the challenging aspect of the Goddess in Gawain's experience: she who will accept only the best combatant to be her champion, whom she will then employ to mediate her extensive powers.

In *Gawain and the Green Knight* and the other texts which deal with this theme, we see the last stages of a ritual that was already ancient, in which the hero, having undergone the ordeal, was admitted into the presence of the Goddess (or her earthly representative) and allowed to enjoy her favours.

Gawain, or whatever name the hero was given in the various transmissions of this tradition, probably mated with Morgain, the Goddess, or Dame Ragnall, after having endured the test of her champion, whose role he then assumed, possibly after a combat in which, wither symbolically or actually, he slew his rival for the favour of the Goddess.

It is this, rather than the more rarified spiritual attainments of the Grail Quest (perhaps represented by the 'new pentangle' of the Gawain poet) which we may see as the outcome of Gawain's test. Having undergone numerous tests and trials, in which he obtained a magical sword, and a shield of power which bore the sign of the Goddess and had an image of her painted on it, he came to her Chapel-in-the-Green, and after braving the Beheading Game, slew or otherwise overcame her champion, finally taking on the role of Green Knight himself, and symbolically, or literally, mating with her.

Thus, as we saw in Chapter 3, Morgan built a valley chapel where only those faithful in love (i.e. to the representative of an eternal feminine, as in the suppliants to the realm of Sophia), could find shelter and be allowed to depart — presumably after having enjoyed the favours of either Morgan herself or one of her 'ladies'.

From this root sprang the idea of Gawain's love of all women, which in the hands of the pious writers of the *Vulgate cycle* transformed him into a libertine. Yet, despite every effort on the part of these writers, they could not completely disguise the original shape of Gawain's quest, or its outcome, any more than they could extinguish the flame of his true personality. In English works like *Gawain and the Green Knight*, *Gawain and Ragnall* etc, the tradition remained stronger, though even in the most extreme anti-Gawain literature of the Continental texts, traces are still to be found, as we have seen, of the original story-line.

Jessie Weston, in her study of Perceval[153] noted an important distinction between the Grail stories in which Gawain was hero and those of Perceval himself.

> It will be well understood that such a story would vary if told from the inside, the mythic, or from the outside, the human, and Initiatory aspect. Gawain belongs to the first, Perceval to the second class of hero, and the versions as we have them are all of this second character; the original *Gawain-Grail* story was probably different. In any case, in view of the evidence. . . I do not think we should any longer withhold from Gawain his rightful place of honour, as first on the roll of winners of the Grail.[53]

This important distinction cannot be over-emphasized. The inner, mythic dimension of which Gawain was a part is precisely what gives him his role in most, if not all, the adventures in which he has a part. The outer, initiative approach could not be his since *he was already part of the inner dimension* — hence the need for another hero — one who would need to undertake a new set of tests and trials, unlike those already achieved by Gawain. With the changing climate of the time those tests naturally assumed a Christian dimension which nonetheless retained aspects of the earlier mysteries.

In this we may perceive a crucial aspect in the origins of the Grail story — a point of interaction where the direction of the story turned from the recital of myth-oriented events, to one of initiation, in which the chosen champion sought the mysterious vessel, and had various tests placed before him. Earlier, it now seems likely, the versions of the tale which went into the making of the first Grail romance, told of a series of tests *already achieved*, in which the hero (Gawain or whoever) was already known to be the successor of previous candidates — the recital being of their retrospective voyage towards the Grail. (Fig 8.)

If we see Gawain as the proto-Grail winner, on an earlier spiral, then this comes full circle in the adventures of his son, Guinglain, who, though never associated with the Grail Quest as such, nonetheless embodies many of the attributes of his more famous father.

The authors of *Gawain and the Green Knight* and *Diu Crône*, perhaps unintentionally, more than any other preserved these ancient traditions,

Text	Hero
Proto-Grail	Proto-Hero
|	|
Gawain-Grail	Gawain
|	|
Major Grail Romances (Chrétien-Vulgate)	Perceval-Galahad
|	|
Guinglain-Grail	Guinglain

Figure 8: *The Succession of the Grail Heroes.*

allowing Morgain her rightful title of 'Goddess' and giving us the clearest picture of the Green Knight in all his elemental power, as well as restoring Gawain to his original role as Grail champion. Even they, however, failed to recognize the Green Knight in Gawain who was, finally, the Champion of the Goddess, as her consort-on-earth.

The presence of the pentangle on the hero's shield, despite the Gawain poet's Christianized glosses, could not disguise the fitness of the symbol in its larger applications. Perhaps the 'people of love' mentioned in *Gawain and the Green Knight* were indeed the last remnant of Goddess worshippers, who saw in the bearer of the pentangle, her true champion — Mary's Knight, who bore the image of the Virgin on his shield, stood revealed to all who could see, as the Knight of the Goddess.

Chapter 7.

The Death of Gawain: A Hero Transformed

THE DEEPEST DEPTHS; THE HIGHEST HEIGHTS

At the end of the *Queste del Saint Graal* Gawain's career seemed to have reached an all time low ebb. In the *Prose Tristan*[41] which was composed some 5 to 15 years later, between 1230 and 1240, this course continues his decline to the darkest depths. The two themes which dominate the role of Gawain and his brothers in this romance are both concerned with vengeance: against King Pellinore and his family, whom the brothers blame for the deaths of their father, King Lot, and their mother, Queen Morgause; and that of Gawain alone for Lancelot and his kin, for the death of his brothers Gareth and Gaheries.

These themes, which lie at the heart of the final tragedy in the Arthurian saga, show Gawain in the worst light of any of the texts we have so far examined. Yet even here, as we shall see, there is a ray of light which prevents his total blackening.

The story is a dark strand in the bright tapestry of the Arthurian story. Pellinore had killed Lot fairly in battle, when the latter led a rebellion against Arthur in the first years of the young king's reign. This sowed the seeds of a feud which continued throughout the years of Arthur's rule. Although both families are represented at the Round Table, there is continuous animosity between Pellinore and his sons, Tor, Lamorack, Agloval, Perceval and Driant, and Gawain and his brothers, Gaheries, Agravain and Mordred (Gareth refuses to have any part in the feud).

In time Pellinore is murdered by Gawain and Gaheries, though the details are not given and for a time there is uneasy peace. Then Lamorack, one of the strongest and best of the Round Table knights, falls in love with Morgause of Orkney, and the two begin a passionate affair which is only ended when Gaheries, in a fit of anger, kills his mother — an act which becomes, in the minds of the Orkney clan, the fault of Lamorack, who dared despoil the wife of the man slain by his own father.

The true state of affairs we may only guess at, since the texts are silent. Certain it is that Morgause, even in her mortal aspect, was a sorceress who would have had no more difficulty in beguiling Lamorack than she had in enticing Arthur into her bed.

The outcome is dark: Gawain, Gaheries, Agravain and Mordred band together and murder Lamorack, striking suddenly from ambush and felling him with a blow (struck by Mordred) from behind. It is the story of Pellinore over again, and once again the brethren seem to go unpunished. The high deeds of the Quest are over indeed, and the beginning of the end for all that Arthur had stood for is in sight. Lancelot, failed in the Grail Quest, returns to his old love for the queen, and Mordred, the bastard child of the king's incest with his sister, begins to plot the downfall of his father.

Against this tragic, overwhelming background, the final chapters in Gawain's career are played out. Yet even here, even now, with the Arthurian kingdom crumbling on all sides, grim and bloody deeds upon his hands, something of the once great hero shines through. Condemn him as they might, the authors of the works which deal especially with these final years — the *Morte Artu* (Death of Arthur)[16] and its variants, the *Alliterative Morte Arthure*[24] and the last books of Malory's masterpiece — cannot disguise the admiration they feel for Gawain. In this way the discrediting of his name brought about by the pious authors of the major Grail texts, is gradually reversed. Gawain becomes a magnificent, tragic hero, human in every respect at last, with most of his otherworldliness purged from him.

In the *Prose Tristan*, the powerful anti-Gawain sentiments are so strong that his hold on our sympathies is almost broken. Though it is Agravain who proposes killing Perceval so that the greatest of Pellinore's line may fall, Gawain does not contradict him. And he is party to the death of Lamorack, as well as Pellinore's other son, Driant.

Gaheries is without doubt the subtlest character in this version of the story. It is he, out of love and fellowship for Lamorack, who kills his mother, and he will have nothing to do with the further persecution of Pellinore's line. (In Malory this motivation is transferred to Gareth, who is the more sympathetic character.) Agravain even contemplates killing Gaheries for this, as though he had taken sides against the Orkney clan rather than shunning them for their violent ways.

Keith Busby[79] draws attention to the last fading spark of loyalty between these Round Table knights in the episode where Lamorack selflessly frees Gawain, who has been imprisoned by the Damoiselle de la Mantagne, remarking later that it was not time for Gawain to die and that he could have scarcely acted differently. Gawain admits to Gaheries that he is grateful, but that he cannot bring himself to love Lamorack because of the feud.

Later in the same text the deaths of Driant and Lamorack are described in more detail. In both cases the Orkney brothers set upon Pellinore's sons without mercy. Gawain wounds an already hurt Driant, and though he then restrains Mordred from decapitating their fallen adversary, all four ride off without a thought for the dying man or his most certain desire for a priest to administer the last rites.

Coming upon an already weakened Lamorack, the same treatment is meted out to him. He is finally slain by Gawain, though he is by then so weak that he faints several times, though refusing to beg for mercy. This time at least, a priest is summoned and allowed to bury the body at a nearby abbey.

Word of the murder reaches Arthur, and the Orkney brothers are specifically named — though oddly not accused — for their part in Lamorack's death. The implication is that Arthur knows what has happened but turns a blind eye — adding further to the shameful actions of his nephews.

Gawain's role throughout the *Prose Tristan* continues to show him in an evil light. He displays a lustful desire for every woman he sees and is not above fatally wounding an unarmed escort in order to have his way. When one damsel accuses him of lightness of love, he makes the extraordinary excuse that he has so many adventures that it is easy to forget one in the excitement of the next! A statement which, remarks Keith Busby, 'might well serve as a preferatory remark to many of his adventures in the corpus of Arthurian literature'.[79]

On top of this Gawain several times fights with already wounded knights, causing at least one death thereby. He seems motivated entirely by jealousy of any knight said to be stronger or better than himself and will use any method to overcome them. Much of his hatred for Pellinore's family may be traced to this same feeling, since all of the de Galles family are mighty fighters, with considerable reputations among the Round Table knights. (As noted earlier, in Chapter 4, this may well originate in the very first adventure of the Round Table Fellowship.)

Tristan, the hero of the work, naturally encounters Gawain several times, and observes his unchivalrous behaviour. Once again, as happened with Perceval, then Lancelot and finally Galahad in the Grail texts, unfavourable contrasts are drawn. Once again Keith Busby sums up:

> The author's attitude could not be clearer: if Tristan is the defender of chivalry, and its judge too, then Gauvain is its enemy. Because Gauvain used to be a good knight, and because others have now surpassed him in terms of prowess and chivalry, he is often seen to be jealous of the reputations of younger and better knights (especially Perceval and Gala-

had). This, together with the revenge motif, is one of the causes of the murders of Lamorack and Driant, and is especially noticeable in the plot against Perceval. It must also be the reason for his constant challenging of knights, his denigration of others and his refusal to admit defeat.[79]

Angered, no doubt, by Tristan's censure, Gawain does not hesitate to vent his spleen on Tristan's love, Iseult, whom he compares, unfavourably, to Guinevere, adding that if one looked hard enough one would certainly find others just as beautiful — a remark almost word for word applied to Galahad — except that he is 'valiant rather than 'beautiful' — earlier in the same text.

Once again, in the matter of the Grail, which is briefly dealt with in the *Prose Tristan*, Gawain is shown to fall far short of the attempt. In a scene which goes even further than the *Queste del Saint Graal* in its denigration of Gawain he is humiliated and sent about his worldly business with not even a glimpse of the Grail allowed him. His name alone is sufficient to exclude him, a fact which, to quote Keith Busby once more, may have added fuel to his feud against the sons of Pellinore:

> His opposition. . . however, is more than just evil pitted against good. As well as a personal vendetta, it is a feud against the lineage of one destined to achieve the Grail (as the feud against Lancelot in the *Queste* had been against a lineage which *had* achieved the Grail in the persons of Galahad and Bohort).[79]

This latter animosity is to flare up again in the final chapters of the Arthurian saga. We take up the story as it is told in *La Mort le Roi Artu*[16] and in Malory.

At the beginning of the text the Quest knights are beginning to straggle home. Of the three who were finally successful only Bors returns. Among the rest Gawain and Lancelot have failed significantly.

Arthur's first action is to have all the adventures recorded, and he makes a point of asking Gawain how many men he has personally killed, even evoking his knightly oath when he hesitates. His answer typifies the later Gawain's blend of honesty and guilt.

> 'My lord', said Sir Gawain, 'you obviously wish to be certain of my great misfortune, and shall I tell you, because I see that I must. I can tell you in truth that I killed eighteen by my own hand, not because I was a better knight than any of the others, but since misfortune affected me more than any of my companions. Indeed, it did not come about through my chivalry, but through my sin. You have made me reveal my shame.' (Trans. J. Cable, *The Death of King Arthur*, 1971)

If he had said that his might came about through being the Champion of the Goddess he could not have said it as clearly. As it is, this has become his 'sin', announced with such disarming honesty that Arthur is reluctant to condemn his nephew's actions.

From this point on, the main theme is the worsening relationship between Gawain and Lancelot, who despite the renewal of his liaison with Guinevere, continues to dominate every tournament and adventure in which he becomes involved. In an episode where Lancelot disguises himself and breaks a lifelong habit by wearing a lady's favour, Gawain, unaware of the identity of the 'Red Knight' himself makes overtures to the girl in question, Elaine of Escalot (Astalot in Malory). When he is refused and discovers that it is Lancelot who is his 'rival', he responds by reporting the fact to Arthur and Guinevere. This remark, though seemingly innocent, provokes trouble which is to have far-reaching consequences.

Guinevere is suspicious of Lancelot's fidelity to her and accuses him publicly of disloyalty to Arthur. Lancelot's kinsmen, including Bors, angrily leave the court rather than listen to such things. It is a pattern that will recur later.

Soon after this Guinevere is falsely accused of plotting the death of one of the knights when she gives him a poisoned apple intended for Gawain. At the same time a black-draped barge appears on the river below the castle, bearing the body of Elaine of Escalot. In her lifeless hand is a letter explaining that her death was brought about by her unrequited love for Lancelot.

Gawain himself bears the news to Guinevere, apologizing for his earlier insinuation. But he still refuses, albeit courteously, to fight in the queen's defence in her trial for murder.

Lancelot then appears, and suddenly Gawain changes his mind. It appears that he sees a chance to score over Lancelot by defending his mistress in front of him. But the combat does not transpire since Lancelot easily defeats Guinevere's accuser and thus proves her innocence according to the laws of chivalry.

This episode leads to the fatal denunciation of the guilty lovers by Agravain, Gaheries and Mordred. Here Gawain and Gareth stand firm against their brethren, Gawain effectively shrugging off the initial accusations to Arthur as unworthy of his consideration.

There follows, however, the trapping of Lancelot and Guinevere in the queen's chamber, and in the scuffle which follows Lancelot kills Agravain and wounds Mordred. Gawain is still on his side at this stage, and continues to support him until, with Guinevere arraigned for treason and sentenced to be burned at the stake, Lancelot rescues her and, in the mêlée, accidently kills both Gareth and Gaheries, who had gone unarmed to provide an honourable guard for the queen.

From this moment Gawain becomes Lancelot's implacable enemy, spurring Arthur on to gather an army against his one-time friend. Yet there is more of a personal vendetta about Gawain's attitude. Vengeance for the death of his brothers means more to him than Arthur's rightful claims against Lancelot and his kin.

In the war which follows Lancelot and Bors prove their superiority over Gawain, whose life is spared by Lancelot when he lies wounded and helpless on the field of battle. Yet when Arthur later draws attention to this noble act Gawain's only answer is one of anger that Arthur should even speak well of their enemy.

Indeed, it becomes evident that Arthur would have preferred to seek peace, while Gawain repeatedly presses for vengeance. Even after Lancelot restores Guinevere to her lord, Gawain insists first that he be banished forever from the realm, and when Lancelot asks whether this will be the end of strife between them, it is Gawain again who insists that the matter will never end while Lancelot lives.

When Lancelot reminds Gawain of an occasion when he had rescued him from a particularly dire imprisonment, Gawain's only response is to accuse Lancelot again of his brothers' death — an ironic reversal of the role in which Gawain has himself so often been cast, as slayer of someone's relative for which they demand reprisal.

From now on the end is hastened by Gawain's obsessional behaviour. More or less forcing Arthur against his inclination to cross to France and attack Lancelot in his own castle, Gawain then tricks the king into allowing him to offer single combat against his enemy. He seems to want to end the war quickly, but in reality cares for nothing other than a personal desire for revenge.

We also learn at this juncture a new version of how Gawain came by the quality of having his strength increase towards midday (see Chapter 1 and supra). In this instance it is due to his father having taken him to be baptized by a hermit who possessed miraculous powers and who, having performed the ceremony of baptism at midday, further endows Gawain with his famous ability. Here, even Gawain's oldest traditional quality, the last remnant of his origins as a cult hero, possessed of otherworldly powers, is taken from him as that very power is given a heavenly origin!

The combat between the two old knights (Gawain's age is given as 76, Lancelot's as 55!) is long and bitter. Both sustain considerable wounds, but Lancelot's might is finally such that he overcomes Gawain, adding insult to injury by refusing to give the *coup de grâce*, though Gawain staunchly refuses to give in.

Then news arrives of a Roman invasion of Gaul and Arthur must turn from the needless war to deal with his true enemies. Gawain, still only half recovered from his wounds, once again proves what a magnificent soldier he is, recalling his standing in Geoffrey of Monmouth's *Historia Regum Brittaniae* and the anonymous *De Ortu Waluuanii*. But the effort proves too much for him as the head wound inflicted by Lancelot opens again.

News now reaches Arthur that Mordred has given out that he is dead and has claimed the throne. Turning towards home the army is delayed by Gawain's worsening condition and fears for his life. Sick and delirious, the old warrior now at last begins to regret his actions towards Lancelot and desires to make amends. In Malory's text he requests pen and paper and writes a moving letter to Lancelot:

> Unto Sir Lancelot, flower of all nobler knights that ever I heard of or saw by my days, I, Sir Gawain, King Lot's son of Orkney, sister's son unto the noble King Arthur, send thee greeting, and let thee have knowledge that the tenth day of May I was smitten upon the old wound that thou gavest me afore the city of Benwick, and through the same wound that thou gavest me I am come to my death-day. And I will that all the world wit, that I, Sir Gawain, knight of the Table Round, sought my death, and not through thy deserving, but it was mine own seeking; wherefore I beseech thee, Sir Lancelot, to return again unto this realm, and see my tomb, and pray some prayer more or less for my soul. And this same day that I wrote this cedle [letter], I was hurt to death in the same wound, the which I had of thy hand, Sir Lancelot; and of a more nobler man might I not be slain... And at the date this letter was written, but two hours and a half afore my death, written with mine own hand, and so subscribed with part of my heart's blood. And I require thee, most famous knight of the world, that thou wilt see my tomb.[32]

We may see from this that Gawain is given to see the time of his own death, as are many otherworldly heroes, and that he does not blame Lancelot for his mortal wound. In *Le Morte le Roi Artu* he begs Arthur's forgiveness, warning him not to fight Mordred and to remember him to the queen. He then requests to be buried next to Gareth and to have an inscription placed on his tomb which reads:

HERE LIE GARETH AND GAWAIN, WHOM LANCELOT KILLED
THROUGH GAWAIN'S FOOLISHNESS[16]

After which, he says nothing more until at the end he commends his soul to Christ.

Gawain thus dies a Christian death with words of repentance on his lips. He is mourned by Arthur and all the court as a great and chivalrous knight. In the *Alliterative Morte Arthure*[24] the king himself delivers the following eulogy over him:

> Then the valiant king looked and was sad at heart, groaned dreadfully, with tears of grief, knelt down by the dead body, and caught it up in his arms, lifted up his visor and kissed him quickly, looked on his eyelids that were tightly closed, his lips like lead, and his pale countenance. Then the royal monarch cried aloud, 'Dear kinsman by blood, I am in sorry plight. For now my honour has departed and my struggle is ended. Here lies the expectation of my well-being, my success in battle. My courage and my valour stemmed wholly from him, my counsel, my succour that sustained my spirit. The king of knights in Christendom, thou wert worthy to be king, though I wore the crown. Mine good fortune, my good name on earth were gained through Sir Gawayne, and through his wisdom alone. Alas,' said Arthur, 'now my sorrow increases. I am utterly destroyed in mine own land. Ah, treacherous, cruel Death, thou lingerest too long! Why dost thou hold back? Thou overwhelmest my spirit.' (Trans. J.L.N. O'Loughlin)

All the recent deeds of blood are thus forgotten — yet even now the ghost of Gawain's past follows the army. On their way home they pass the Castle of Beloé, whose lord hates Gawain because of his great abilities. His lady, on the other hand, had secretly loved Gawain for a long time, and when she learns that he is dead, laments him loudly. Her husband, hearing this, savagely kills her. As she dies she begs to be buried alongside Gawain, for love of whom she has met her death.

A battle then ensues between Arthur's men and those of Beloé, and the lord is killed. Thus even after his death Gawain's reputation continues to bring disaster upon his companions.

The last we hear of him is in a dream that Arthur has before he is due to meet Mordred in battle. Gawain is shown surrounded by poor people who declare that they have secured his admission to heaven because of his great generosity and charity towards them. (In Malory this becomes a crown of fair ladies for whom Gawain has fought in his lifetime — somehow a more appropriate setting for one who should, in all probability, have returned to the otherworldly realm rather than the Christian heaven.)

His last words are a renewed warning not to fight Mordred and to call upon Lancelot for aid. But Arthur refuses and Gawain is lost to sight. The once great knight is dead and (presumably) forgiven. Yet at the end the author of *La Morte le Roi Artu* seems uncertain how to judge Gawain (as indeed have most modern commentators). There is so much ambiguity in his characterization. From the *Conte del Graal* onwards, some blacken him, others seek to find favourable aspects in his life. But he remains, at last, enigmatic.

We may seek the reasons for this in the changing attitudes of the medieval culture which adopted Gawain for its premier hero and transformed him from an otherworldly character and Champion of the Goddess into a chivalrous knight of the Round Table — a role in which he never seems wholly comfortable. His very evident magical qualities remain, however, very much part of him — hence the many curious adventures, ranging from those in *La Mule Sans Frein* to *Gawain and the Green Knight*. The curious stories surrounding his birth and early deeds, in which he rose to become very nearly Emperor of Rome, seem constantly to contradict each other. Yet this paradox is what gives Gawain his most lasting characteristics: the unequivocable bravery and courtliness which enable him to achieve the Beheading Game and the test of Lady Ragnall, his generosity towards his fellows which dates back to the earliest records, and his devotion to women which earned him a reputation as a rake.

Considered in the light of our investigation of Gawain's career, the fitness of these adventures is clear. In *Gawain and the Green Knight* the hero successfully overcomes a great trial at the hands of a powerful, elemental guardian, whose role he then assumes. In *Gawain and Ragnall* the reward for this is further extended when Gawain marries the earthly representative of the Goddess (or maybe even the Goddess herself). Finally, in *Diu Crône*, he is given the opportunity of releasing the dead courtiers of the Grail king and of freeing the Waste Land.

Beyond this, he could not really go. Having attained the highest of the heights, he had now to descend to the deepest of the depths, his otherworldliness gradually eroded until he became little more than a cowardly, bullying, criminal — his original role almost totally forgotten.

Norris J. Lacy in his essay 'The Character of Gawain in *Hunbaut*'[103] insists that Gawain is a 'stock' character. That this is very far from the case has surely been illustrated throughout this book. That he changes radically throughout his literary career must also be obvious, and the reasons for this have been discussed at some length. As a representative of a pagan goddess, Gawain was, consistently and determinedly, degraded from a person of foremost heroic attributes, to one of often immoral and distasteful attributes. Yet, as we have seen, he was originally a hero who far outstripped Lancelot, the premier champion of the later Arthurian romances. Also before the story of the Grail became Christianized, and a new hero, Galahad, (who was in fact Gawain under a different guise) was devised to achieve this greatest of tasks, it was Gawain who achieved these mysteries.

The other tasks of the hero, which included bringing back the spring, restoring to life the 'sap' frozen by winter's fury; the curing or restoring of the Wounded King, were all once part of Gawain's story, as Jessie Weston noted long ago. What has always been missing from this understanding is the fact that the hero frequently acted as the *agent of the Goddess*, whether by becoming her initiated champion, her lover or her son. As John Spiers indicated in his great book, *Medieval English Poetry, the Non-Chaucerian Tradition*,[139] *Gawain and the Green Knight* is a Christian poem, 'But it is Christian rather in the same way as some of the medieval Christmas carols are, as Christmas itself is; Christian in harmony with pre-Christian nature belief and ritual, a Christian re-interpretation of these. It is Christian to about the same depth as it is a courtly romance'.

It is this continual tension between his original point of origin and his later development which give the character of Gawain his enduring strength and fascination. As E.S. Dick notes in a recent article[88] Gawain is 'the perfect knight who is not perfect enough to settle in either of the two ideal worlds, too human and too superhuman at the same time'.

⌐ᴈᴄᴏ୨ᴚ⌐

THE GREEN KNIGHT AT CAMELOT: THE STORY OF GAWAIN RESTORED

It only remains now to fit together the pieces of the jigsaw we have seen gradually emerge from the tangled forest of the Arthurian literary *oeuvre*. Much remains tentative still, and will continue so until further work is done on certain of the texts, such as *Diu Crône* and the *Prose Tristan*. A full translation of the entire *Vulgate cycle* is an eagerly awaited event.

But though much work remains to be done, we can at least make an attempt — more positive in some areas than in others — at a reconstruction of the original Gawain story, as it may have been before time and cultural change fragmented it.

What we have observed to emerge from the often seemingly impenetrable tangle of text and story, is a tale which, though its elements are never found in one place, nevertheless possesses a remarkable degree of coherence and consistency. We have traced the story of Gawain, in all its manifold forms, down many a crooked byway, from birth to infancy to manhood and finally death or transformation. And we have seen him rise to the greatest heights attainable to a Round Table knight, while at the same time his literary career plummeted to the deepest depths. And we have traced, concurrently, another kind of Quest, in which he was also supremely successful, and which lead him, finally, after many tests and trails, to become the Knight of the Goddess.

What follows is, by its very nature, simplistic and drastically foreshort-ened. The reality is far more subtle and has been traced throughout the pages of this book. For almost every one of the incidents described here there are numerous other possibilities, other combinations, of the episodes which the story-tellers who first told of Gawain's history could have drawn upon. What you read here is the synopsis of a tale which might have been told, over many nights, in a smoke-filled hall, before ever the authors and compilers turned it into a literary form. For there are many stories of Gawain, and this is but one.

The Story of Gawain

Gawain is born of the union between the God-King Arthur and the Goddess Morgain. Like all heroes his birth is clouded by mystery and he is sent away from both parents to be educated in the realm of Faery by otherworldly women on an island beneath a lake. (Alternatively he is brought up under the aegis of a masculine priesthood and rises to become the champion of Rome's emperor.)

Acknowledged at last as the nephew/son of the king he takes his place among the heroes of the Round Table and undertakes his first great adventure, the Quest for the White Hart. During this he is sworn to serve all women, and from this point continues to rise to a position of supreme champion, both of the Round Table and of Queen Guine-vere, who looks upon him with favour.

His next great task is the freeing of the Besieged Lady, who turns out to be his mother, Morgain, and whose lover he becomes before he knows her true identity. Driven temporarily mad by this knowledge he is found and restored by one of her maidens, and returns to Cam-elot in time to undertake his greatest adventure, the Challenge of the Green Knight and the test of the Beheading Game. This has been engineered by Morgain herself to test her son and through him all of Arthur's knights. Its successful accomplishment means that the hero will become the new Champion of the Goddess, superseding the old; his reward is the winning of the Flower Bride, the otherworldly maiden whose consort he becomes for a time.

Gawain succeeds in this test but his trials do not end there. Before he can rightfully wear the green baldric awarded to him by the Flower Bride he must succeed in another adventure the outcome of which will award him a true bride. He next encounters the Lady Ragnall, another of the great archtypes of the Goddess who play such a major part in his life. To her he grants the right of freedom of choice which trans-forms her from hideous damsel to beautiful woman. She in turn offers Gawain, and through him Arthur, sovereignty — both over her own, human heart, and symbolically over the land itself. He is thus installed as the new champion, a role he maintains for at least five years, at which time Ragnall is lost to him, as she returns to the Otherworld from which she came. (Guinglainn, the son of Gawain and Ragnall, later emerges from the realm of faery to take up his father's role, but this is not told of anywhere in the texts and can only be inferred.)

From here Gawain proceeds to the greatest achievement open to him as a Round Table knight — though still aided by the Goddess. He achieves the Quest for the Grail and sets free the many souls which have been held captive, and the Grail country itself, which had lain waste under the curse of an impotent king.

His greatest adventures now over, Gawain remains the supreme champion of Camelot despite internecine strife and an ancient feud which drives him at least to a further bout of madness and a desertion of the way of the Goddess for a path of human vengeance.

Finally death claims him and we see him last in Arthur's dream, ensconced in the Otherworld surrounded by lovely faery women, a true knight of the Goddess at last received into his true home.

In this story Gawain stands forth at last as the true 'Green Knight' of Camelot. Not the huge, boisterous and terrifying Green Man with his mighty axe, who challenges the chivalry of the Round Table, but rather a man who serves the principle of nature in the guise of the Goddess; whose right to wear the green baldric extends to the right to call that colour his own.

This is the crux of our argument, behind which lies a far more profound quest than that for a literary context. Though versions have been discussed throughout this book, it is hoped that readers will perceive the deeper significance of Gawain's story and if necessary read *between* the lines.

The reasons for the decline of Gawain in medieval literature are manifold, too many to enter into here. We have seen that the status of women, as earthly representatives of the Goddess, remain surprisingly constant, despite every effort to represent them as enchantresses or as the providers of amorous entanglements. Gawain himself, despite — or perhaps because of — his all-embracing passion for women, saw clearly beyond this to the mystical realization behind the myth. Gawain himself reigns for a time only, after that his son succeeds him. The line of champions continues to the present and the position is open to all.

Gawain's story, in the end, is a triumphal one, in which his marriage to Ragnall becomes much more than a physical union. There are many aspects of the Goddess, and of this marriage comes a breath of hope for the future. If we choose to see it — a future that may see at last a healing of the long divided masculine and feminine aspects of the human psyche. The image of the pentangle on Gawain's shield says it all, for it represents, above all, harmony, a unity of the spirit which is so desperately needed in the age we are living through. If we survive this age, it will be because of the lessons that archetypal stories such as Gawain's have to teach us. From him we may learn how to enter the Courts of Joy.

Appendix 1.
The Childhood of Gawain

There follows the first English translation, by Prudence Jones, of the fragmentary thirteenth-century poem *Les Enfances Gauvain*.[14] It is remarkable for the insights it offers into the early days of the hero, which though they are presented elsewhere within the context of larger romances (see Chapter 2) here stand alone. It is impossible to say with any certainty now, but it may well be that the poem represents part of a much larger work, dealing with Gawain's career from birth to death. It makes fascinating reading and has remained unobtainable in English for too long.

THE CHILDHOOD OF GAWAIN

Trans. Prudence Jones

First Fragment

'I dearly want to go there for two months, or perhaps seven or five or six or four, to relax and amuse myself. I very much want to do that, with only my lady-in-waiting and the squire. You can be sure that I shall conduct myself so that you will not be shamed, and you will only hear good things of me. I want only a chaplain, who will chant Mass to me every morning, one with white hair like hoar-frost. Grant me this, fair and honest lord: a seneschal and a cook and a porter, and a cleric and a cellarer. This is the number of people I would like, and in truth I will never want more. And in order to reassure you, I shall make the porter swear that no one shall enter within, unless accompanied by you yourself, or unless he is known to be a man of good character.'

In this way the maiden deceived her brother, so that he did not know what to say, but bursting into laughter, assured her that he would do everything she had asked. And she, in order to beguile him even more, began to embrace him, and then said, 'By your leave, I do not wish to remain here any longer.'

There was no opportunity to dally. Morcadès put her plan into operation, and made her way to the spot. The castle had bread and wine and meat already, being well provisioned, so that she never suffered from the lack of anything which might be necessary or useful. For seven full months she carried the child.

. . . Morcadès, if she had known how to breastfeed the infant safely. But this could never be. Lot, the squire, was at the birth of the infant to the damsel, but no trace of this was known. No-one had heard it or seen it: everyone was totally deceived. Nobody knew but Lot, who had made her pregnant. Now some ingenuity was needed, and the task had to be carried out with care, so that the deed should be concealed, and she should not lose the name of maiden.

Between the sea and the forest lived a wise knight, known as Gawain the Brown. He was a remarkably upright and honest man, wise and gentle. He had had a rich manor built, but still he had no child, not heir, nor a wife, I will tell you truly. He loved to go hunting for deer, and he claimed by inheritance the house and the woodland which he owned. And he had often sent some game to Morcadès, as an offering, for he loved the lady-in-waiting so much, that he did favours for the mistress. For a long time he had wanted to marry the girl and share the heights of love with her. He was so consumed with love that he had proposed to her several times, but she did not want to hear anything of it. For it is foolish to speak of one's love to someone who has no inclination for it. Hence the maiden continued arguing with Gawain for a long time, and he had no satisfaction from her.

> (Here we lack column c) of the obverse,
> column a) of the reverse, and the first
> 6 lines of column b) of the reverse, i.e.
> 98 lines in all.)

'. . . as my heart desires'. And now having decided on a route, the maiden and the infant departed. She did not leave by the main gate: she left Morcadès and Lot together and went by a postern gate, holding the infant concealed. Then by chance she met [. . .] where Gawain lived [. . .] who came along hunting birds. When he came across her, Gawain was so overjoyed at their encounter that he immediately dismounted from his horse and took her gently in his arms. So delighted was he merely to meet her, that he could not help himself. And as he was greeting the maiden warmly, embracing her, the squirrel fur lifted from off her robe and he saw the infant. He had no squire with him, no huntsman, only four dogs: thus God willed it, for so it was well.

He asked her where she was going, and what she was going to do with the baby, where she had found it, who had given it to her, why she was wandering in that place. For he knew well that it was not hers, since she was his true beloved. She could do whatever she liked with it, or whatever she commanded him to do. There was nothing under Heaven that he would refuse [. . .] which she would wish to do.

And when the maiden heard him, she took her own counsel. So he had discovered the truth, and if he wished to have her love he would have to conceal the facts which I have begun to describe.

When she returned, she told Morcadès what she had done; but this is how she parted from Gawain. It truly pleased her, she said, that she should take him as her beloved and be betrothed to him, once Morcadès had finished her lying-in, and he had had the infant christened. And thus their journey ended, and Gawain agreed to do as she asked.

The little baby of which I tell, which was now in Gawain's household, was not yet a Christian. But he had it christened, and called Gawain. Afterwards, he was so thorough in carrying out the agreement, that a wet-nurse was found (for the child), and he was swaddled. Nor did Gawain want to remove the beautiful cloth of silk from the child's pillow, nor the bezants: he did not want to have them. But he added more words to the letter, like a man who would overlook nothing. Then he put these things in a drawstring bag, and replaced them in the cloth of silk.

Afterwards he had a small tun brought, and put the infant inside it, the infant whose features were aristocratic. For in this way he wanted Chance to take over. In the base man's words: Neither flood nor frost can avert the path of Destiny. And may God accompany the infant, insofar as he is able, willing, and aware!

At the same time it was arranged for the barrel to be made ready. Gawain called one of his sergeants, who knew nothing of what had happened, and ordered him to take the tun to the shore without delay.

Second Fragment
Oh, women have to give birth. And so love-play and longing exist, to put an end to adventures.

The child, of noble nature, grew bonny and fair, and the good lady fed him so well that he could come and go as he pleased and she could not hold onto him. When he was 10 years old, he went fishing with his father, who loved him dearly. But he didn't want to hear anything of this trade, nor did he make any attempt to learn it. It was very difficult to get him out to sea, but the fisherman beat him, and so forced him to go out there, and to learn to strike sail, to paddle, to throw the nets, and to draw them in when he was ready and had enough fish.

When he was older than 10, his father was taken ill: and the worthy man made his confession. He vowed to go on pilgrimage, as the priest had recommended, to Monseigneur St Peter in Rome, as soon as he was recovered. He wanted to go to some trouble over this, and so wished to take the child with him. If it pleased God that he should become a holy man, they would give the child to the Pope.

He loved the child dearly, and always called him 'dear son'. He still had the bezants and the ring, which were not heavy, the silken cloth and the clasp, for he had supported himself by his trade. He had neither known great hardship, nor fallen into poverty. For that reason he still had all the goods, as I believe. He had not yet seen the letter, which had been in his possession for a long time: he had not looked in the drawstring bag when he put the ring in it, for he was never a scheming man. And so according to plan his wife Gill asked for [the] money [she needed], and so he went on his way, and took the child with him.

And if I am to tell you all, he took the child and the goods, and in the drawstring bag discovered the letter, which he asked a cleric far away from his country to read. And so such a tale was discovered! When the cleric had read the letter, pored over it from top to tail, he told him openly what he saw in it, and told him well. But he did not discover the identity of the child. He read it as well as he could. He read the letter aloud, that's all he did.

'The youth is the son of a nobleman. Both mother and father are of high birth; he is of extremely noble lineage. And he has been christened, thanks be to God, but I do not find his name anywhere here. The letter says that he has the right to be a knight, when he is old enough; and that the man that finds him ought in truth to have the bezants. The ring, the golden buckle and the silken cloth ought to be given to him when he is knighted: and on the cloth a coat of arms. I can find no more information in the letter, except that he was both conceived and born in secret: furtively, but through love. So he does not have a full title, but by the ring he will recognise his father, and by the buckle his mother. She was put to great suffering and trouble for him, and great pain when he was born, for nobody knew that he existed.' The cleric said, 'Well, now you have him, with good recompense.'

The fisherman wept with joy, and set off on his way immediately. And you must understand that he loved all the more the child who had had no taste for fishing, whom he had had to drag by force to the sea. He was all the more able to love the child from his heart, and because he had been baptized, he felt attached to him. Now St Julian gave the fisherman such good lodgings, and the Lord God guided him in such fashion, that he made his way to Rome. There he found many clerics, old, young and white-haired, all before the Pope, who had his seat at the Capitol.

He was not able to have an audience immediately, for he was not allowed to go forward. But he bore with the situation until there was space for a private audience, and so he made his confession to the Pope three days before Ascension Day. When the Pope heard the fisherman's story, he was overjoyed. Having heard the roundabout fortunes of the young man, he received him graciously, and said that he would never abandon the young man, him, but would give him without fail all that he needed, however matters might turn out, and would make him his nephew, for he might well have great ability.

And so the fisherman took leave of the holy man, and he took the bezants, that is to say all of them, as his reward. And you may be sure he used them well, for he had kept the child for a long time, and that with good grace. The Pope had the ring, the buckle and the pall, made of Thessalonian cloth, tied all together, and wrapped more tightly. And he said that he would give them all to his nephew when the time came for him to be made a knight. And now he sought out a master who would take good care of him. First the master taught him swordplay, so that he would not become short of breath. Then he put a lot of effort and attention into teaching him how to hunt in the forest, and to fish, and about the games of hawk and hound, which he had to learn to be properly educated as a knight. He taught him to spur his horse and to mount it. And the Pope loved the boy well, for he called him nephew, and valued him greatly. Everyone, in truth, cherished him and did him great honour. And he merited this so greatly that he was in no way gauche, but extremely courteous and debonair, so that no-one could be ashamed of him. Hence he was well-turned-out in every respect, and so you can be quite sure that there was no squire as valiant as he in the country, nor so greatly honoured, nor more honest nor more loyal. His worth can be attributed to his lineage, and his deeds sprang from his nature rather than from his upbringing. If he had acted in accordance with his upbringing, he would never have risen to such renown as you will hear about in what follows, before this story draws to its close.

I will leave the Pope and tell you about King Arthur, the greatly honoured king. But now more about the fisherman, who has returned to his house and immediately told his wife about what he has learned from the letter. He has told her everything from beginning to end, just as I have told you already. But I shall not tell it all again, as most people would complain and would find me irritating. She was delighted with the story she heard: her meals had certainly helped the boy, and the concern she had lavished on him. She was not in the least bit grieved to have been given the bezants, for she knew full well that she would now have all she needed for as long as she lived: she could never fall into poverty if she used them wisely. Her heart was happy and joyful.

I will now leave the fisherman, saying no more than that he lived on. He could and did endow himself well, and his wife with him. Now let us return to where we left King Arthur, and Morcadès, who was dear to him.

The damsel Morcadès was still in her castle. She covered her tracks as well as she could, like one who knew well enough how to do so. She covered her tracks well, she hid herself well. When the time came for her confinement to end, no-one knew anything about it, apart from the damsel who had also known about the other business. Thus Morcadès had not been seen by the king whilst she was discommoded. Once he had come to visit, believing that she was out of sorts, but as one skilled and practised in such behaviour, she had deceived him so greatly that he was unable to reproach her. The king had plenty to do at the time, so the story tells me, for it was time for him to take a wife, and he dearly wanted to do so.

The king of Ireland had a sister, of great renown, beautiful, wise, and highly esteemed. Arthur called his messengers and sent them to the king of Ireland. They rode with such haste, through forest and plain, that they obtained audience with the king without too much trouble. They asked the king for what they wanted: they wanted to have his sister for the lord of Britain. The king found no difficulty in doing what they asked, but rejoiced at the command when he heard it, and freely offered what had been requested by Arthur, lord of the Britons. In this matter there is nothing to say, but that he was grand and fair and noble.

Without asking advice from his people, willingly he gave Guinemars the esteemed, the renowned. Thus he retained his sister in name, he loved her with all his heart. She did not demur in any way, and you know she was right to do so, for if she had objected, whether she had wanted to or no, the deed would have been done anyway. And so she would have made more enemies. And so they set off on the return journey.

And when Arthur the king knew that she was coming, he courteously went to meet her, and thus received her with great honour, as he was bound to do, and took her to Dinasdaron. Then he commanded the presence of all around him, both knights and ladies, and held a magnificent wedding celebration, which lasted for a fortnight. His sister Morcadès was there also, having for the occasion left her castle Bel Repaire, where she had been taking her pleasure, having recovered from her confinement, and would have been enjoying herself still more if she had stayed there longer, and she had not been afraid of getting pregnant. Her beloved Lot, who was so dear to her, had been a knight since reaching his majority, and left her service, so he could neither come nor go nor hold audience with her in private, as he was accustomed to, but by every possible means conveyed his eyes to her heart. When he was unable to visit her, he made his heart speak to her, telling her of his love, his joy and his pain. Thus he had her heart and she had his, which communicated with her and told her of his worth.

And so for a long time they loved each other, and often spoke together. And the king loved his wife so much that she was his mistress as well as his lady: his mistress in that he loved her, but often called her lady. And he must have loved her a great deal to have called her both lady and mistress. She was indeed so worthy and wise that she would never have agreed to harm him, never consented to any wickedness or villainy against him. She would have preferred to bring shame upon herself than to do anything which would anger him, or bring dishonour on him.

The good queen was richly gifted. She was so loyal and refined that she would rather her own heart was broken than do anything to hurt him. She loved whoever he loved, and for that reason King Arthur called her his lady, which was not to be wondered at. Her complexion was so rosy that among all the royalty there no lady was as beautiful as she, of such worth and integrity, or who loved her lord so much. And equally she loved Morcadès, so was with her all the time. What baser minds would say about this courtesy is that the man who loves the master, loves the dog; for to be sure, no-one who loved me would ever injure my dog.

Now the chamber was thrown open for the good and renowned lady, and all the knights came within. Lot was not in the least grieved, to be able so often to see her who delighted him, but on the other hand he was sad that he could do no more than speak to her, unable to kiss or embrace her, except stealthily, in secret, and that not so often. When everyone else was away, he never went to her room. Now it is a foolish man who puts off till the future the enjoyment he has in hand today, and can have his pleasure of now, who chases after what he does not have, and waits for the lark to settle in his hand tomorrow. He lets what he has escape him, and then he suffers what he cannot lay hold of it. To be sure, such a one is not to be pitied.

Lot soon took what he wanted, he did what was wise, demanding neither respite nor delay. I have often seen such respite given, and many a tear be shed afterwards. I should prefer 100 sous, if I had them in the morning (I know as much in Latin), than 100 marks four days from now. Do you think I am mad? And Lot preferred three weeks [of todays] to a month of tomorrows. So pay attention all: I prefer a fistful of what I fancy, of my joy and my pleasure, doing something that pleases me, than any amount of what others can tamper with. And what I have bought is worth twice as much to me as anything I rent.

Guinemars, the noble queen, and Morcadès became companions, they would come and go together. And the king's sister married off the maiden, who in truth loved Gawain the Brown, who had loved her. She was pleased to be married to him, for he was very rich and served her courteously.

Now I shall leave King Arthur and Gawain the Brown, of whom I shall tell no more at this stage. And now of the young squire, who was growing up in accordance with his nature, it is right that I should tell the tale. The Pope loved him greatly, for he was never seen to be vainglorious or arrogant, but honest, gentle and valiant. Never had there been a finer squire. After he was 12 years old, he was so fully grown and tall that he was nothing if not a marvel. But still he did not know his name.

The squire served the Pope willingly at all his meals, though only by carving for him. The [Holy] Father appreciated his skill at this. No-one was better than he, no squire, indeed, have I seen who carved as well as he did. No-one did it better than he, and thus his attention was everywhere, as well as whatever acts of courtesy and good breeding a squire was supposed to do. He showed favour to no-one, for he never did wrong to anyone, and he never outraged anyone, and so he always remained within the conventions. Nor, when anyone has harmed him, was he ever seen to attack them. He always did well that which he had to do, this courteous youth, and so he believed that the Pope, in truth, who had plenty of good sense and understanding, was truly his uncle, for he loved him so strongly. But he was never boastful because of this.

While he was still a squire he acquired such prowess and such loyalty that the Pope was emboldened to make him a knight. And know that he was apparelled in all that a knight usually wears: he had silken cloth tied everywhere.

On St John's Eve, one of the most joyful days of the year, he was dubbed knight in truth. And I shall be brief enough in describing his knightly deeds, but afterwards he was a grand seigneur and feared in many lands. The Pope had demanded of him everything which is proper to a knight, and held him in great affection. And he was right to hold him so dear: if he had known what was to come, he would have valued him even more. The story does not end here: St John is a very good saint, there is none higher now or in the future. There is no other saint for whom such a feast is held, for, so the story tells us, no more noble man was ever born of a mother; and Zacharias was his father, a very holy priest. And St John, who dressed in animal skins, the martyr, was of such great power that all rejoiced at his birth. Elsewhere, like the Christians, pagans celebrate [his feast].

And our new knight, who in his time gained much recognition, was the best who bore arms (so the story tells us at its end) who ever carried painted lances to the joust. So the whole world honoured him, who was empty of baseness and full of great courtesy. He had prowess and valour in his grasp, and bounty was his mother, who gave him great honour, and he would never be the companion of a rich man who was foolish and cowardly.

A faint-hearted rich man has no courage, so I cannot love him at any price. He cannot have a worse fault, or a worse mark of avarice. A poor knight is more worthy than a rich one with a hundred bushels* of deniers who scorns fame and valour: a poor knight who acts honourably, as far as he is able, with the humble as with the great, who is wise in word and deed, and who would talk courteously when in good company, who promises and performs deeds of courtesy, without pride and without baseness, than is the wicked rich man, who is inhospitable and rude, who speaks ill of people and is full of hatred, and who never invites anyone to his lodgings either to drink or to eat, since he hates them all and insults them with his thousand bushels** worth of goods, and who often bars his door, for he cannot see any noble people or worthy men who would like to sit with him. Such a man is, in fine, shamed by God and shunned by all honest men! For his wealth is not his own, but the Devil's who will reclaim his goods in future. God says so, I know it. Whoever says this is not dreaming: either we serve God or we serve the Devil. No-one who amasses wealth in great amounts would let himself be beheaded or hanged for daring to spend only three deniers: either he will be a slave to his money or he will

---

* Text: one muid — the bushel equivalent of this measure varied over the years but here is translated figuratively, as 100 bushels.
** Text: 10 muids.

not dare spend it. As usurer therefore, without doubt, who will do his own will in everything.

What does the slave do? His legacy lies heavily upon him, and he believes in it more strongly than in Jesus Christ. It is his great pleasure to caress it, to fondle it gently. This, he says, is pure paradise, and thus he says he wants everybody to live. He does not think about any other way of being, for he is not concerned about death, which will suddenly come upon him for certain. If he dies unprepared and his soul goes to the cunning Devil, he will find in Hell what he has done, but he will not find one jot of good, for here on earth he did nothing: but of evils, he has done aplenty. His worldly goods will now pass to whoever has been his lord, and his revenues will go to the doctor, while his soul will languish in great torment, where it will remain eternally.

This is what the slave will do with money if he is wicked. But the man who is lord and master of wealth, and is able to do what he wishes with it, in him both God and world conquer, and thus he goes to holy paradise. So he has both worldly honour and celestial joy. This man has two strings to his bow who accords with God by having wealth; this man ought to maintain the state of the world, to know how to come and how to go. And when he comes to the end of his life, he will not die, it is not death. Then he will begin to live. Thus says Oedes in a book of his.

On this I would have spoken at some length if I had not wished to hear more of other things. Let us go back to the knight, who was worth, clearly, more than 1,000 cowardly missing deniers [sic]. He was a good and distinguished knight, as indeed here, like the man who takes account of this work.

The Pope loved him dearly. Whatever he needed, he gave him, so that he was able to maintain his arms, for he was never found to be base, nor was he known to choose a companion who was not of excellent character. So they went on their way together, and lost their way so often, as it seems to me, and here and there through many a land, conquering by prowess and by honour, wherever they knew there would be a tourney, at which their services would be of use. Our new knight, who was so fair and attractive that he was the talk of all the world, for he never went to a tourney but he carried off all the prizes, and was never taken prisoner or captured, journeyed for two and a half years, and in that time made many friends.

At this time the emperor died, having neither son nor brother who could take over the empire after him. And so there was great concern among those who had served him for a long time, and those who had a large following. There was enough of trouble and sorrow for those who had lost their good lord.

Appendix 2.

The Arming of Gawain

A number of the most important Gawain texts deal in some detail with the hero's arming, and with his possession of certain specific weapons. In particular, as we saw in Chapter 6, the symbolism of the pentangle on his shield is of considerable interest.

In fact the pentangle, or pentacle as it is sometimes called, is such an ancient symbol that no one knows its exact origin. It was first found scratched on fragments of pottery from Ur of the Chaldees (c. 2000 BC) and is associated thereafter with the realms of magic and mysticism. Its attribution to Solomon, on whose seal it was said to be carved, is itself interesting, since to medieval audiences he would have been known as a magician rather than an all-wise king.

In the Pythagorian system, which stemmed from Classical Greece, the pentangle represented marriage of the first, masculine number, three, with the first feminine number, two, and thus became representative of the marriage of upper and lower, the human and the divine, masculine and feminine — precisely the meaning, mystically expressed, of the Grail, and therefore eminently suitable to be found in the possession of a successful Quest knight.

In alchemy, the pentangle represented the *quintessentia*, the four elements — earth, air, fire and water — with the addition of a fifth element, spirit, from which all creation was formed. Gawain is thus shown to be a totally balanced individual, possessed in equal measure of the elemental qualities which, in the medieval mind, expressed the humanity and excellence of the personality. Marked thus with the sign of perfection, no task, no adventure was too great for the hero.

In several other works Gawain is associated with certain weapons, the possession of which would mark him out as above average in the hero stakes, while the Vulgate *Merlin* tells in a notable passage how he won his famous steed.

This wondrous steed is sometimes called Gingalet, Le Gringalet, Guingalet of Kincaled, all of which seems to mean 'of good staying power'. It is repeatedly stolen and finally killed by Galerou of Galloway in *The Adventures of King Arthur at Tarn Watheling*. Weston thinks it was a sun-steed and adds that Gawain's other 'solar' attributes included the possession of Excalibur. This occurs in Chrétien without explanation, while in the *Merlin* Arthur gives the sword to Gawain, who apparently wields it thereafter, preferring one he has taken from King Rions. Here Excalibur is not in the gift of the Lady of the Lake as elsewhere, but it should come as no surprise to find Gawain in possession of a weapon which came from the Otherworld.

Indeed, since this version makes Excalibur the same sword which Arthur pulled from the stone to prove himself worthy of kingship, it is thus another symbol of his sovereignty! While if, as both Heinrich Zimmer[155] and Jessie Weston[151] have suggested, Excalibur derives ultimately from Caledbolg, Cuchulainn's sword, once again it can be seen that matters have come full circle to the sword's original owner.

The association of Gawain with Cuchulainn, is, as we saw, of primary importance. It is further strengthened by heraldic evidence. We have already noted that Guinglain, Gawain's son, can be identified as a type of Cuchulainn, and this is born out in *Wigalois*, where the hero carries a black shield with a golden wheel (intended to represent Fortune's Wheel); while Cuchulainn is known to have borne a dark red shield with five wheels of gold.[105] Gawain in turn has a golden pentangle on a red ground. All of these are remarkably close. The golden wheels emphasize Cuchulainn's solar attributes, as does the description, in the *Tain*[54] of him changing, during the heat of battle fury, into a 'crimson wheelball from his crown to the ground', and his ability to draw in every hair of his head until a drop of blood stood out on each one — a description which Professor Rhys saw as a bizarre depiction of the sunset.[134]

In *Gawain and the Green Knight* and *De Ortu Waluuanii* Gawain's solar attributes are again emphasized. In the former the description of his arming suggests his summer strength; in the latter, on the day he receives arms from the Roman emperor Gawain dons a red surcote over his armour. Subsequently, he performs so well in the tournament that since he had no other name, he became known as 'the Knight of the Surcote'.

Thus as Mildred Leake Day points out, in *Gawain and the Green Knight* when the hero dons the 'royal-red' surcote 'the garment is replete with the associations of a youth who fought brilliantly in tournaments in Rome, slew the notorious king of the pirates, brought peace to Jerusalem by single combat, unhorsed the great Arthur at the ford near Caerleon, and rescued the Lady of the Castle of Maidens'.[87]

In all the details of Gawain's armour and weapons help substantiate the argument put forward in the foregoing pages; namely that he was the Green Knight of Camelot and the Champion of the Goddess.

Appendix 3.

The Chapel in the Green

There have been several attempts to discover the site of Gawain's greatest adventure — some of them fanciful, others worthy of serious consideration. The question one must ask however, is can we expect to find a physical location for a place of otherworldliness and magic? The Green Chapel, together with its occupant, are part of a very deep-seated and ancient tradition. Entrances to the Otherworld certainly do exist, both in this dimension and in the inner worlds of the minds. Sites such as the Eildon Hills, Glastonbury Tor, Breen Down or Wayland's Smithy (to name but four) all possess their unique signature, to which the sensitive visitor may swiftly be aware.[144] So that if we seek to find not the actuality of the Green Chapel, but rather a place which may have inspired it, we may indeed discover a possible site.

The Gawain poet's geographic descriptions are quite specific, and it has long been recognized that he travelled North through the country to Wales, on to Anglesea, along the Welsh coast and on into Cheshire ('the Wilderness of Wirrell') and that Bercilak's castle Hautdesert must lie somewhere close to the Welsh border. The passage concerning what Gawain found when he arrived at last at the place where he was to meet the Green Knight is precise:

> Then spurred he Gringolet, and betook himself along the path by the side of a wood, and rode over a rough hill into the valley... At length a little way off he caught sight of a round hillock by the side of a brook, and there was a ford across the brook, and the water therein bubbled as though it were boiling. The knight caught up the reins and came to the hill, alighted, and tied up the reins to the branch of a tree. Then he went to the hill and walked round about it, debating within himself what place it might be. It had a hole at one end and on either side, and it was overgrown with tufts of grass and was all round and hollow within. He thought it nought but an old cave or a crevice. Within and without it there seemed to be a spell... (Trans. J.B. Kirtlan)[46]

This does indeed sound like a real place. Bertram Cosgrave, writing in the journal *Antiquity* for 1948[83] suggested that an early Bronze Age chambered tomb, known locally as the Bridestones, might fit the bill.

It lies a few miles west of Congleton, among the hills of the Peak District. Certainly it is a wild and lonely spot, which could easily have suggested to the poet a suitable site for the Green Knight's abode.

Another suggestion comes from Mable Day, in the introduction to the 1940 Early English Text Society edition of *Gawain and the Green Knight*. Miss Day suggested that a cave near Wetton Mill in the northeastern corner of Staffordshire (O.S. Sheet iii; Grid ref. SK 0956) fitted all the requirements. She went on to say:

> If Sir Gawain, approaching as he would from the West, came down from Butterton Moor by the Hoo Brook, he would see [the cave] on the left side beside the weir when he reached the bottom of the valley. The bank on which the Green Knight stood would be the cliff just below the Hoo Brook on the opposite side of the [River] Manifold to the Green Chapel. From the top of this cliff a passage, mentioned by Plot [*The Natural History of Staffordshire*, Oxford, 1986] and still traversable, communicates with a cave at the foot, the 'hole' of 1.22221. Issuing from thence, the Green Knight crossed the Manifold to the level ground in front of the mill, where the Beheading Game took place.

This is unequivocable. Miss Day also points out that local tradition names the cave *Thurshole* meaning, 'fiend's house'. If we consider that this is certainly a reference to Thor, the Norse god of thunder and lightning, whose attributes fit very well with those of the Green Knight, we begin to see how appropriate this site may be.

Wetton Mill. *Photo by Tim Cann.*

R.E. Kaske[98] has investigated this further and has shown that virtually every detail described in the poem corresponds to the situation and the general structure of the cave at Wetton. The recent illustration below left gives an idea of the atmosphere which still surrounds the site.

One other possible contender was put forward more recently by R.W.V. Eliott.[90] This is a cave known locally as 'Lud's Church'. It lies only a few miles from Wetton Mill and the Hoo Brook, but although the name is interesting for the suggestion it brings of another otherworldly association — Lud is a corruption of the Celtic god Lugh, with whom once again Gawain has associations — it lacks the close physical identity with the description found in the poem.

Taken together, even if neither site actually inspired the Green Chapel, the association of the names Thor and Lud suggest that the area was rich in the traditions of the Otherworld. In the end we cannot be sure, nor perhaps should we wish to be, as to the site of the Green Chapel.

Appendix 4.

The Sweet Sorrow

The poem which follows was collected by the great folklorist Alexander Carmichael on the Hebridean island of South Uist in 1865.[81] It is a corrupt text and sometimes difficult to follow. In it Arthur has a dream of a woman 'put upon him' by a witch. But it is Gawain who goes to fetch her, a theme of great antiquity in Celtic tradition, as we may judge from numerous stories. He encounters the woman sitting in a chair of gold and apparently (the text is oblique and difficult at this point) accepts a challenge from a giant with whom he plays the Beheading Game. The remarkable similarity between this text and certain of those we have discussed in the foregoing account of Gawain's career, makes it important. Not only for its intrinsic merit, but because it represents a continuing tradition in which Gawain figures as the obtainer of sovereignty for Arthur. I have chosen to reproduce the text here because of its interest and its relative obscurity. Behind its occasional difficulties lies a world of meaning and reference to the Knight of the Goddess.

A DAY that Arthur of the waves   (leg. *slaugh*, hosts?)
   Went to the hill of triumphs to hunt,
There was seen coming from the plain
   A maid of fairest form under the sun.
There was a harp in the hand of the young damsel
   Of sweetest kiss and brightest mien;
And sweetly though she played the harp,
   Sweeter the voice which accompanied it.
It was at the sound of her sweet harpstrings
   That the king sank into gentle sleep;
And when he awoke from his slumber,
   Quickly his hand reached for his weapons.
Concerning the girl who had played the music
   Who had not been seen alive or dead,
Sir Gawain spoke right generously,
   'I shall go myself to seek her for thee,
Myself, my lad and my hound,
   The three of us the woman to seek.'
He set off with his lad and his hound,
   And with his fair, white-sailed, lofty ship.

He was seven months at sea
Ere he saw solid earth
Where he could bring the ship to land.
He saw in the brightness of the sea
  Stones of price with green water-cress,
Windows of glass on the gable,
  Plenteous there were cups and horns.
Sir Gawain was at its base,
  A black chain was suspended from above,
And the chain which did not quiver
  Carried him aloft at a run.
He saw the tender gentle maid
  On a chair of gold within,
A carpet of silk beneath her soles,
  And the hero greeted her fair face.
'Has God blessed thee, man?
  Deep is the love that has brought thee across
    the waves;
If the lord of this castle be in health
  He knows no mercy or pity.'
'I am most impatient that he comes not,
  I shall do battle with him speedily.'
'How wouldst thou do that when thou
  Art not the best warrior under the sun?
For no weapon will draw blood from the man
  But his own bright white sword.'
'Let us promote speech and abate wrath,
  Let us lay a trap for the giant;
Let us steal his sword from the man,
  So will we take off his head.'
I saw newly come from the sea
  A young warrior wounded by weapons;
He had a golden spur on his right foot,
  Full elegant were his dress and form.
He had another spur about his left foot
  Of royal silver or inlaid (?) gold;   (fial, fine?)
I made to seize his spur,
  But if I did, it was not good sense;
He grasped his weapon and to be
  Near him was to be a dead man.
'A truce! a truce! great warrior,
  I am alive and near my weapons,
Tell me of a truth thy tidings,
  Who thou art or what thy name.'
'I am the victorious fortunate Bile,
  It is I who shall have the house of melody;
Is there any doubt I shall be king?
  Over against me were the Greeks.
It is I shall have the wife
  With fairest cheek and whitest teeth,

It is I shall have the ship
  Which will leave the wash behind;
It is I shall have the horse
  Which swiftest struck hoof on grass,
It is I shall have the hound
  Which malice or violence will not affect.'
They moved to the house on the
    rock,
  There thou canst verify my tale;
That is how I rode the horse
  Of swiftest and most prancing pace.
Riding furiously across the ocean,
  Cantering over the surface of the sea,
I saw the hound-loving battalion of three
  In close combat about the woman.
I shall still the combat,
  I shall take it on myself to check them,
The three brothers, my sad tale!
  In sad combat about the woman.
I am the hero who was never affrighted,
  The eldest son of the King of France;
By me fell the two sons of the King of Greece,
  It is they themselves who killed the third one.
If thou desirest to take me with thee,
  Dig a grave for the King of Greece's children;
That is how I dug the grave,
  Since it is the work of a madman
To dig, at the request of a captive (?) woman,
  A grave to please herself.
She leapt down into the pit,
  The wise woman of fairest hue;
The soul sprang out of her body,
  Alas! tonight it is woe.
If only I had then a leech,
  I had used him at that time,
I had brought her to life once more,
  I had not left my love in the grave.
On the mount of the way of the true words,
  On Thy right hand, O Son of God,
May I be on the Day of Doom.
That is the end of my tale,
  And how the Sweet Sorrow was sung.

Appendix 5.
Aspects of the Goddess in the Major Texts

Because of the complexity of the argument it was felt that a tabulation of the various aspects taken by the Goddess in certain of the texts discussed above may prove helpful. The table shows the remarkable degree of similarity between the various versions of the story, as well as the way that the themes have remained to a large extent constant. The aspect taken by the Goddess is matched with the characters who represent her. Her function in the story, as bestower of either a life-enhancing or sovereignty-bestowing gift, as a tester or challenger, is listed next, followed by the outcome of the hero's encounter. Finally the hero himself is listed, showing that in almost every case this is Gawain. By no means every text discussed is included in this chart; to have listed them all would have been unnecessary and tedious for the reader. What follows is a simplified guideline only, which should be used in conjunction with the text, in particular Chapters 3-5.

Text	Aspect	Character(s)	Life-enhancing sovereignty-bestowing gift	Nature of test	Reward/outcome	Hero
Gawain and the Green Knight	Lovely woman/hag	Lady Bercilak/Morgane the Goddess	Baldric	Chastity/Beheading Game	Enhanced status	Gawain
La Mule Sans Frein	Lovely woman	Damsel of the mule	Bridle	Combat	Kingdom/bride	Gawain
Diu Crône	Lovely woman/hag	Lavanet/Guinevere/Dame Fortune	Life-enhancing vessel/baldric	Combat	Bride/kingdom	Gawain
Le Morte d'Arthur	Triple aspect	3 women at the spring		Combat/adventure	Enhanced status/life lesson	Gawain/Uwain/Pellinorre
Perlesvaus	Triple aspect	3 women at the spring	Life-enhancing vessel	Combat/adventure	Enhanced status	Gawain
Gawain & Ragnall	Lovely woman/hag	Ragnall	Kiss	Sovereignty test	Enhanced status/marriage	Gawain
Pwyll	Fairy women	Rhiannon/Creiddelyadd		Combat/exchange	The kingdom	Pwyll
Turk and Gawain		Putative wife/daughter of host	Cauldron (2)	Combat	The kingdom	Gawain
Le Chevalier de la Charette	Lovely woman	Guinevere		Combat	The kingdom	Gawain/Lancelot
Le Chevalier à l'Epée	Lovely woman	Daughter of hospitable host		Combat	The kingdom (?)	Gawain
Hunbaut	Lovely woman	Daughter of hospitable host/lady of Gant Destroit		Combat	Fealty of King of Man	Gawain
The Carl of Carlisle	Lovely woman	Carl's daughter		Combat/Beheading Game	Marriage	Gawain
Vulgate cycle	Faery woman	Florée		Combat	Marriage	Gawain

Figure 9: *Aspects of the Goddess in the Major Texts.*

Bibliography

(All titles were published in London, unless otherwise stated. Learned articles appear in inverted commas e.g. Krappe, A.H. 'Who *was* the Green Knight?' in *Speculum*, vol. XIII, (1938), pp206-215.

Publications of the Modern Language Society of America is abbreviated throughout as PMLA.)

1. TEXTS

1. 'The Adventures of the Sons of King Daire' trans. W. Stokes, in *Academy* vol. 1042, (1892)
2. 'Arthur and Gorlagon' trans. F.A. Milne, with notes by A. Nutt, in *Folklore* vol. 15, (1904), pp40-67
3. *Le Bel Inconnu ou Giglain, fils de Messire Gauvain et de la Fée aux Blanches Mains* ed. C. Hippeau, Paris, Aubrey, 1860
4. 'The Birth of Arthur', ed. and trans. J.H. Davies in *Y Cymmroder* vol. 24 (1900), pp249-264
5. *From Cuchulainn to Gawain* trans. E. Brewer, Cambridge, D.S. Brewer, 1973
6. *I Cantari de Carduino* ed. P. Rajna, Bologna, Romagnoli, 1873
7. Chaucer, G. *The Canterbury Tales* Oxford, Oxford University Press, 1912
8. Chrétien de Troyes *Arthurian Romances* trans. D.D.R. Owen, J.M. Dent, 1987
9. Chrétien de Troyes *The Knight of the Cart* trans. D.W. Rogers, New York, University of Columbia Press, 1984
10. Chrétien de Troyes *Perceval: The Story of the Grail* trans. N. Bryant, Cambridge, D.S. Brewer, 1982
11. *Compert Cuon Culainn and Other Stories* ed. A.G. von Hamel, Dublin, Dublin Institute for Advanced Studies, 1968
12. *The Continuations of the Old French Perceval of Chrétien de Troyes*

ed. W. Roach, Philadelphia, American Philosophical Society, 3 vols. 1949-52

13. Cross, T.P. and Slover, C.H. *Ancient Irish Tales* Dublin, Figgis, 1936

14. 'Les Enfances Gauvain' ed. P. Meyer, in *Romania* vol. 39 (1910), pp1-32

15. *The Four Ancient Books of Wales* trans. W.F. Skene, Edinburgh, Edmonston and Douglas, 1868

16. *From Camelot to Joyous Guard: The Old French 'La Morte le Roi Artu'* trans. J.N. Carman, Lawrence, University Press of Kansas, 1974

17. *The Complete Works of the Gawain-Poet* trans. J. Gardner, Carbondale, Southern Illinois University Press, 1975

18. *Gawain on Marriage (De Coniuge non Ducenda)* ed. A.G. Rigg, Toronto, Pontifical Institute of Mediaeval Studies, 1986

19. Geoffrey of Monmouth *History of the Kings of Britain* trans. S. Evans, J.M. Dent, 1958

20. *Gliglois* ed. C.H. Livingston, Cambridge, Mass., Harvard University Press, 1932

21. Hall, L.B. *The Knightly Tales of Sir Gawain* Chicago, Nelson-Hall, 1976

22. Heinrich von dem Turlin *Diu Crône* ed. G. Scholl, Amsterdam, Rodopi, 1966

23. *The High Book of the Grail (Perlesvaus)* ed. N. Bryant, Cambridge, D.S. Brewer, 1978

24. *King Arthur's Death: The Middle English Stanzaic Morte Arthur and Alliterative Morte Arthure*, Exeter, University of Exeter, 1986

25. *The Knight of the Parrot (Le Chevalier du Papegau)* trans. T.E. Vesce, New York, Garland Publications, 1986

26. *Lancelot of the Lake* trans. C. Corley, Oxford. Oxford University Press, 1989

27. Butler, I. 'Lai de Cort' in *Tales from the Old French* Boston, Houghton Mifflin, 1950

28. *Libeaus Desconus* ed. M. Kaluza Leipzieg, Reisland, 1890

29. *Life of Merlin* trans. B. Clarke, Cardiff, University of Wales Press, 1973

30. *Livre d'Artus* see 60 below *The Vulgate Version* vol. VII (1913)

31. *The Mabinogion* trans. J. Gantz, Harmondsworth, Penguin, 1976

32. Malory, Sir T. *Le Morte d'Arthur* New York, University Books, 1966

33. Marie de France, *French Medieval Romances* trans. E. Mason, J.M. Dent

34. *Merlin, roman en prose du XIIIe siècle* eds. G. Paris and J. Ulrich, Société des Anciens Textes Franẑais, Paris, Firmin Didot, 1886

35. 'De Ortu Waluunii: An Arthurian Romance' now first edited from the Cotonian ms. etc, by J.D. Bruce in *Publications of the Modern Lan-*

guage Association of America pp 365-456

36. 'Pedwar Marchog as Hugain Llys Arthur, (The 24 Knights of Arthur's Court)' trans. R. Bromwich, in *Transactions of the Honourable Society of Cymmrodorion* (1956), pp 116-32

37. *The Quest for the Holy Grail* trans. P.M. Mattarasso, Harmondsworth, Penguin, 1969

38. Raoul de Houdenc, *La Vengeance Raguidel* ed. C. Hippeau, Paris, Aubry, 1862

39. *The Rise of Gawain, Nephew of Arthur (De Ortu Waluuanii Nepotis Arturi)* trans. M.L. Day, New York, Garland Publishing, 1984

40. de Boron, Robert *Le Roman de l'Estoire dou Graal* ed. W. Nitze, Paris, Champion, 1927

41. *Le Roman de Tristan en Prose* ed. R. Curtis vol. I Munich, Hueber, 1963; vol. II, Leiden, E.J. Brill, 1976

42. *The Romance of Hunbaut: An Arthurian Poem of the Thirteenth Century* ed. M. Winters, Lugduni Batavorum, E.J. Brill, 1974

43. *The Romance of Perceval in Prose: A Translation of the 'Didot Perceval'* trans. D. Skeels, Seattle, University of Washington Press, 1966

44. *The Romance of Yder* trans. A. Adams, Cambridge, D.S. Brewer, 1983

45. *Le Romans de Durnmart le Galois* ed. E. Stengel, Tübingen, Bibliothek des Literarischen Vereins in Stuttgart, 166, 1873

46. *Sir Gawain and the Green Knight* trans. Rev. E.J.B. Kirtlan, Charles H. Kelly, 1912

47. *Sir Gawain and the Green Knight* trans. Brian Stone, Harmonesdsworth, Penguin, 1959

48. *Sir Gawain and the Green Knight, Pearl and Sir Orpheo* trans. J.R.R. Tolkein, Allen & Unwin, 1975

49. *Sir Gawain and the Green Knight* ed. J.R.R. Tolkein and E.V. Gordon, Oxford, Oxford University Press, 1967

50. *Sir Gawain and the Lady of Lys* trans. J. Weston, D. Nutt, 1907

51. *Sir Gawain at the Grail Castle* trans. J. Weston, D. Nutt, 1903

52. *Sir Perceval of Gales* eds. J. Campion and F. Holthausen, Heidelberg, Carl Winter, 1917

53. *Syr Gawayne* eds. F. Madden, Richard and John E. Taylor, 1839

54. *The Tain* trans. T. Kinsella, Oxford, Oxford University Press, 1970

55. *The Tale of Balain* trans. D.E. Campbell, Evanston, Northwestern University Press, 1972

56. *Trioedd Ynys Prydein (The Welsh Triads)* ed. and trans. R. Bromwich, Cardiff, University of Wales Press, 1961

57. *Two Old French Gauvain Romances (Le Chevalier à L'Epée & La Mule Sans Frein)* eds. R.C. Johnston and D.D.R. Owen, Edinburgh, Scottish Academic Press, 1972

58. Ulrich von Zatzikhoven, *Lanzelet* trans. K.G.T. Webster, New York,

Columbia University Press, 1951
59. 'Vita Gildae' trans. S. Baring-Gould in *The Lives of the British Saints* Edinburgh, Grant, vol. I (1872), pp 440-42
60. *The Vulgate Version of the Arthurian Romances* ed. J.O. Sommer, Washington, The Carnegie Institution, 8 vols, 1908-16
61. Wace and Layamon *Arthurian Chronicles* trans. E. Mason, J.M. Dent, 1962
62. Wirnt von Grafenberg, *Wigalois: The Knight of Fortune's Wheel* Lincoln, University of Nebraska Press, 1977
63. Wolfram von Eschenbach, *Parzival* trans. A.T. Hatto, Harmondworth, Penguin, 1980

2. CRITICAL STUDIES

64. Adler, A. 'Sovereignty in Chrétien's *Yvain*' in PMLA vol. XLII, no. 2 (June 1947), pp 281-305
65. Arthur, R.G. *Medieval Sign Theory & Sir Gawain and the Green Knight* Toronto, University of Toronto Press, 1987
66. Baird, W. 'The Three Women of the *Vengeance Raguidel*' in *Modern Language Review*, vol. 75 (1980), pp 269-274
67. Bartrum, P.C. *Early Welsh Genealogical Tracts* Cardiff, University of Wales, 1966
68. Blaess, M. 'Arthur's Sisters' in *Bulletin of the Board of Celtic Studies* vol. 8 (1956), pp 69-77
69. Bogdanow, F. 'The Character of Gauvain in the 13th Century Prose Romances' in *Medium Aevum*, vol. 27 (1958), pp 154-161
70. Bogdanow, F. *The Romance of the Grail: A Study of the Structure and Genesis of a Thirteenth Century Arthurian Prose Romance* Manchester, Manchester University Press, 1966
71. Bromwich, R. 'Celtic Dynastic Themes and the Breton Lays' in *Etude Celtique*, vol. 9 (1960-1), pp 439-474
72. Bromwich, R. 'Scotland and the Earliest Arthurian Tradition' in *Bulletin Bibliographique de la Société Internationale Arthurienne*, vol. 15 (1963), pp 85-95
73. Bromwich, R. 'Trioedd Ynys Prydein: the Myvyrian Series' in *Transactions of the Honorable Society of Cymmrodorian*, part 1, 1968, pp 299-301; part 2, 1969, pp 127-156
74. Brown, A.C.L. 'Arthur's Loss of Queen and Kingdom' in *Speculum*, vol. 15 (1940), pp 3-11
75. Brown, A.C.L. *Iwain* Boston, Ginn & Co., 1903

76. Bruce, J.D. 'Arthuriana: Gawain's Slaying of the Knights of the Grail-Quest in the Early Prints of Lancelot du Lac' in *The Romanic Review*, vol. 3 (1912), pp 173-193

77. Bruce, J.D. *Evolution of the Arthurian Romance* 2 vols, Gloucester, Mass., Peter Smith, 1958

78. Buchanan, A. 'The Irish Framework of Sir Gawain and the Green Knight' in PMLA vol. 48 (1932), pp 315-338

79. Bush, K. 'The Character of Gauvain in the Prose Tristan' in *Tristania* vol. II (1977), pp 12-22

80. Busby, K. *Gauvain in Old French Literature* Amsterdam, Rodopi, 1980

81. Carmichael, Alexander *Carmina Gadelica* vol. V, Edinburgh, Oliver and Boyd, 1954

82. Chadwick, H.M. *Early Scotland* Cambridge, Cambridge University Press, 1949

83. Colgrave, B. 'Sir Gawayne's Green Chapel' in *Antiquity*, pp 351-353

84. Cosman, M.P. *The Education of the Hero in Arthurian Romance* Chapel Hill, University of North Carolina Press, 1965

85. Cross, T.P. 'A Welsh Tristan Episode' in *Studies in Philology* vol. 17 (1920), pp 93-110

86. Dalton, G.F. 'The Ritual Killing of the Irish Kings' in *Folklore* vol. 81 (1970), pp 1-22

87. Day, M.L. 'Scarlet Surcoat & Gilded Armor: The Literary Tradition of Gawain's Costume in Sir Gawain and the Green Knight & De Ortu Walluuanii' in *Interpretations* vol. 15, no. 2, pp 53-58

88. Dick, E.S. 'The German Gawein: Diu Crône and Wigalois' in *Interpretations* vol. 15, no. 2, pp 11-17

89. Eisner, S. *A Tale of Wonder* Wexford, John English & Co., 1957

90. Elliott, R.W.V. *The Gawain Country* Leeds, University of Leeds, 1984

91. Goetinck, G. *Peredur: A Study of the Welsh Tradition in the Grail Legends* Cardiff, University of Wales Press, 1975

92. Gowans, L.M. *Cei and the Arthurian Legend* Cambridge, D.S. Brewer, 1988

93. Greenlaw, E. 'The Vows of Baldwin' in *Publications of the Modern Language Association* vol. XXI, no. 3, pp 575-636

94. Griffith, R. 'Bertilak's Lady: The French Background' in *Annals of the New York Academy of Arts* vol. 314 (1978), pp 249-266

95. Hartley, M.P. 'Faulkners, Medievalism and Sir Gawain and the Green Knight' in *American Notes and Queries*, vol. 21 (1982-3), pp 111-114

96. Heller, E.K. 'Story of the Magic Horn' in *Speculum* vol. 9 (1934), pp 38-50

97. Jonassen, F.B. 'Elements from the Traditional Drama of England in *Sir Gawain and the Green Knight*' in *Viator* vol. 17 (1984), pp 221-254

98. Kaske, R.E. 'Gawain's Green Chapel and the Cave at Wetton Mill' in *Medieval Literature and Folklore Studies* eds. J. Mandel and B.A. Rosenburg, New Jersey, Rutger's University Press, 1970, pp 111-121

99. Kelly, D. 'Gauvain and Fin'amors in the Poem of Chrétien de Troyes' in *Studies in Philology* vol. 67 (1970), pp 453-460

100. Kittredge, G.L. *A Study of Gawain and the Green Knight* Peter Smith, Gloucester, Mass., 1960

101. Korrel, P. *An Arthurian Triangle* Leiden, E.J. Brill, 1984

102. Krappe, A.H. 'Who Was the Green Knight?' in *Speculum*, vol. XIII (1938), pp 206-215

103. Lacey, N.J. 'The Character of Gawain in Hunbaut' in *Bulletin Bibliographique de la Société Internationale Arthurienne* vol. 38 (1986), pp 298-305

104. Loomis, R.S. *Celtic Myth and Arthurian Romance* New York, Haskell House, 1967

105. Loomis, R.S. 'Gawain, Gwri and Cuchulinn' in *PMLA* vol. 43 (1928) pp 384-396

106. Loomis, R.S. 'Morgue La Fée in Oral Tradition' in *Romania* vol. LXXX (1959), pp 337-367

107. Loomis, R.S. 'Some Names in Arthurian Romance' *PMLA* vol. XLV (1930), pp 416-443

108. Loomis, R.S. *Wales & the Arthurian Legend* Cardiff, University of Wales Press, 1956

109. Lozachmeur, J.C. 'Guinglain et Perceval' in *Etudes Celtiques*, vol. 16 (1979), pp 279-281

110. Lozachmeur, J.C. 'Origines Celtiques des Aventures de Gauvain au Pays de Galvoie dans *Le Conte du Graal* de Chrétien de Troyes' in *Actes de 14ième Congrès Internationale Arthurienne* Rennes, 1985

111. Lutterell, C. 'The Folktale Elements in *Sir Gawain and the Green Knight*' in *Studies in Philology*, vol. 77 (1980), pp 105-127

112. Markman, A.M. *Sir Gawain of Britain* Michigan, University Microfilms, Anne Arbour, 1965

113. Matthews, C. *Arthur and the Sovereignty of Britain: King and Goddess in the Mabinogion* Arkana, 1989

114. Matthews, C. *Mabon and the Mysteries of Britain: An Exploration of the Mabinogion* Arkana, 1987

115. Matthews, C. and J. *Hallowquest: Tarot Magic and the Arthurian Mysteries* Wellingborough, Aquarian Press, 1990

116. *An Arthurian Reader* ed. J. Matthews, Wellingborough, Aquarian Press, 1988

117. *At the Table of the Grail* ed. J. Matthews, Arkana, 1987

118. Matthews, J. 'The Family of the Grail' in *Avalon to Camelot* vol. I, no. 3 (1984), pp 9-10

119. Matthews, J. *The Grail: Quest for the Eternal* London, Thames & Hudson, 1981

120. Matthews, J. and Green, M. *The Grail-Seeker's Companion* Wellingborough, Aquarian Press, 1986

121. Matthews, J. and Stewart, R.J. *Warriors of Arthur* Poole, Blandford Press, 1988

122. Meyer, K. *The Voyage of Bran Son of Febal* D. Nutt, 1895

123. 'Approaches to Teaching *Gawain and the Green Knight*' eds. M.J. Miller and J. Chance in *Modern Language Association of America*, New York, 1986

124. Morgan, G. 'The Significance of the Pentangle Symbolism in *Sir Gawain and the Green Knight*' in *Modern Language Review*, vol. 74 (1979), pp 769-790

125. Newstead, H. 'The Besieged Ladies in Arthurian Romance' in *PLMA* vol. LXIII (1948), pp 803-830

126. Newstead, H. *Bran the Blessed in Arthurian Romance* New York, Columbia University Press, 1939

127. Newstead, H. 'Joie de la Cort Episode in Erec and the Horn of Bran' in *PMLA* vol. LI (1936), pp 13-25

128. Nickel, H. 'The Arming of Gawain' in *Avalon to Camelot* vol. 1, no. 2 (1983)

129. Nickel, H. 'Why Was the Green Knight Green?' in *Arthurian Interpretations* vol. 2, no. 2 (1988)

130. Pearce, S.M. 'The Cornish Elements in the Arthurian Tradition' in *Folklore* vol. 85 (1974), pp 145-163

131. Pennick, N. *Earth Harmony* London, Century, 1987

132. Ray, B.K. *The Character of Gawain* Oxford, Oxford University Press, 1926

133. Rhys, J. *Celtic Britain* Society for Promoting Christian Knowledge, 1904

134. Rhys, J. *Lectures on the Origin & Growth of Religion as Illustrated by Celtic Heathendom* Williams & Norgate, 1888

135. Rhys, J. *Studies in the Arthurian Legend* Oxford, Clarendon Press, 1891

136. Ritchie, R.L.G. *Chrétien de Troyes and Scotland* Oxford, Clarendon Press, 1952

137. Schofield, W.H. *Studies on the Libeaus Desconus* (Studies and Notes in Philosophy & Literature vol. IV) Boston, Ginn & Co., 1895

138. Shictman, M.B. 'Malory's Gawain Reconsidered' in *Essays in Literature* vol. XI (1984), pp 159-176

139. Speirs, John *Medieval English Poetry* London, Faber and Faber, 1957

140. *The Book of Merlin* ed. R.J. Stewart, Poole, Blandford Press, 1987

141. *Merlin and Woman* ed. R.J. Stewart, Poole, Blandford Press, 1988

142. Stewart, R.J. *The Mystic Life of Merlin*, London, Arkana, 1986

143. Stewart, R.J. *The Prophetic Vision of Merlin*, London, Arkana, 1986

144. Stewart, R.J. and Matthews, J. *Legendary Britain: A Quest*, London, Cassell, 1989

145. Stokoe, William C. jnr. 'The Sources of Sir Launfal: Lanval and Grealent' in *PLMA* vol. LXIII (1948), pp 392-404

146. Sturm, S. 'Magic in *Le Bel Inconnu*' in *Esprit Createur*, vol. 12 (1972), pp 19-25

147. Thompson, R.H. 'Gawain Against Arthur' in *Folklore* vol. 85 (1974), pp 113-121

148. Thompson, R.H. 'The Perils of Good Advice' in *Folklore* vol. 90 (1979), pp 71-76

149. Vinaver, E. 'A Romance of Gaheret' in *Medium Aevum* vol. 1 (1932), pp157-167

150. Webster, K.G.T. 'Arthur and Charlemagne' in *English Studies*, vol. 36 (1906), pp241-242

151. Weston, J.L. *From Ritual to Romance* New York, Doubleday, 1957

152. Weston, J.L. *The Legend of Sir Gawain* D. Nutt, 1897

153. Weston, J.L. *The Legend of Sir Perceval* D. Nutt, London, 1909

154. Whiting, B.J. 'Gawain: His Reputation, His Courtesy and His Appearance in Chaucer's *Squire's Tale*' in *Medieval Studies* vol. 9 (1947), pp189-234

155. Zimmer H. *The King of the Corpse* Princeton, Princeton University Press, 1971

Index

Entries in *italic* type refer to texts.